with many thanks for your
and hospitality on my
Malvern and Worcester

[signature]

January 1985

ALL IN THE MIND

By the same author

THE SHROUD OF TURIN

Ian Wilson

All in the Mind

REINCARNATION, HYPNOTIC REGRESSION, STIGMATA, MULTIPLE PERSONALITY, AND OTHER LITTLE-UNDERSTOOD POWERS OF THE MIND

DOUBLEDAY & COMPANY, INC.
GARDEN CITY, NEW YORK
1982

Library of Congress Cataloging in Publication Data

Wilson, Ian, 1941–
All in the mind.

Previously published as: Mind Out of Time?
Includes bibliographical references and index.
1. Reincarnation.   2. Hypnotism.   3. Multiple personality.
I. Title.
BL515.W53   1982   154.7'7
AACR2
ISBN: 0-385-17915-4
Library of Congress Catalog Card Number 81–43420

Contents

List of Photographs

Following page 52

List of Illustrations in the Text

List of Tables

Preface

THROUGHOUT THE CENTURIES men and women from all walks of life have reported strange experiences when they seemed to see people, places, and events through the eyes of another individual, and from times before they were born. Some who have described such experiences have been deeply hypnotized. Others have been, to all appearances at least, fully conscious. Various explanations have been suggested, among them inherited memory and, most popularly, reincarnation, yet underlying these the fundamental question has remained. Do the experiences represent real flashbacks from some prebirth past? Has the mind, in a quite literal sense, been "out of time"? If such a question could be answered with a positive "yes," at the very least our approach to history would be revolutionized. Given the development of reliable means of inducing such flashbacks and an orderly approach, mysteries that have beleaguered historians for centuries could conceivably be resolved by new eyewitness accounts. Lost languages and how they were spoken could be retrieved. At a stroke a fresh and exciting chapter could be opened up in our understanding of man's mind.

But can the mind *truly* go out of time? Are the flashback experiences real or illusions in the recipient's mind? This book is the first serious and comprehensive attempt to answer these questions, and I have based it on a searching out of the best rather than the most dubious material. There is, for instance, a lively literature of out-of-time memories from the happy hunting grounds of Atlantis, Ancient Egypt, and Tibet. Such cases I have generally avoided as—on the most charitable interpretation—difficult to check. Nor have I chosen to regurgitate at second hand material that is mere anecdote. Into this category fall most examples of *déjà vu*, the "I've been here before" feeling. Although a remarkably high proportion of the population have experienced this feeling at one time or another, reported cases are invariably so flimsy and subjective that serious study is impossible.

I have therefore concentrated on well-attested cases. In the United States the psychiatrist Dr. Ian Stevenson has collected from all over the world hundreds of past-life memories on the part of children, generally under the age of six. In Britain, Dr. Arthur Guirdham, a retired National Health Service psychiatrist, has written a series of books detailing Cathar past lives remembered by himself and pseudonymous patients and friends. Throughout the world dozens of hypnotists and hypnotherapists have reported instances of their subjects remembering past lives while under hypnosis. These cases have usually been reliably tape-recorded and a positive plethora of examples has been published in recent years. There are also extraordinary cases of individuals (like the former BBC playwright Ada F. Kay, today A. J. Stewart) whose lives have apparently been taken over by a previous personality. If there is anything to the out-of-time experience we should be able to deduce it from a rigorous firsthand investigation of cases of this kind.

Perhaps not surprisingly, some of the chosen reincarnationists were more amenable to my approach than others. Dr. Ian Stevenson consented to my visiting him at Charlottesville, Virginia, but otherwise insisted on remaining aloof from a book directed toward the general reader. Dr. Arthur Guirdham proved affable and hospitable at his Bath home, but closed up like a clam when I raised the question of even the most discreet approaches to his Cathar patients and friends. Most of the hypnotists and hypnotherapists were agreeable to being interviewed, but few were prepared to provide sufficient details for the master index of past-life regression cases I had originally envisaged. By far the most helpful were Derek Crüssell of Bromley, who allowed me complete freedom to attend the experimental regressions he held each Sunday, and Joe Keeton of Hoylake, who made available his entire tape collection of past-life hypnotic regressions and the names and addresses of his subjects for me to explore in total liberty.

Having gained an entrée into this intriguing world, my first and most prevailing impression was of the integrity of those with whom I became most closely involved. There could be no doubting their basic honesty and sincerity, diverse as many of their attitudes were. Nor was there any possibility of fraudulent collusion between hypnotists and those remembering past lives under regression. In some cases I was able to watch individuals known to me go under hypnosis for the first time and reveal past lives as astonishing to themselves as to everyone around them.

But hardly had I satisfied myself of this than the whole course of the investigation began to take on a complexion and direction quite different from anything I had anticipated. I had carefully selected, wherever possible, cases in which the past life remembered was known to have existed. The task of checking the factual accuracy of past-life material against available historical sources seemed a straightforward one, and I had confidently expected that my degree in history would be the only qualification I needed. It was only when I checked these out in depth that I began to realize not only that there was something wrong, but that to even begin to understand it I was going to need some help from the realms of psychology, a field in which I had not the slightest academic qualification.

It was a predicament in which I was fortunate to have one natural advantage, in the person of my wife Judith, a qualified psychologist trained at Sheffield University in the early 1960s. While the interpretations made in this book are my own, it has been Judith who carefully checked each chapter from the psychologist's point of view and saved me from some of the more obvious layman's mistakes. I have also greatly benefited from similar vetting of the manuscript by Dr. Chris McManus of Bedford College, University of London, Dr. David Stevenson of the Liverpool School of Tropical Medicine, and Jon Beer of Professor Richard Gregory's Brain and Perception Unit at Bristol University. Yet more specialist advice about the workings of the mind has been kindly given by Professor Lionel Haward of the University of Surrey, Dr. Ray Cooper of the Burden Neurological Institute, Bristol, and Professor Ernest Hilgard of Stanford University, California.

While the book would have lost much authority without such help, it would have been absolutely impossible without the cooperation of the hypnotists and the subjects of the cases chosen for investigation. To these, and in particular Joe Keeton and Derek Crüssell—on whose cases I have relied particularly heavily—I wish to acknowledge my heartiest thanks. Among the other hypnotists who should be mentioned I owe much gratitude to Harry Hurst, Tom Barlow, Leonard Wilder, Wilf Proudfoot, and the late Arnall Bloxham, all of whom assisted in varying ways. Of the past-life subjects both hypnotic and nonhypnotic, I am particularly grateful to those who allowed their real names to be used, among these Sue Atkins, Carol Dow, Edna Greenan, Graham Huxtable, Michael O'Mara, Alfred Orriss, John Pollock, Mona Reynolds, David Rolfe, Dr. Tom Troscianko and, not least, A. J. Stewart, as well as those who, like "Jan" of Merseyside, freely gave information during interviews but chose, for understandable reasons of privacy, to remain anonymous.

A full list of those individuals and organizations who provided information on the cases featured (and not featured) in this book would be virtually impossible, but special thanks are due to the following: Professor William Feindel of the Montreal Neurological Institute for providing valuable background on the work of the late Dr. Wilder Penfield; Louise Moody for help in locating crucial photographs from the work of her late husband, Dr. Robert Moody; Ray Donovan of Blackpool, Madeline Harper of Ovingdean, Denzil Lush of Bristol, and John Ray of the Cambridge University Faculty of Oriental Studies for information relating to the "Rosemary" case; Francis Freitas of Bombay, Michael Green of the Department of the Environment, London, and Renée Haynes and Eleanor O'Keefe of the Society for Psychical Research, London, for background to various of Dr. Ian Stevenson's cases; Jeffrey Iverson and Magnus Magnusson for advice relating to the work of Arnall Bloxham; Dr. Vernon Harrison for a specialist appraisal of the handwritings of Carol Dow and

A. J. Stewart; Monica O'Hara, wife of Joe Keeton, for much assistance relating to her husband's work; the University of Oulu, Finland, for providing an important paper by Dr. Reima Kampman; the Columbus *Dispatch*, Ohio, for providing press cuttings of the Billy Milligan case; Father Joseph Crehan of the Society of Jesus for providing a long-out-of-print German pamphlet by Dr. Alfred Lechler; Stanley Ellis of Leeds University for an expert appraisal of voice recordings of Joan Waterhouse; June Tims of the *Surrey Comet* for help relating to the Philip Gaston case; Brenda Walklate, Lily Brown, V. Rhodes, Tom Williams, and the Manchester *Evening News* for information on Elsie Cain; James Brabazon, Caroline Bingham, Hugh Macandrew of the National Gallery, Edinburgh, and Stephen Rees-Jones of the Courtauld Institute of Art, London, for background relating to A. J. Stewart and James IV; the Reverend Barry Trotter of Frenchay, the Reverend Edward Bailey of Winterbourne, John Lucena of the Frenchay Preservation Society, and the Bristol *Evening Post* for information on Dr. Nehemiah Bradford.

The help of several libraries and archive collections has also been particularly valuable in a work of this kind, and I would like to record thanks to the staff of the Bristol City and University libraries; the British Library, London; the Newspaper Library, Colindale, London; the University of London library; the Lambeth Palace library; the Society for Psychical Research library; the Lady Lever Art Gallery and Library, Port Sunlight; the Public Record Office, Kew; the Somerset County Record Office, Taunton; the Muniment Room, Guildford; the Bristol *Evening Post* editorial library and the Mary Evans Picture Library, London. Not least I am deeply indebted to Iris Sampson of Backwell for translating from the German the entire text of Dr. Alfred Lechler's *Das Rätsel von Konnersreuth*, and to the indefatigable Anna Evans, already a veteran of *The Shroud of Turin*, for the innumerable typewriting tasks that work on this present volume has entailed.

Finally I would like to say this, both to the reader and to those who have actively assisted in this book. Writing *All in the Mind* has been a far from easy task, not least of my problems being that I found myself tearing apart the material of many of those who openly and kindly made this available to me for investigation.

Conscious of this, I have tried very hard to make the book more than a prejudiced and negative-minded debunk. One of the most refreshing aspects of my interviews with specialists in the study of the mind has been the honest admission of the best of them that it is a field in which science remains still in the Dark Ages. If I have succeeded in casting the merest glimmer of light into that darkness then my endeavors will have been more than worthwhile . . .

Bristol, England
October 1980

Author's Note

WHEREVER POSSIBLE THROUGHOUT this book it has been my policy to quote the authentic, legal names of all those referred to, even when hitherto these have been more familiarly known by pseudonyms. This has been the case with Virginia Tighe (pseudonym Ruth Simmons), Claire Brenner (pseudonym Christine Beauchamp), and Chris Sizemore (pseudonym Eve of *The Three Faces of Eve*). In some instances I have been obliged to follow the pseudonyms adopted by others (e.g., Dr. Arthur Guirdham's Mrs. Smith and Miss Mills), while in others, ignorant of the individuals' real names, I have invented pseudonyms of my own. The latter device has generally been employed to avoid a medical paper's tedious repetition of the words "the subject," and occurs only in the case of those subjects referred to in the text as Harry, Mary, Alec, Cynthia, and Niki.

From the purist point of view I would have preferred to use quotation marks when referring to "past lives," and to alleged past-life and multiple personality entities by name—e.g., "Bridey Murphy," "Ragen," and so on. While such a styling has the advantage of reminding the reader of the hypothetical nature of these descriptions, used extensively it becomes a hindrance, and on my publisher's advice has been omitted.

CHAPTER 1

An American Psychiatrist
and Reincarnation

Do WE, EACH OF US, carry hidden memories of times before we
were born? Are we individuals who have lived and died many
times in previous centuries? Does reincarnation exist?

If one day science pronounces an overwhelming "yes" to these
questions, the most likely place from which this will come is an
unpretentious old colonial-style building in Westland, Charlottesville, Virginia. Here, thoughtfully off-campus, the University of
Virginia houses its Division of Parapsychology, a tiny research
team specially dedicated to the investigation of claimed memories
of past lives. And no individual exhibits that dedication with
greater professionalism and tenacity than the division's director,
Canadian-born psychiatrist Dr. Ian Stevenson, who for more than
twenty years has set himself single-mindedly to proving that reincarnation exists, that it is scientifically demonstrable.

Today it might not seem so very remarkable for a scientist to
be trying to prove the existence of reincarnation. In most Western countries interest in Eastern cultures and beliefs has grown
significantly since World War II. Throughout the United States
there are many hypnotists, including some qualified psychologists,
actively "regressing" subjects into what are popularly supposed to
be past lives. Scientologist L. Ron Hubbard claims to have carried

out "an official scientific survey on forty-one persons," providing "absolute proof" of reincarnation.[1] In Australia an experimenter by the name of Gerry Glaskin claims past-life memories can be stimulated by a special technique of massaging the head.[2] Recent surveys by popular U.S. newspapers have shown belief in reincarnation to be particularly high among college students;[3] and among adults, if the trend is the same as in the United Kingdom, around one third of the population believe in reincarnation in some form.[4]

But what makes Dr. Ian Stevenson so special is that he is undeniably one of the most senior and by background orthodox of scientists to have become attached to a belief that many would dismiss as an oriental superstition. Bespectacled, very "English" in voice, in his reserved manner and his formality of dress, Stevenson was born in Montreal on Hallowe'en, 1918. As a young man, he qualified in medicine at McGill University and after minor posts in Phoenix and New Orleans became an assistant professor at Louisiana State University in 1949. Appointed full professor in psychiatry and neurology at Charlottesville in 1957, he showed, in the following year, the first significant public signs of the unusual new direction he was to adopt for his career. He entered the American Society for Psychical Research's competition for the best essay on the survival of the human personality after bodily death. His entry, "The Evidence for Survival from Claimed Memories of Former Incarnations,"[5] was adjudged the winner, and this success seems to have sparked in him a resolve to improve on the secondhand, already-published cases of past-life claims on which he had been obliged up to that time to rely. Aided by some generous financial sponsors, from 1961 he began the collection of his own firsthand material, utilizing every available moment of vacation time for visits to far-flung countries of the world, all with a view to seeking out individuals with conscious memories of past lives, together with witnesses and others able to support or verify the information thus gathered.

So successful were these "field trips," as he calls them, that by 1966 Stevenson was able to publish the first textbook of his findings, *Twenty Cases Suggestive of Reincarnation*.[6] Highly detailed, closely written, and clinical in its approach, this immediately set an altogether-new standard for books in this field, and

arriage breakdown. Then, extraordinarily, came the first indica-
on that his prayers just might be answered.

One night early in 1958, as they lay in bed, Florence an-
unced, "I know this will please you, but it doesn't please me.
n pregnant." Unwaveringly John told her that she would have
in daughters, and that this was going to be God's way of re-
ning Joanna and Jacqueline to them and giving John the sign
t he had asked for. With all logic on her side Florence Pollock
uld have none of it. The normal odds against having twins are
nty to one, with even greater odds against twin daughters, and
re was no history of twins in either Florence's or John's
ilies. Furthermore, when Florence consulted a gynecologist
was told categorically in the presence of her family doctor and
wife that there was only one heartbeat and one set of limbs.
re was no way in which her husband could be right.

ut somehow John Pollock *was* right. On the morning of Octo-
4, 1958, while her husband was still on his milkround,
ence gave birth to twin daughters, Jennifer and Gillian. Her
and John lost no time in announcing the event in the very
issue of the Hexham *Courant*:

LLOCK. To John and Florence at 29 Leazes Crescent,
xham, on October 4th, God's most precious gift of twin
ghters, Jennifer Mary and Gillian Theresa. Thanks be to
d and to our Blessed Lady.

Pollock's first sight of the twins in his wife's arms the same
ng was even more satisfying. The girls had been born
ten minutes of each other, Gillian first, then Jennifer, who
erefore the "younger" of the two. And as he studied Jen-
arefully, his eyes became drawn to a faint but unmistakable
hite line running down her forehead. Immediately he knew
seen that thin white line before—on the forehead of
ine, the younger of the two dead sisters. At the age of two
ine had fallen off her tricycle, gashing her forehead. By the
e was six the scar had healed to a thin white line identical
at visible on the newborn Jennifer. Then Florence Pol-
ainst her every inclination, spotted another feature, also
ifer. The dead sister Jacqueline had had a brown pig-
nevus or birthmark, strongly resembling a thumbprint.

has since been followed by similar volumes of even greater
thoroughness.[7] A particularly unexpected and ostensibly convincing aspect of this material is that instead of being based on
adults' hypnotic memories of past lives—the usual variety of modern past-life claims—the typical Stevenson subject is a child between the age of two and six who has professed *conscious* memories of having lived before. Such a child may talk and behave as if
he has different parents and belongs to a different location to that
in which he finds himself. He may recognize and name objects,
places, and people he claims to have known in a previous life. He
may "relive" the circumstances of a violent past-life death. Above
all, he may produce so much detail about the deceased person he
seems to have been that it becomes possible to identify that person and check information with surviving members of the past-
life family. For a case that demonstrates many of the classic
Stevenson features there can be no better example than one from
Britain involving the daughters of a now sixty-year-old Englishman, John Pollock.[8]

The son of a Scots father and a Jewish mother, John Pollock
has had for almost as long as he can remember an intense belief
in reincarnation. In 1941, when living in Bristol in southern England, he was converted to Roman Catholicism, but at this point
instead of abandoning his previous ideas—regarded as heresy by
the Roman Church—he insisted on retaining them, even to the
priests who heard his confessions. At night he would pray to God
for some proof of reincarnation, so that one day he might be able
to show the priests that they were wrong and he was right.

In the course of time John married Florence, a deeply religious
girl from a devoutly Baptist family. Although Florence found herself unable to accept her husband's strange obsession with reincarnation, she did accept, on the birth of her daughters Joanna and
Jacqueline, that they would be brought up in her husband's faith.
When the family moved north to Hexham in Northumberland,
where John set up business as a milkroundsman, Florence happily
sent Joanna and Jacqueline to the local Roman Catholic school.
Here the girls became popular pupils, and every Sunday, in company with their friend, nine-year-old Anthony Layden, they would
walk from their home to St. Mary's Church for the special Mass
held for the school's two hundred and fifty children. It was on

just such a Sunday, May 5, 1957, that Joanna, aged eleven, and Jacqueline, aged six, set out with Anthony Layden for what was to be the last time in their lives.

No one in the Pollock family could have known that four miles down the road, in the grand mansion called Horsley Hall, a fifty-one-year-old widow, Mrs. Marjorie Wynn, had suffered yet another night of the depression and insomnia she had endured for the last five years. Acutely depressed, at 5 A.M. she knocked on the door of the room in which her sister-in-law was sleeping, complaining that she had been unable to get any rest. Her sister-in-law eventually persuaded her to go back to her room. Mrs. Wynn was a Christian Scientist and had previously refused to have anything to do with doctors or any drugs they might prescribe, but shortly before nine o'clock she got dressed, swallowed fourteen aspirin and three phenobarbitone, and walked out of the house intending, as she later confessed, to end it all. She took the powerful dark-green Wolseley she had purchased not long before, headed out of her drive onto the A69 toward Carlisle, and let the drugs she had taken have their longed-for effect. Little more than moments later, a farmer, Charles Harrison, who was driving in the same direction, noticed the erratic behavior of the Wolseley ahead of him. As he followed, the car displayed disconcerting variations of speed, and at Battle Hill he saw it suddenly swing onto the wrong side of the road, exaggeratedly avoiding a parked van and causing an oncoming car to brake violently. Harrison realized that there must be something seriously wrong and decided to intercept the vehicle by overtaking it. He pulled almost alongside the Wolseley and was able momentarily to glimpse Mrs. Wynn in the driving seat before she swung out once more, forcing Harrison to drop back.

As the two cars sped through Hexham's Shafto Leazes, with houses on either side of the narrow road, Harrison—with a surge of horror—saw the Wolseley swing over to the wrong side of the road again, mount the opposite pavement, straighten up, then speed along the pavement, the driver's side of the car scraping the stone garden walls of the houses. In the merest fraction of a second before impact he spotted the three children walking along the pavement, helplessly facing Mrs. Wynn's oncoming vehicle. In the middle was the taller figure of Joanna Pollock, with little

Jacqueline on one side of her and Anthony Layde[n] closest to the wall. All three children were hand i[n] in his Sunday suit, the two girls in their school bla[zer] with the gold badges gleaming in the sunshine. [Nei]ther braked, nor tried to slow down. The nex[t] Phyllis Stafford, a housewife waiting at a bus sto[p] side of the road, saw the children tossed into the[ir] balls." A second later the Wolseley crossed back of the road and traveled on for some two hun[dred] eventually coming to a halt and beginning to r[oll] hill, with Mrs. Wynn slumped in the driver's s[eat] scious from the drugs, but otherwise uninjure[d] the car, applied the handbrake, and removed before rushing with Mrs. Stafford to where lying. But there was nothing either could do. [Jo]line Pollock had been killed instantly from th[eir] injuries. Anthony Layden, who had been thro[wn by] the impact, was found to be dead on arrival three had been the only children in the stree[t]

It was a sickening tragedy which made he[adlines in the] press the next day and, with the ensuing in[quest on the] unfortunate Mrs. Wynn, occupied the colum[ns of the] weekly *Courant* for several months to com[e. With great] courage, somehow John and Florence Po[llock managed to ex]punge feelings of bitterness and even to se[nd messages of] condolence and forgiveness to Mrs. Wynn[, who remembered] nothing of the incident and was by now g[iven over to psy]chiatric care. Shortly afterward, Floren[ce Pollock,] grateful for the kindness shown to her by of St. Mary's Church, made the decision the Roman Catholic faith. Meanwhile, th[e trauma of] the tragedy had made John Pollock even beliefs. Almost immediately he decide[d that the death of his] daughters was God's judgment on him f[or his belief in re]incarnation. He became convinced th[at God was] going to answer his prayer, and that r[eincarnated versions of] Joanna and Jacqueline would in due ti[me be returned to him.] Florence Pollock's genuine distaste he guise this belief, and for a while there

An identical mark, in an identical place, was clearly visible on the newborn Jennifer's left hip. What was strange was that there was no similar birthmark on twin Gillian. Intrigued and in his own mind powerfully fortified in his reincarnationist beliefs, John Pollock lost little time in making the case known in parapsychological circles. It was in this manner that it came to the attention of Dr. Ian Stevenson in Charlottesville.

After contacting and interviewing the Pollocks, Stevenson asked for a pathologist to take blood samples from the twins. The samples established a 98.8 per cent probability that the twins were monozygotic, i.e., from one single egg cell. To Stevenson this discovery was particularly important from the point of view of the brown birthmark and forehead line being found only on Jennifer. As he has commented:

> With identical twins you would expect both to have these birthmarks. If they cannot be attributed to a genetic factor, reincarnation becomes a plausible hypothesis.[9]

Four months after the twins' birth the Pollocks moved to Whitley Bay on England's Northumberland coast, where John had acquired a shop, and for the first three years of their infancy the girls never revisited Hexham. This fact gave Ian Stevenson an idea for a further test. Why not, he suggested to John Pollock, try taking Gillian and Jennifer back to areas of Hexham that their dead sisters had known well as a check on whether past-life memories might be reactivated?

To Florence Pollock's distinct unease, John welcomed the idea and so, when Gillian and Jennifer were about three years old, they were driven the thirty miles back to the town where their sisters had lived and died. They immediately behaved as if they had known it all their lives. As John Pollock has described the experiment:

> In Battle Hill, Hexham, we let them walk ahead of us, not guiding them. Suddenly one said: "The school's just around the corner." They couldn't have seen it because it was hidden by St. Mary's Church. But her sister said: "That's where we used to play in the playground." We went past Hexham Abbey. One said: "The swings and slides are over there." But

the swings and slides were in the park on the other side of
the hill, out of sight. And as we passed our old house they
both said: "We used to live there."

Only the dead Joanna and Jacqueline had gone to the school.
Only the dead Joanna and Jacqueline had ever played in the play-
ground. And how could the twins possibly remember the house
which they had left when they were just four months old and
never seen again? Dr. Stevenson asked to be kept informed of any
further relevant incidents which might occur, and accordingly
John Pollock kept a watchful eye for these. One such concerned
the dead Joanna and Jacqueline's old toys. The Pollocks had not
been able to bear to part with these and so when the family
moved from Hexham the cardboard box in which they were
packed was stored out of sight in the loft of the new premises at
Whitley Bay. Gillian and Jennifer were never told about the contents of this box, nor, at Florence Pollock's insistence, were they
told anything of their father's strange reincarnationist views. All
they knew of their dead sisters was that they had "gone to
heaven." But when the twins were four John suggested, not, one
suspects, without a certain degree of contrivance, that it would be
wasteful not to allow them at least some of the toys that Joanna
and Jacqueline had possessed. Accordingly two old dolls together
with a toy wringer were left outside their bedroom door.

It was Florence Pollock who witnessed the scene. The moment
Jennifer spied the two dolls she said, "Oh, that's Mary. And this
is my Suzanne. I haven't seen her for a long time." Then, turning
to Gillian, "And there's your wringer." Quite unprompted Jennifer had correctly given the names by which the dead sisters had
known the dolls, and equally correctly from the reincarnationist
point of view had attributed the wringer to the "older" sister's
ownership.

Another incident at about the same age took place one day
when the twins were out playing in a yard at the rear of the
Whitley Bay house, one backed by a lane used for parking cars.
Suddenly John Pollock heard hysterical screaming. Running out,
he found the pair crouched in a corner of the yard, huddled in
each other's arms, and repeating, "The car! The car! It's coming
at us!" Looking to where the twins were pointing, he saw in the

lane a car that had just started up, directly facing the twins, and theoretically presenting the very same aspect as Mrs. Wynn's Wolseley as it had swung fatally toward Joanna and Jacqueline.

The most macabre incident of all was an occasion on which Florence Pollock had left the twins quietly playing in their playroom while she worked downstairs. Unobtrusively returning to the room to check that they were all right, to her astonishment and horror she found Gillian cradling Jennifer's head in her hands and saying, "The blood's coming out of your eyes. That's where the car hit you." When John Pollock returned home to hear the story, it was accompanied by floods of tears from his wife, who was increasingly unable to bear such incidents. They appalled her and challenged her religious principles to the very foundations.

Fortunately for Florence Pollock, not long after the twins' fifth birthday the incidents ceased as mysteriously as they had begun. Today Gillian and Jennifer claim no trace of any memories purporting to be those of Joanna and Jacqueline, although Gillian still has a tendency to act as the older sister. John Pollock kept to his word that he would not ever discuss his reincarnationist ideas with them while they were young, and it was not until they were thirteen that Gillian and Jennifer learned anything from their parents of the strange circumstances surrounding the deaths of their former sisters and their own births and childhood. To this day the twins remain as puzzled by the story as any outsider to the family.

Effectively their dilemma is our dilemma. Can they really be the dead Joanna and Jacqueline reborn, the dead sisters' minds somehow having been translated into new bodies? Might some form of genetic memory be responsible? Alternatively, might they have been tuned into their dead sisters' memories by some peculiar property of time, their minds literally being "out of time"? For a serious scientist such as Stevenson, one of the first issues has to be that of determining exactly how much information can be relied upon. It is, for instance, indisputable that eleven-year-old Joanna and six-year-old Jacqueline Pollock were killed by Mrs. Wynn's Wolseley on Sunday, May 5, 1957, as the newspaper reports and inquest and trial records of the time describe only too graphically. Twin daughters Gillian and Jennifer were born to

John and Florence Pollock on October 4, 1958, as a check at Britain's General Register Office confirms. Although Jennifer's original forehead "scar" seems to have been erased by time, the brown thumbprint-like birthmark on her left hip, claimed to be identical with the one on the dead Jacqueline, is certainly still there and was displayed to millions of viewers during a British television program on the Pollock case in 1979. Beyond this, however, Stevenson acknowledges that there are many features inadmissible as real evidence. Dramatic though the twins' "replaying" of Joanna and Jacqueline's memories might have been, the only witnesses were John and Florence Pollock, and not always together. Florence died in 1979 and despite the openness and honesty with which John Pollock tells his family's story, he cannot by any stretch of the imagination be regarded as an unbiased witness. He has collected every conceivable book about reincarnation and the occult, and has recently begun dabbling in spiritualism. Ian Stevenson would therefore give the Pollock case no more than an intermediate rating, it having, in his words "the weakness that both girls are members of the same family, and that Mr. Pollock believes firmly in reincarnation."[10]

But, as Stevenson would also argue, it does not stand alone. Its credibility is immensely enhanced by other cases, many with tantalizingly similar features, all carefully recorded in the Stevenson files at Charlottesville.

CHAPTER 2

Some Difficulties
of Dr. Stevenson's
Reincarnation Evidence

I<small>AN</small> S<small>TEVENSON IS UNDER NO ILLUSIONS</small> that in order to succeed in establishing a clear scientific case for reincarnation he has a task as daunting as Charles Darwin's last-century arguing for the theory of evolution. With the same thoroughness as Darwin, over the past twenty years Stevenson has repeatedly traveled worldwide in search of his material—Alaska, Brazil, Turkey, Lebanon, Britain, and elsewhere in Europe, and most particularly to the more obviously reincarnationist countries such as India, Burma, and Sri Lanka. From the past-life-memory claimants he has come across, he has assembled files on some two thousand cases, many of these abundant with detail and corroborated by witnesses' testimonies. Where practical he has fed detailed statistical data into a computer, illuminating in respect of percentage trends. He has published in immense detail more than seventy of his cases, each tackled with admirable objectivity and thoroughness and written up in a dry-as-dust style directed single-mindedly at a scientific rather than a lay readership. And although he would wish for better, he is gradually being taken more seriously in some academic circles, with periodicals of the international prestige of the *Journal of Nervous and Mental Disease* having in recent years accepted pro-reincarnationist articles by him.[1]

But the serious question that arises is whether his judgment matches the standards of his methodology.

Undeniably there is justification for Stevenson's adopted field of study from the point of view that many of the characteristics of the Pollock case occur in many other examples, especially those to be found among the more reincarnationist countries. While one of the less impressive aspects of Gillian and Jennifer's past-life "memories" is that they derived from incidents that happened within their own family, more normally, and less explicably, many of Stevenson's cases are of children claiming to belong to a different home and different parents—"I am the son of Shankar of Vehedi" was announced by a three-and-a-half year old Indian boy whose father was actually one Girdhari Lal Jat from Rasulpur.[2] Such details can often be traced to someone who has indeed once lived. Among children of this type, Gillian and Jennifer's strange "reliving" of the death of their dead sisters is by no means unusual. Particularly during the evening or early morning many seem to lapse into a form of trance or delirium "reliving," complete with a change of voice, episodes meaningless or foreign to their observing parents. This condition may also occur spontaneously, perhaps when a child's family is traveling through an unfamiliar village, the child thereupon naming certain landmarks and claiming once to have lived there. Gillian and Jennifer's recognition of their dead sisters' dolls is repeated in numerous instances of past-life object and people recognition among Stevenson cases. Being wheeled along in his stroller, a two-year-old from Alaska burst out, "There's my Susie," pointing out an apparently unknown woman passerby.[3] Allegedly, the woman was the child's stepdaughter in his previous life.

The Gillian and Jennifer type birthmarks are similarly a feature of a high proportion of other past-life examples. Besides repetition of moles or nevi, commonly occurring in cases among the Tlingit Indians of Alaska, Stevenson reports having examined, on more than two hundred present-day subjects, replicas of knife, spear, and bullet wounds allegedly sustained by their deceased personalities,[4] also seventeen cases with birthmarks in the form of surgical scars, some complete with stitch-marks allegedly from operations undergone by the previous incarnations.

The particularly violent past-life death recalled by the twins is another common element among other, worldwide cases, over 75 per cent of Stevenson's Lebanese and Turkish examples and nearly 60 per cent of all his cases claiming to have died similarly violently in their past lives.[5] Symptoms of such a memory often manifest even before the child is able to talk, taking the form of seemingly inexplicable terrors, as in the case of one little Sinhalese girl, Shamlinie, who from birth could not bear to be bathed, and when she was six months old cried uncontrollably throughout her first bus journey. Allegedly, when she was able to talk, Shamlinie exhibited past-life memories corresponding to those of an eleven-year-old girl drowned after an oncoming bus had forced her off a narrow road into a ditch by a paddy field.[6]

Most persistently of all, just as in Gillian and Jennifer Pollock, whatever past-life memories the child has had tend to fade rapidly after the age of four or five so that by the age of ten virtually everything will have been forgotten apart from scraps that may have been learned from parents.

With the intermingling of all these features, it is instructive to appreciate in more detail other specific Stevenson cases alongside that of the Pollocks. One certainly very representative example is that of Ravi Shankar,[7] an Indian boy born in July 1951 in one of the sprawling suburbs of the city of Kanauj in Uttar Pradesh. His father was called Ram Gupta, but when he was only two years old Ravi Shankar began to claim that he was the son of a barber called Jageshwar from Chhipatti, a neighboring district of Kanauj. He said that in his past life he was murdered by one Chaturi, a washerman, and Jawahar, a barber, who cut his throat. He kept asking for toys he had possessed in his previous life and added special credence to his story by pointing out a long linear mark, strongly resembling a knife wound, allegedly visible around his throat since birth. This he claimed was the scar from the murder. Since the Chhipatti district is only half a mile from the Shankar home, it was not long before Ravi Shankar's claims came to the ears of a barber called Jageshwar; he visited Ravi Shankar's parents and revealed that he had once had a son, Munna, who at the age of six had been murdered in precisely the circumstances described by Ravi Shankar. The murder suspects were indeed a washerman named Chaturi and a barber named Jawahar, but although they were arrested and at one stage Chaturi made an unofficial confession, they were never brought to justice because there was insufficient evidence. The date of Munna's murder was just six months before Ravi Shankar's birth.

By the time Ian Stevenson heard of the case, Ravi Shankar's father had died and Ravi Shankar himself, now eleven, had forgotten most of the details. Nonetheless, a schoolmaster had written down some of Ravi Shankar's utterances as early as 1956 and from these, together with what relatives and neighbors could remember, Stevenson managed to piece together some twenty-six items of factual information that seemed to support Ravi Shankar's case as a genuine reincarnation memory. Particularly impressive was the still-visible birthmark scar which Stevenson has described from an examination he made of it in 1964:

> Under the ridge of the chin, somewhat more on the right side than the left, I observed a linear mark crossing the neck in a transverse direction. It ran about 2 inches long and was about ⅛ to ¼ inch wide. It was darker in pigment than the surrounding tissue and had the stippled quality of a scar. It looked much like an old scar of a healed knife wound. This, I was told, was what remained of a considerably longer mark which, during early childhood, had also lain lower in the neck about one third the distance between the sternal notch and the chin.[8]

Another typical case of Stevenson's, but in which he was able to be on the scene much earlier, has come from the beautiful, predominantly Buddhist island of Sri Lanka, formerly Ceylon. On August 7, 1969, in a hospital not far from Colombo, the capital, was born a boy by the name of Sujith.[9] When the child was a few months old his parents divorced and his mother took him to live at her mother's home in Mount Lavinia, three miles south of Colombo. But before he was two, Sujith began to say that his proper home was at Gorakana, eight miles to the south. He gave his name as Gorakana Sammy, and said his father was called Jamis and that he had a bad eye. Sammy himself worked with the railways, and also made money by selling arrack, a particularly powerful alcoholic spirit made from fermented coconut juice. He was killed by a passing lorry as he walked away after a quarrel with his wife Maggie one day.

As before, Stevenson found that there actually was a deceased individual who matched Sujith's story. A Buddhist monk friendly with Sujith's family discovered that just six months before the child was born a fifty-year-old arrack merchant named Sammy Fernando died at Gorakana in precisely the circumstances described. The son of a man called Jamis who had a slightly disfigured eye, Sammy Fernando was sacked from the Ceylon Government railways early in his working life. Turning to the profitable—though illegal—manufacture and sale of arrack, Sammy produced a particularly potent variety which he imbibed a little too excessively in the course of his trade. Bouts of drunkenness accompanied by violence and obscene language blotted an otherwise happy marriage to a local beauty named Maggilin ("Maggie") Alwis, and during one such episode, after he had pursued Maggilin from the house, Sammy was killed by a passing lorry as he paused unsteadily at a roadside kiosk for some cigarettes.

In this case, after exhaustive interviews with Sujith's family, Stevenson managed to accumulate no less than fifty-nine statements from the young Sujith which seemed to check out with information supplied by Sammy Fernando's widow Maggilin, and others who had known the original Sammy. Although Sujith had no relevant birthmarks to display, the child seemed to compensate for this by some rather quaint behavioral peculiarities. For example, besides his addiction to arrack and outbursts of obscene language, Sammy Fernando smoked Four Aces cigarettes and was particularly fond of hot spicy foods. These tastes the young Sujith expressed in various ways. Whenever anyone was going out shopping he would implore them to buy him arrack and Four Aces cigarettes. Although he would invariably receive nothing more intoxicating than a Coca-Cola or lemonade, he would sit drinking this from the bottle in a manner said to be identical with that remembered of Sammy Fernando, complete with the arrack drinker's characteristic belch. He would swear volubly and obscenely in a manner quite untypical of his mother and grandmother, and he would voice strong demands for *wade* (a highly spiced patty), manioc and hot curries—all dietary preferences typical of the arrack drinker and most unusual in young children.

The dossier of cases that Stevenson has built up is, then, osten-

sibly an impressive one. He has been careful everywhere to list
each statement attributed to his subjects, and to set out the
verifications he has been able to make, the names of his informants, and any conflicting or corroborating elements that may be
relevant. However, the crucial question that arises is: Has he
found something truly new and scientific or has he been cruelly
misled by a series of tall stories and acting performances of the
Sujith type? To try to establish the more likely of these alterna-
tives is by no means easy, yet there are some valuable guidelines
to be gleaned from looking above and beyond the evidence
Stevenson has presented, also from even superficial inquiries into
the sort of individuals Stevenson has chosen to rely on for both
the searching out and the actual subject matter of his material.

One of the first difficulties for any overall validity of Stevenson's material is the absence among his published cases of any discernible rules that might govern the hypothetical existence of reincarnation. We might expect, for instance, to be able to
determine whether there is some kind of waiting period or
"limbo" between one life and the next, or whether we are somehow reconceived in a new body the moment the old one dies. Unfortunately, no ready guideline seems evident. Some of Stevenson's subjects seem to wait five years or more between lives; in
some cases, the past-life personality does not die until as little as
two weeks before the birth of the new personality, and an instance even occurs of the past-life personality seeming not to have
died until three and a half years *after* the new one was born (see
table, page 17).[10] Similarly, when we would expect to be able to
determine whether or not we shift nationality and/or geographical region between one life and the next, Stevenson's cases
reveal no logical pattern (see table, page 19).[11] Some personalities appear to migrate three hundred miles or more between
lives; others stay within the same village or even within the same
family. There are also alarmingly inconsistent patterns between
one culture and the next: almost all Tlingit Alaskan Indian cases,
for instance, purportedly reincarnate within the same family,
while almost all Asian Indian cases outside it.

If these attempts at broad statistical evaluation reveal grounds
for distrust in substantial numbers of Stevenson's cases, this becomes yet more acute when we begin to look at some of the indi-

viduals upon whom he has leaned most heavily for the supply of his material. Among his acknowledgments of those who assisted him in Sri Lanka and India there stands out one strikingly Anglo-Saxon name, that of Francis Story. An Englishman born in 1910 and therefore eight years Stevenson's senior, Story accompanied Stevenson on many field trips and "added greatly to the gathering of data and their analysis" until his death in 1971.[12] Some mea-

THE INCONSISTENCIES OF THE DEATH TO REBIRTH TIME INTERVAL AMONG IAN STEVENSON'S PUBLISHED REINCARNATION CASES

Subject	Alleged Past Life Personality	Death Date	Birth Date	Death to Birth Interval			No Interval Suggesting possession?
				Suggesting preconception waiting period	Suggesting instantaneous death-conception	Suggesting period when fetus unoccupied	
Indian Cases							
Prakash	Nirmal	April 1950	Aug 1951	1 yr 4 mths			
Jasbir	Sobha Ram	May 1954	Late 1950				3½ yrs after birth
Sukla	Mana	Jan 1948	March 1954	6 yrs 2 mths			
Swarnlata	Biya	? 1939	March 1948	9 yrs*			
Ravi Shankar	Munna	Jan 1951	July 1951			6 mths	
Mallika	Devi	? 1949	Dec 1955	6 yrs			
Parmod	Parmanand	May 1943	Oct 1944	1 yr 5 mths			
Gopal Gupta	Shaktipal	May 1948	Aug 1956	8 yrs 3 mths*			
Sunil	Sri Khrishna	April 1951	Oct 1959	8 yrs 6 mths			
Jagdish Chandra	Jai Gopal	Oct 1922	March 1923			5 mths	
Bishen Chand	Laxmi Narain	Dec 1918	Feb 1921	3 yrs			
Kumkum Verma	Sundari	? 1950	March 1955	5 yrs			
Rajul Shah	Gita Thacker	Oct 1959	Aug 1960		10 mths		
Puti Patra	Lolita Bera	? 1956	Nov 1964	8 yrs			
Dolon Mitra	Nishith	July 1964	Aug 1967	3 yrs 1 mth			
Veer Singh	Som Dutt	? 1937	? 1948	11 yrs			
Ramoo & Rajoo	Bhimsen & Bhism	April 1964	Aug 1964			4 mths	
Sri Lankan Cases							
Gnanatilleka	Tillekeratne	Nov 1954	Feb 1956	1 yr 3 mths			
Wijeratne	Ratran Hami	July 1928	Jan 1947	19 yrs			
Ranjith	Unidentified Englishman	?	? 1942		*Unknown*		
Shamlinie	Hemaseelie	May 1961	Oct 1962	1 yr 5 mths			
Gamini	Palitha	July 1960	Nov 1962	2 yrs 4 mths			
Disna	Babanona	Jan 1958	April 1959	1 yr 3 mths			
Lalitha	Nilanthie	Feb 1953	Aug 1962	9 yrs 6 mths			
Ruby Kusuma	G. G. Karunasena	July 1959	Sept 1962	3 yrs 2 mths			
Indika	Weerasinghe	Dec 1960	July 1962	1 yr 7 mths			
Sujith	Sammy Fernando	Jan 1969	Aug 1969			7 mths	
Mahes	Jolly de Silva	June 1964	March 1965		9 mths		
Warnasiri	Ananda	Oct 1956	Nov 1957	1 yr 1 mth			
Wijanama	Unidentified Kandy Moslem	?	Aug 1959		*Unknown*		
Tlingit Cases							
Jimmy Svenson	John Cisko	Mid-1950	Nov 1952	2 yrs 6 mths			
William George Jr	Wm George Sr	Aug 1949	May 1950		9 mths		
Corliss Chotkin	Victor Vincent	Spring 1946	Dec 1947	1 yr 6 mths			
Norman Despers	Henry Despers	? 1937	? 1944	7 yrs			
British Cases							
Gillian & Jennifer Pollock	Joanna & Jacqueline Pollock	May 1957	Oct 1958	1 yr 5 mths			
Lebanese Case							
Imad	Ibrahim Bouhamzy	Sept 1949	Dec 1958	9 yrs 3 mths			

*Possible intervening life claimed

The inconsistencies of the death-to-rebirth time interval among Ian Stevenson's published reincarnation cases.

sure of Stevenson's regard for Story may be gained from the fact
that the volume of his Sri Lankan cases is dedicated to Story's
memory, and from his eulogistic introduction to Story's posthu-
mously published *Rebirth as Doctrine and Experience*.[13] Yet once
this and other of Story's writings are studied a particularly
disquieting feature becomes obvious. At the age of sixteen, Story
was converted to Buddhism, and followed this reincarnationist
religion obsessively from that age on. He remained a bachelor all
his life and spent altogether some twenty-five years in Asian countries, immersing himself more and more deeply in the Buddhist
way of thought. This in itself might be regarded as not necessarily
detrimental to his objectivity, but such a charitable view is not
sustained by the actual content of his writings. In *Rebirth as
Doctrine and Experience*, among many anecdotal and quite
uncheckable past-life cases, Story refers to one independently
known, that of Mary Cohan (actually "Cohen"), deriving from a
regression conducted by the British hypnotist Henry Blythe. According to Story, "the authenticity of this case has been established beyond reasonable doubt."[14] Henry Blythe is now dead,
and, according to his son Peter, "nothing can be found to corrob-
orate and prove that . . . Mary Cohen . . . ever lived before
upon this earth. We should not allow wishful thinking to mag-
nify and distort the very flimsy evidence."[15]

A similarly slipshod approach to the recording of data is indicated elsewhere in the same work by two references to an Indian child, Pramod, as having been born on March 15, 1944.[16]
Story not only quotes these as deriving from a sworn statement,
but also notes jubilantly that this gives an interval of "just nine
months and six days"[17] after the death of the boy's alleged previous personality—which we are no doubt intended to interpret as
a case of instant reconception. But a cross-reference to the case of
the same child (in this instance referred to as "Parmod") in
Stevenson's *Twenty Cases Suggestive of Reincarnation* reveals a
birth date of October 11, 1944,[18] a discrepancy that Stevenson has
omitted to explain and which inevitably leaves one wondering
who and what to believe. Such inaccuracies may seem petty, but
if they occur in cases we can check, then we may justifiably suspect them in those we cannot. It is perhaps relevant to note that
despite twenty-five years of living in the East, Story never learned

GEOGRAPHICAL DISTANCE BETWEEN SUBJECT'S BIRTHPLACE AND ALLEGED PAST-LIFE PLACE OF DEATH				
Subject	Alleged Past Life Personality	Place of Death	Place of Birth	Estimated Geographical Distance
Indian Cases				
Prakash	Nirmal	Kosi Kalan	Chhatta	6 miles
Jasbir	Sobha Ram	Vehedi	Rasulpur	20 miles
Sukla	Mana	Bhatpara	Kampa	11 miles
Swarnlata	Biya	Katni	Shahpur	100 miles
Ravi Shankar	Munna	Kanauj	Kanauj	½ mile
Mallika	Devi	Vellore	Madras	70 miles
Parmod	Parmanand	Moradabad	Bisauli	90 miles
Gopal Gupta	Shaktipal	Mathura	Delhi	100 miles
Sunil	Sri Khrishna	Budaun	Aonla	22 miles
Jagdish	Jai Gopal	Benares	Bareilly	300 miles
Bishen Chand	Laxmi Narain	Shahjahanpur	Bareilly	30 miles
Kumkum Verma	Sundari	Darbhanga	Bahera	25 miles
Rajul Shah	Gita Thacker	Uttumnagar	Vinchhiya	60 miles*
Puti Patra	Lolita Bera	Salgachya	Kapasberya	1 mile
Dolon Mitra	Nishith	Burdwan	Calcutta	60 miles
Veer Singh	Som Dutt	Sikarpur	Salikheri	5 miles
Ramoo & Rajoo	Bhimsen & Bhism	Uncha Larpur	Sham Nagara	10 miles
Sri Lankan Cases				
Gnanatilleka	Tillekeratne	Talawakele	Hedunawewa	16 miles
Wijeratne	Ratran Hami	Uggalkaltota	Uggalkaltota	No distance
Ranjith	Unidentified Englishman	Kotte or England	Kotte	1½ miles or 5400 miles
Shamlinie	Hemaseelie	Galtudawa	Gonagela, Colombo	1 mile
Gamini	Palitha	Nittambuwe	Colombo	20 miles
Disna	Babanona	Wetewa	Udubogawa	3 miles
Lalitha	Nilanthie	Colombo	Pilyandala	10 miles
Ruby Kusuma	G. G. Kurasena	Aluthwala	Galle	10 miles*
Indika	Weerasinghe	Colombo	Pilyandala	10 miles
Sujith	Sammy Fernando	Gorakana	Homagama	18 miles
Mahes	Jolly de Silva	Colombo	Colombo	4 miles
Warnasiri	Ananda	Kimbulgoda	Kirikita	5 miles
Wijanama	Unidentified Kandy Moslem	Kandy	Wehigala	16 miles
Tlingit Cases				
Jimmy Svenson	John Cisko	Klukwan	Sitka	100 miles
William George Jr	Wm George Sr	at sea	Unrecorded	Indeterminable
Norman Despers	Henry Despers	Dundas Bay	Hoona	35 miles
Corliss Chotkin	Victor Vincent	Angoon	Sitka	40 miles
British Cases				
Gillian & Jennifer Pollock	Joanna & Jacqueline Pollock	Hexham	Hexham	No distance
Lebanese Case				
Imad	Ibrahim Bouhamzy	Khriby	Kornayel	25 miles

Geographical distance between the subject's birthplace and alleged past-life place of death.

a single modern Asian language.[19] For Stevenson to have chosen him as an investigator and data analyst seems, at the very least, questionable.

Another investigator chosen by Stevenson has been Dr. Jamuna Prasad. Dr. Prasad, described early in Stevenson's work as "Deputy Director of Education, Uttar Pradesh" and later as "Director, Bureau of Psychology, Allahabad," apparently stage-managed most of Stevenson's field trips to India, and acted as his "principal interpreter" during most interviews with the subjects and witnesses of Indian cases. In this role he must be regarded as one of Stevenson's major informants, and Stevenson records that the staff of Dr. Prasad's Bureau of Psychology found many of his subjects for him. Just as Story was an ardent Buddhist, so Prasad is an ardent Hindu, with a particular interest in spreading Hindu beliefs in reincarnation. Inquiries made in Allahabad reveal that his bureau is little more than a counseling service for high school students and it would appear to be coexistent with what is described as "The Allahabad Institute for Kundalini Research" of which Prasad is also director. Prasad's own blurb describes this as founded by "the pious wish and zeal of a team of Psychologists and Educationists who have for some time past been interested in researches on Yoga and psychic powers and other paranormal phenomena."[20] From this description, can one expect Prasad and his colleagues—sincere though they undoubtedly are—to have an objective approach to reincarnation?

There are further misgivings when Stevenson's subjects themselves are the object of scrutiny. Although Stevenson has long promised a volume devoted to some American and European examples supporting his theory,[21] such a work has not yet appeared —he has not even published the Pollock case—and the vast majority of his material derives from the traditionally reincarnationist countries of the East, peoples culturally a world apart from his own. To communicate with such individuals, Stevenson has been obliged all too frequently to resort to interpreters—not the best means for gauging subjects' trustworthiness. And to compound the difficulties, reliable records by which verbal testimonies might be independently corroborated are all too rare in oriental countries.

These very same circumstances make it difficult for any independent Western investigator to cross-check Stevenson's cases, but there is one essentially armchair test which can be applied which does rather critically reveal that there has to be something seriously wrong. It is a sad fact that the vast majority of India's millions live in the most abject poverty while the wealthy, who are often excessively so, are very few and far between. By any normal law of averages one might therefore expect the vast majority of Stevenson's Indian cases, whatever their present-day social circumstances, to possess past-life memories as poor people. We might also expect it to be very rare indeed to find any child remembering a life of high birth and riches. Yet as the table on page 22 reveals, the very reverse is the case. When we analyze the economic and social background of all thirty of Stevenson's most fully published Indian and Sri Lankan cases it is quite apparent that in no less than twenty of these the past-life individual concerned was either wealthy or from a higher caste than the family of the present-day child. Millionaires, factory owners, and high-caste Brahmins proliferate among the previous incarnations, while the present-day child frequently belongs to a low-caste family of particularly precarious means. And perhaps most pertinent of all, among Stevenson's published Indian and Sri Lankan cases there is not a single example in which a child from a present-day rich or even middle-class family remembered a former life of grinding poverty, and only one in which the past life was socially inferior in any way.[22] From this information the possibility can scarcely be ignored that poor families may have tried to pass off their children as reincarnations of dead offspring of the rich in order to reap some financial advantage.

It cannot be said that Stevenson has not considered fraudulence. Quite frequently he alludes to it, only to reject it on insubstantial grounds. He argues, for instance, that the emotional displays by the subjects are too convincing—though the desperate and unscrupulous among Eastern peoples are as versatile in convincing histrionics as their compatriots elsewhere in the world. He also argues that he can see no clear motive, yet his cases of Gopal Gupta, Veer Singh, Sunil, and Jagdish Chandra, each of whom insisted that in their past life they were of a higher caste than that into which they were born in their present existence, look like four rather unpleasant little boys putting on a thinly dis-

Subject	Social Circumstances	Alleged Past Life Personality	Social Circumstances	Markedly More Affluent Past Life
Indian Cases Prakash	Lived in mud hut	Nirmal	Family prosperous shopkeepers living in brick house	✓
Jasbir	Father a low caste peasant	Sobha Ram	Family high caste Brahmin	✓
Sukla	Father a railway worker	Mana	Family wealthy and well-known	✓
Swarnlata	Father relatively poor office assistant	Biya	Living in well-appointed house	✓
Ravi Shankar	Unspecified	Munna	Father a barber, but case of notoriety value	N
Mallika	Unspecified but seemingly middle class	Devi	Unspecified but seemingly middle class	✗
Parmod	Father a Sanskrit professor	Parmanand	Prosperous shopkeepers	✗
Gopal Gupta	Father kept a petrol filling station	Shaktipal	Father a millionaire	✓✓
Sunil	Father poor and often unemployed	Sri Khrishna	Very wealthy factory owner	✓✓
Jagdish	Father a lowly lawyer	Jai Gopal	Father a wealthy Brahmin	✓
Bishen Chand	Father a railway clerk	Laxmi Narain	Father a wealthy landowner	✓
Kumkum Verma	Father a homeopathic physician	Sundari	Blacksmith caste	✗
Rajul Shah	Well-to-do Jain family	Gita Thacker	Hindu grain merchant with own shop	✗
Puti Patra	Father very poor laborer	Lolita Bera	"Distinctly more prosperous" but also notoriety value	✓N
Dolon Mitra	Father relatively humble poultry supervisor	Nishith	Extremely wealthy family	✓✓
Veer Singh	Father low caste Jat	Som Dutt	Father a high caste Brahmin	✓
Ramoo & Rajoo	Brahmin farmers	Bhimsen & Bhism	Brahmin farmers but notoriety value	✗N
Sri Lankan Cases Gnanatilleka	Family lived in jungle	Tillekeratne	Family had house in valley with paved roads	✓
Wijeratne	Farming family	Ratran Hami	Of same family but notoriety value	✗N
Ranjith	Unspecified	?	Unidentified Englishman	✓
Shamlinie	Father poor agricultural worker	Hemaseelie	Father worked at a bakery	✗.
Gamini	Junior bank employee	Palitha	Family markedly more wealthy with car and electricity	✓
Disna	Father a merchant	Babanona	Middle class, had income	✗
Lalitha	Father partly educated. Lower middle class	Nilanthie	Family lived in very much larger home than Lalitha's	✓
Ruby Kusuma	Father a poor vegetable seller	G. G. Karunasena	Wealthy landowner	✓✓
Indika	Father a poor cultivator	Weerasinghe	Wealthy owner of building contracting business	✓✓
Sujith	Mother a divorcee of uncertain means	Sammy Fernando	Well-known successful crook	✓
Mahes	Air Force instructor	Jolly de Silva	Wealthy upper middle class alcoholic	✗
Warnasiri	Father a relatively humble farmer	Ananda	Father an affluent school headmaster	✓
Wijanama	Father a poor carpenter	?	Unidentified wealthy Kandy Muslim	✓

✓✓ Past life personality of quite exceptional wealth
N Case having notoriety value—i.e. past life personality a murder victim, or murderer

Comparative social circumstances of Ian Stevenson's published Indian and Sri Lankan cases.

guised act to earn themselves better food and an exemption from drudgery. From Stevenson's own evidence Veer Singh, for example, openly asked for one third of the property of his past-life father Laxmi Chand, then subsequently lost interest when Chand, through a reverse in fortunes, became considerably poorer than Veer Singh's present-life father.[23] Gopal Gupta's father seems to have taken a suspicious delight both in encouraging potentially lucrative newspaper interest in his son and basking in the attention and liberality of the visitors that streamed to his door in the wake of the publicity.[24] Specific accusations that parents coached their children in the past-life memories are mentioned but dismissed both in this instance and in respect of Dolon Mitra,[25] Sunil,[26] Ravi Shankar,[27] Puti Patra,[28] and Shamlinie[29]—and there may well have been others. No less than three of Ravi Shankar's neighbors alleged that the child had been taken by his father to visit the barber Jageshwar on one occasion before making his reincarnation claims. And it seems suspiciously more than coincidence that no less than three different relatives or friends of Sammy Fernando lived within 250 yards of the home of Sujith's mother, one of these literally backing onto the Sujith household.[30] While in both the Ravi Shankar and Sujith cases the families involved denied prior knowledge of each other, it cannot be overlooked that Stevenson, so prolific with other information, invariably tells us all too little about the characters and background of the parents, the most vital informants in each case. Such an omission does not inspire confidence.

But although these circumstances reveal serious grounds for believing that Stevenson may have let through rather more fraudulent cases than he would care to concede, there are considerable numbers of his cases where such an interpretation cannot be justified. As I have said, a single Indian example does involve an actual downgrading of caste. The child in question, Kumkum Verma,[31] the daughter of an educated and prosperous landowner from Bahera, seems to have remembered a life as a woman from a lower, blacksmith caste, one Sundari of the nearby city of Darbhanga who died five years before Kumkum was born. How can a case of this sort be explained?

What is of interest about Kumkum is not so much her identification with a past-life personality, but her striking behavior when recalling her memories, particularly during the evenings, when there was usually only one person around. She seems to have gone into states of near delirium so intense that her parents, fearing for her health, positively discouraged her from summoning up memories of her past life. One persistent feature, which her mother could not fail to notice during these attacks, was the child's frequent references to snakes and her lack of fear of these in ordinary life—one day when a live cobra fell out of a tree at her school Kumkum even went up to it and stroked it on the hood. While Stevenson only saw in this a parallel with the life of the dead Sundari, who had kept a live cobra as a kind of guard dog for her valuables, Kumkum's mother saw a significance of a different sort. Despite having five other children she clearly remembered that during this pregnancy she dreamed vividly and memorably of a girl child surrounded by snakes. During this pregnancy she also developed pica-type[32] cravings for milk, fruit, and salted foods, all of which tastes were subsequently displayed by Kumkum, and had not been possessed by the dead Sundari. A case such as this, with its less-detailed memories, accompanying delirium, and an obviously related dream experienced by the mother during pregnancy is by no means alone.

Another typical Stevenson case is that of a Burmese girl, Tyn Aung Myo, who had deliria involving memories of a World War II Japanese soldier:

> She remembered being near a pile of firewood and about to cook a meal when an airplane came over. She recalled that at that moment the Japanese soldier she claimed to have been was wearing short pants and a big belt, but had taken off his shirt . . . The pilot of the airplane spotted the Japanese soldier and dived at him, spraying machine-gun bullets. The Japanese soldier ran around the pile of firewood in an effort to escape, but a bullet struck him in the groin. He died immediately.[33]

Tyn Aung Myo's memories were even vaguer than Kumkum's, offering no clue to the identity of the Japanese soldier, and no town or family name. But what suggests a powerful parallel to the Kumkum case is that Tyn Aung Myo's mother recalled a dream during her pregnancy which was likewise unmistakably linked with her daughter's subsequent memories. As she told Stevenson, toward the end of her pregnancy she dreamed three times at five- to ten-day intervals of a stocky Japanese soldier wearing short pants and no shirt who kept following her and saying he was coming to stay with her. These maternal "announcing dreams," as Stevenson calls them, feature in other Burmese cases,[34] and also across the other side of the Pacific Ocean among the Tlingit Indians of Alaska.[35]

Herein, then, lies the other and potentially far more authentic aspect of Stevenson's material. While it is likely, even demonstrable, that by insufficient criticism Stevenson has let in rather more fraudulent reincarnation claims than he would care to concede, conversely, his work seems to include, unrecognized by him, striking potentially genuine evidence for a mother's mental imagery somehow being transmitted to her unborn child. Sadly, in no case does Stevenson seem to have attempted to trace the real-life traumas that might have given rise to the maternal dream, a most regrettable omission. A maternal dream transmitting mechanism could, for instance, explain much of the otherwise so puzzling Pollock case. It can scarcely be doubted that during her pregnancy with the twins Florence Pollock must have played and replayed in her mind the events of the life and death of her earlier daughters Joanna and Jacqueline, and it seems by no means inconceivable that she passed these on to the fetal Gillian and Jennifer.

Adding credence to this idea are some intriguing recent findings in gynecological research. English obstetrician Dr. Michele Clements of the City of London Maternity Hospital has recently demonstrated beyond reasonable doubt that the fetus not only hears stimuli external to the womb, such as music, as early as four months after conception, but also reacts to these and unconsciously retains the memories into adult life.[36] Independently, Dr. Carl Sagan has argued that a considerable portion of a fetus's uterine existence is spent in dreams, dreams which can scarcely derive from the fetus's own life experiences.[37] It is but a short step to the view that during pregnancy a mother's mental traumas, of whatever origin, may be unconsciously transmitted to the unborn child, so that the child subsequently takes on what is merely the illusion of past-life memories by identifying itself with the victim of the traumas. Such a view is well supported by the in-family nature of the past-life memories in many of the more credible Stevenson cases (such as the Pollocks and those among the Tlingits), and by the disproportionately high number of Stevenson children who identify themselves with the victim of a murder or a similar sudden, violent death. Although one objection to this explanation may be the difficulty of birthmarks being created by maternal dreams, as we shall see from a later chapter even this is not as implausible as it first appears. It should, in any event, be observed that while in his publications during the past twenty years Stevenson has referred to numerous cases involving birthmarks, he has yet to publish a single supportive photograph.[38]

"Either he is making a colossal mistake, or he will be known (I have said as much to him) as the Galileo of the twentieth century."[39] Almost certainly this assessment of Stevenson, made by a medical colleague, is far too simplistic. A moderate view of Stevenson's material is that it is neither totally spurious nor the basis for scientific acceptance of reincarnation as a law of nature that the psychiatrist has long hoped for. Stevenson's prime error would seem too great an absorption in the reincarnation hypothesis, with too little attention given to an unfettered exploration of the undeniably fascinating aspects of the human mind that his work touches on. And even this muted criticism must be set against the high standards Stevenson has set in a field hitherto all too dominated by the dubious and the uncheckable—as demonstrated even by the two ostensibly sound British examples we are about to consider.

CHAPTER 3

Two Unacceptable
British Cases

"AH-YITA-ZHULA!"

It was with these words, uttered in Blackpool, England, on August 8, 1931, that a young woman known as Rosemary allegedly began speaking in Ancient Egyptian.[1] Listening to her intently was a fifty-one-year-old doctor of music, Frederic H. Wood, who had over many years become increasingly immersed in spiritualism.

As Wood already knew, Rosemary, whom he had consulted as a spiritualist medium, claimed to be the reincarnation of a young temple dancer called Vola, living in the reign of the eighteenth-dynasty pharaoh Amenhotep III. Supposedly Vola was the voice-piece of a Babylonian princess named Nona, one of the harem of the pharaoh, who drowned while escaping from some Egyptian priests. Originally Vola communicated only in English, but when she began speaking what seemed to be Ancient Egyptian, which she claimed to hear from Nona as she passed from "semi-trance" to normal consciousness, nothing could have been a greater source of excitement for music teacher Wood. A few months earlier, after he had written an article about Rosemary for a psychic magazine, Wood had received a letter from a professional Egyptologist, inquiring if actual Ancient Egyptian words ever came through during the consultations. The Egyptologist, Alfred J. Howard Hulme, who lived in the South of England, near Brighton, had impressed Wood by his obvious interest in spiritualism, and by the fact that he was apparently so conversant with the language of Ancient Egypt that he had already compiled a unique Esperanto-Egyptian grammar and dictionary.

Wood made a careful phonetic transcription of Rosemary's strange utterance and sent this off to Hulme. To his delight he learned by letter a few days later that it was indeed Egyptian, and on September 5, 1931, Wood attended Rosemary once again. Another strange message came through, this time including the Egyptian word *ankh*, meaning life. Wood again wrote out the sounds phonetically, sent off the transcript to Hulme, and received the same assurances that the language was that of Ancient Egypt. More and more phrases followed, to total some nine hundred in the course of the next five years. All these, analyzed by Howard Hulme, turned out to be "infallible" Egyptian. Every phrase received was carefully numbered by him and transcribed into its original hieroglyphics. The eventual outcome was a book, *Ancient Egypt Speaks*, published in 1937, and written jointly by "A. J. Howard Hulme, Hons. Cert. in Egyptology, Univ. of Oxford," and "Frederic H. Wood, Mus. Doc. Dunelm, Hon. R.C.M.," which claimed to have "completely restored the spoken language of Ancient Egypt."

This was a remarkable claim, for then and now. Although the hieroglyphics of written Ancient Egyptian have been decipherable for some one hundred and fifty years, these convey only the consonants of Egyptian words, not the vowel sounds, which can only be guessed at. Since no living person knows how Ancient Egyptian was spoken, for Rosemary's utterances to be verified as genuine would effectively constitute the most dramatic possible evidence for some form of transmission from the dead, the kind of evidence that Ian Stevenson has long dreamed of finding. So what is the truth behind Rosemary's Egyptian? The clue lies in the manner Hulme has described his findings. Given that Nona, from whom Rosemary heard the words, was supposed to be a Babylonian living in Egypt, Hulme might have used this as an excuse to explain any grammatical errors in the received language.

Instead, he chose to eulogize Nona's "infallible use ot Egyptian grammar." As Hulme explained patronizingly for the benefit of the uninitiated:

> It is difficult to show and explain to the ordinary reader the purely technical and most convincing features: such as period characteristics, survival of archaisms, grammatical accuracy, peculiar terms, ordinary elisions, figures of speech, etc., *but they are intensely evidential.*" [Hulme's italics][2]

To show off just how conversant he was with the language of Ancient Egypt, Hulme pointed out with impressive technicality how, for instance, Nona had used the Egyptian "Old Perfective" ("a quaint style of almost prehistoric age") which would allegedly have come easily to her because it was related to the "Permansive" of Akkadian, her native Babylonian tongue.[3] He acknowledged self-deprecatingly that it had taken him twenty hours to draw up twelve questions to put to Nona in Ancient Egyptian, whereas Nona had given sixty replies to these in just an hour and a half. This he calculated was seventy-three times faster than his own composition. As on the very next page he described Nona speaking "at a speed seventy times the capacity of the world's best Egyptologists" it might reasonably be inferred by the uninitiated layman that Hulme himself was close to being one of the world's best Egyptologists.

But was he? And in particular, just how competent was his Ancient Egyptian? Even back in the 1930s these questions did not go unasked. Battiscombe Gunn, Oxford University's Professor of Egyptology, was never sent a review copy of *Ancient Egypt Speaks* but he studied the book with a knowledgeable eye as soon as its publication was brought to his attention. In June 1937 Gunn published in the *Journal of Egyptian Archaeology*[4] a stinging review of *Ancient Egypt Speaks* that has seemingly passed unnoticed by reincarnationist writers. With biting sarcasm Gunn not only showed up clearly and unequivocally the amateurishness of Hulme's grasp of Egyptian grammar, but also how clumsily this "Hons. Cert. in Egyptology, Univ. of Oxford" had twisted what he received from Wood's transcriptions to fit his own imaginings of what the original Egyptian may have been:

Nona said, for instance, *ā vā' stee vóng tu*. Most scholars would have made nothing of that, but Mr. Hulme saw that it must be ⟨hieroglyphs⟩ , meaning "to enumerate, now, the items." But he saw also that Nona's pronunciation was not quite all that it should be (after all, she was a foreigner), or else that Dr. Wood had not got it quite right—we do not know which; for he amends this utterance to *eph ê; stirf ó(ng) tu*. Again, confronted with *ah donk zeet y ra von(k)*, he perceived that Nona, speaking as always with "infallible use of Egyptian grammar," had said ⟨hieroglyphs⟩ "so that the ear may give it life," which she ought to, or must, have really pronounced *ā'(r)di onkh zi't, iraf, (ng)ā' nkh*.

Even without a knowledge of Ancient Egyptian the general reader can appreciate for himself how Hulme manipulated the sounds he heard. But could Gunn's attack have been unfair, a piece of spiteful academic prejudice? Hulme's workings were kindly rescrutinized for me by John Ray, Reader in Egyptology at the University of Cambridge, and translator of the recently published Ancient Egyptian text *The Archive of Hor*. As John Ray was able to confirm, there could be no mistaking Hulme's incompetence. In a number of sentences Ray found inexcusably bad grammar, and he pointed out that Hulme had frequently confused Middle Egyptian and Late Egyptian in his translations of Nona's phrases, despite the fact that these languages were as distinct as classical Latin and present-day Italian. In any phrase sent to him by Wood, Hulme had in fact a wide choice of Egyptian words that could be made to fit the consonants to give his preferred meaning. To give an English example: if the word "bend" were received, for instance, the possible words to be matched against this would be any with the letters "b", "n", and "d". Thus Hulme's possible choices would include band, bend, bind, bond, banned, and boned to name but a few. And if even then he was not satisfied with his choice he could always argue that Rosemary had pronounced incorrectly when hearing the original, or Wood had transcribed incorrectly when listening to Rosemary,

and thus alter his translation to fit. On this basis Hulme could conjure up an Ancient Egyptian meaning for any set of sounds produced by Rosemary. Of course, if all Hulme's reconstructions made faultless sense it would be a different matter, but this is far from being the case as a casual glance at the pages of *Ancient Egypt Speaks* makes clear.

If there may remain just the glimmer of a possibility that despite Hulme's bunglings of the translations, Rosemary may somehow have been genuinely tuned in to Ancient Egypt, this too can be discounted by John Ray's expert analysis. Rosemary described visions she had seen of life in eighteenth-dynasty Thebes, among these a colorful street scene with camels being used as transport and people traveling in tents on the camels' backs. As Professor Gunn had observed and John Ray has confirmed, at the period of the eighteenth dynasty the camel was not used in Egypt as a beast of domestic transport.[5] In short, the whole Rosemary saga, language and visions, would seem worthless fiction.

So who were Wood, Rosemary, and Hulme to have involved themselves in such an affair? Dr. Wood, who was born in India in 1880, was undoubtedly a sincere man and talented musician, much respected as the organist and choirmaster at Blackpool's Church of St. John the Evangelist for forty-five years until his death in 1963. Shock and grief at the sudden death of his brother Dennis in a London car accident in 1912 seem to have driven him to take an interest in spiritualism. According to Mr. Ray Donovan of Blackpool, Wood's literary executor, he had arrived at the hospital too late to see his brother alive. Standing by the body, he vowed he would let nothing obstruct his attempts to find his brother in the "spirit world."

Wood, impelled into spiritualism in this manner, would seem in his turn to have encouraged Rosemary in her mediumship. The twentieth-century Rosemary shared with Wood an interest in music and singing, but in the late 1920s she became disturbed by trance-like spells when her hand seemingly wrote by itself. Wood interpreted this as the sure sign of natural psychic powers. This led to his using Rosemary to contact his dead brother (together with the nineteenth-century Prime Minister William Ewart Gladstone!) and ultimately to the circumstances of *Ancient Egypt Speaks*.

We know Rosemary was "always slightly aloof" in manner, so no doubt it was at her insistence that her true identity remained concealed in connection with this case. Certainly Wood guarded the secret well but when she died in 1961, just two years before Wood, it was revealed that she was Ivy Carter Beaumont, born in Blackpool on June 7, 1893, and a schoolmistress by profession until her retirement in 1955. She remained a spinster throughout her life. Almost certainly her utterances, some of which were recorded on a Gramophone disc, were similar to the speakings in tongues commonly claimed among pentecostals and charismatics, which when investigated rarely turn out to be any true language either living or dead. The only difference is that these were identified as genuine Ancient Egyptian by a man making himself out to be a professional Egyptologist. It is in this key area—the credentials of Alfred J. Howard Hulme—that the regrettable spuriousness of the Rosemary saga at last becomes clear.

A. J. Howard Hulme's photograph stares out from the pages of *Ancient Egypt Speaks* as that of a serious and scholarly looking young man—but even this is not all that it appears. A casual glance at the date on the back reveals that the photograph was taken in 1914, nearly a quarter of a century before the publication of the book, when Hulme was, in fact, sixty-seven years old. A harmless enough piece of vanity, maybe, but then we notice that while Dr. Wood's photograph shows him in his University of Durham academic robes, Hulme appears in no such garb. Another trivial point, perhaps, but not when we find that obscurity surrounds any "Hons. Cert. in Egyptology" issued by the University of Oxford, and further mystery surrounds any A. J. Howard Hulme ever having been a member of that University. The plain fact of the matter is that Hulme could never have been a properly qualified Egyptologist in any academically recognized form. As Wood himself should have realized, no serious scholar, on the basis of the single phrase "Ah-yita-zhula!" could conceivably have identified Rosemary's utterances as Ancient Egyptian, when the vowel sounds of Ancient Egypt's spoken language were then, and still are now, quite unknown. Furthermore, given a breakthrough in retrieving the spoken language of Ancient Egypt, from however unorthodox a source, would not any self-respecting academic have consulted colleagues and sought to have his data cross-checked? The members of the British Egyptological fraternity are few in number at any one time, and they all know each other. It is plain that not only did Hulme fail to consult anyone else, but, as Professor Gunn specifically noted, he did not even invite Oxford's Egyptologists when there was a lecture on his findings in that city shortly after *Ancient Egypt Speaks* was published.[6]

So who was he? Suffice it to say that his real name would seem not to have been even Howard Hulme, but merely A. J. H. Howard. Born in 1870, his prime interest in life was a love of art, and it would seem to be this that brought him to the attention of the wealthy Port Sunlight industrialist Lord Lever, who in 1911 put Howard in charge of his growing art collection.[7] This included a small museum containing some, though not many, Egyptian antiquities. Interest in these probably prompted Howard to acquire, from Gardiner's *Egyptian Grammar*, published in 1927, the scanty knowledge of Ancient Egyptian he displayed, though it is just possible that Lever sent him on some privately arranged crash course to Oxford, thus justifying the mysterious "Hons. Cert." At all events, the present Lady Lever Art Gallery's very limited knowledge of Howard suggests that he achieved no great impact on the Lever collection. By 1922 a Mr. S. L. Davidson had been appointed curator of an improved and more permanent collection, such Egyptian antiquities as Lord Lever possessed had been sold, and Howard, by now married, had moved south[8] to end his days in a cottage set high on the hillside of Ovingdean, just outside Brighton in Sussex. The title deeds of the cottage—which he renamed "Egypt's Way"—describe him as an artist and this seems corroborated by an interview reported in the *Brighton and Hove Herald* of January 8, 1938, in which he is referred to as a retired art teacher. The older inhabitants of Ovingdean remember him and his wife more for their recluse-like habits and interest in spiritualism. Why he should have chosen to add Hulme to his surname from the time he left Port Sunlight is anyone's guess, the ghost of a clue perhaps lying in the fact that this was Lady Lever's maiden name.[9] But we can be certain that nothing in Howard's career justified the arrogant "professional Egyptologist" stance he took for *Ancient Egypt Speaks*. It would be unfair to suggest he deliberately intended to deceive. He was sensitive, artistic, and, like Wood, overly interested in spiritualism. More than likely his only crime was to allow his active imagination far too much license in applying to Rosemary's utterances his minimal knowledge of Ancient Egyptian. But that he was never the recognized, properly qualified Egyptologist that he tried to appear is no longer in doubt. He died, aged eighty-one, at Brighton on September 29, 1951.

From a case in which the main character was certainly not all that he appeared, we turn now to one in which, by contrast, the key individual's credentials are impeccable. Dr. Arthur Guirdham[10] was born in Cumberland, England, in the year 1905. Like Dr. Ian Stevenson he has been a psychiatrist; he was educated at Oxford and was senior consultant in the Bath clinical area for more than twenty years until his retirement ten years ago. Like Stevenson he has become associated with reincarnation, in his case in respect of a thirteenth-century French heretical sect called the Cathars or Albigensians, of whom, with others, he now claims to have reincarnation memories. But it is there that the comparison with Ian Stevenson ends, for the truly perplexing issue with Guirdham is the incompatibility of the presentation of his case with the professional standards that might be expected from someone of his background and training.

It was in May 1962 that a West Country doctor referred to Guirdham an attractive housewife in her early thirties, suffering from persistent nightmares. The housewife, whom Guirdham has called Mrs. Smith for reasons of medical anonymity, described to the psychiatrist how the nightmares took the form of a man entering a room in which she was lying on the floor. The man's approach would fill her with terror, and she would wake up screaming so loudly that her husband was concerned that she would wake the street. These nightmares were now occurring two or three times a week. From interviewing Mrs. Smith and studying her case notes, Guirdham learned something of her unusual early history. She was of Roman Catholic parentage and had nearly died from peritonitis during her early teens, her condition having been so serious that to her terror a priest and nuns actually arrived to administer the Last Sacrament. In the wake of the peritonitis she became delirious and during this babbled repeatedly about having another baby (which was subsequently interpreted as a reference to a childbirth in a previous existence). Not long after she recovered from the peritonitis she began to suffer occasional but dramatic bouts of unconsciousness, which were not unlike epileptic fits.[11] At about the same time the problematic nightmares started, initially at two- to three-month intervals, but now of a quite unendurable frequency. According to Guirdham, Mrs. Smith's nightmares ceased after his very first consultation with her, although he was initially unaware of this, and in accordance with his usual practice advised further visits. During the next four years, via consultations and lengthy correspondence, Mrs. Smith heaped upon Guirdham information about mental torments which she confessed she had never previously told anyone. Some were odd precognitive experiences, but by far the most arresting were "memories" of a life among the Cathars in the Languedoc region of France during the early thirteenth century. Mrs. Smith told Guirdham that at school she had frequently lapsed into bouts of reverie in which she seemed to be with a lover of the French Cathar period named Roger. On her exercise books she would scrawl scraps of Provençal poetry which she heard from Roger. By the time she was eighteen or nineteen years of age Roger had become in her dreams an almost real and constant part of her life and in 1954, following a visit to France, she began, and as quickly abandoned, a novel about it all.

It so happened that Guirdham had been fascinated by the history of the Cathars for many years, and he became more and more involved with what Mrs. Smith disclosed. He found certain items of information which she produced extraordinarily impressive. She described, for instance, the Cathars wearing dark-blue robes when according to most historical sources the Cathar habit was black. A consultation by Guirdham with a French expert on the Cathars, Professor Duvernoy, revealed new findings that the Cathar robes had indeed been dark blue at the time Mrs. Smith described. Then she spoke of her thirteenth-century lover taking loaf sugar for a chest complaint. Initially Guirdham found himself unable to believe this, but then he discovered not only that loaf sugar was rare though known in France at the period, but also that it was specifically recommended for diseases of the chest by Arab doctors, whose influence was particularly strong in the Languedoc at the time of the Cathars.

For Guirdham perhaps the most convincing of all Mrs. Smith's strange reminiscences were those dealing with the persecution of the Cathars by the official Roman Catholic Church, during which Roger died in prison and the thirteenth-century Mrs. Smith was led out to be burned at the stake. During her late teens, she recorded a dream of her Cathar death:

> The pain was maddening . . . I thought of Roger and how dearly I loved him. The pain of those wicked flames was not half so bad as the pain I felt when I knew he was dead. I felt suddenly glad to be dying. I didn't know when you were burnt to death you'd bleed. I thought the blood would all dry up in the terrible heat. But I was bleeding heavily. The blood was dripping and hissing in the flames. I wished I'd had enough blood to put the flames out. The worst part was my eyes . . . I tried to close my eyes but I couldn't. They must have been burnt off.[12]

Guirdham, approaching sixty when Mrs. Smith began confiding her strange dreams, says he is known among his family as a Doubting Thomas. Although he has acknowledged an already latent interest in past-life-type experiences, this intriguing patient and her outpourings undeniably dramatically intensified his leanings. Like Guirdham, Mrs. Smith had a marked antipathy toward Roman Catholicism, in her case because of a particularly strict upbringing in this faith, her traumatic Last Sacrament experience, and an excommunication following her marriage to an Anglican. Like Guirdham, Mrs. Smith had French ancestry. And, like Guirdham, she had this strange fascination with the Cathars.

Although he had hitherto had no past-life memories of his own, Guirdham now came to believe that he himself had been the Roger of Mrs. Smith's dreams, historically Roger-Isarn de Fanjeaux who died in prison in 1243. Mrs. Smith too seems to have recognized this—which was why her nightmares ceased so abruptly on her first consultation with Guirdham; she had rediscovered her lost *amour*. Two lovers from thirteenth-century France had found themselves seven centuries later as patient and psychiatrist in Bath, England. And so, after his retirement from the Health Service, Guirdham wrote *The Cathars and Reincar-*

nation, a by no means unconvincing account of the whole extraordinary saga, with Mrs. Smith's real identity carefully protected.

Had Guirdham halted there or, even better, accompanied his popular account of the affair with an in-depth psychiatric study of the case—so far as this was possible once he had declared his own involvement—it might yet have been possible for his claims to be treated with due seriousness. Instead, however, he met other people who not only reinforced his belief that he had once been a Cathar, but also convinced him that they, too, had been with him at that time. In the autumn of 1968, while Guirdham was convalescing from an illness, a seemingly chance acquaintance was struck up with a breezy, fresh-faced, blond-haired woman who happened to be passing his house in her car one day. This was Clare Mills (another Guirdham pseudonym), a spinster in her early forties, who already had an interest in psychic occurrences as subsequent events were to prove. She was on no more than nodding acquaintance with Guirdham before she asked him pointedly whether the words "Raymond" and "Albigensian" meant anything to him. Of course they did. Albigensian was another word for Cathar. Raymond, which might have meant anything to anybody, was for Guirdham the name of the young Count of Toulouse who gave protection to the Cathars. Although Guirdham insists he did not encourage her, Clare Mills, like Mrs. Smith, began to pour out to Guirdham her strange dreams and reveries about life among the Cathars. Like Mrs. Smith, she said her problems had begun shortly after a near-death illness (diphtheria at the age of five). Like Mrs. Smith, she started to have a powerful recurring dream shortly after the illness—she dreamed she was walking barefoot toward a stake and heaped faggots, accompanied by others, while someone struck her back with a burning torch. Miss Mills could actually go one better than Mrs. Smith with her dream injury. She could produce evidence. One day, not long after she had met Guirdham, she asked him if he would examine a distressing muscular pain in her hip, which had persisted for the past two months. The cynical might question why she had not consulted her GP, but the request, with which Guirdham complied, had the useful result of revealing to the as-

tonished psychiatrist Miss Mills's most unusual birthmark. As
Guirdham described it:

> . . . When I looked at her left hip I saw slightly above it a
> belt of strange protuberances arising from her skin. I have
> never in my life seen anything comparable. Some of these
> structures were an inch long. Some were bladder-shaped and
> at first sight resembled polypuses, but they were without
> stalks and attached to the skin by a relatively broad base. In
> shape and appearance they looked like large blisters produced
> by burns. The difference was that there was no fluid in their
> interior and they were semi-solid. The distribution of these
> semi-solidified vesicles was significant. They extended from
> above her hip across her back to the mid-line.
> "I suppose this is part of your dream. This is where the
> burning torch hit you?" I spoke lightly and not at all insis-
> tently.
> "Yes," she said simply.[13]

If Guirdham had not been hooked already, he was now, and so
his relationship with the enigmatic Miss Mills, though always totally platonic, deepened. Throughout 1971 Miss Mills continually
recounted names and phrases that kept popping inexplicably into
her head, names invariably discovered by Guirdham to have some
connection with the Cathars.

Like Rosemary, Miss Mills had experienced spells of automatic
writing in the form of messages that would appear on a pad at
her bedside during her sleep. By now these had stopped and instead Miss Mills began to see recognizable faces in dreams and visions, people in dark-blue robes who inevitably had to be Cathars.
A Cathar woman named Braïda appeared to her and taught her
special Cathar natural healing techniques. From what was revealed Miss Mills came to believe that in the thirteenth century
she had been Esclarmonde de Perella, a redoubtable woman who,
though crippled, played a key part in the Cathars' defense of their
spectacular Pyrenean fortress of Montségur in 1244. When the
besieging Roman Catholics forced them to surrender, Esclarmonde and two hundred others had chosen to die at the stake
rather than recant. It was on her way to the stake that she

allegedly received the burning brand injury so enigmatically still visible on the body of the twentieth-century Miss Mills.

If the emergence of these three reincarnated Cathars in the form of Mrs. Smith, Miss Mills, and Guirdham is a little hard to believe, more was to follow. In *We Are One Another* (a follow-up to *The Cathars and Reincarnation*), Guirdham describes how a friend of Miss Mills's came onto the scene in October 1971. Betty Butler had just been to France to recuperate after the death of her husband and she returned enchanted with the Montségur region. When Betty died of a stroke not long after this, her mother found among her effects a drawing book in which she had scrawled, apparently at random, while recovering from a severe attack of scarlet fever at the age of seven. New study of the jottings revealed that they were not at all meaningless. These were shown to Guirdham and he recognized them as unmistakable Cathar names and details about the murder of two Inquisitors and their entourage by Cathar sympathizers at Avignonet in 1242. It seemed that Betty too had been a Cathar, and was subsequently identified as Hélis de Mazerolles, Guirdham's thirteenth-century sister. Further revelations followed in quick succession. As a result of these, Guirdham came to believe that Betty Butler's mother, who died not long after her daughter, had been the reincarnation of Bruna de la Rocque d'Olmes, wife of a Montségur sergeant-at-arms; another friend of Miss Mills's, Jocelyn, the widow of an Army officer, also from Bath, was found to be the reincarnation of the Braïda appearing in Miss Mills's night visions; Miss Mills's eighty-year-old retired businessman father was found to have been Bertrand Marty, a Cathar bishop; a former boyfriend of Miss Mills's had been Pons Narbona, another sergeant-at-arms, and a Cathar convert. Uniting all these individuals was their Catharism, which Guirdham painted as harking back to a pure, primitive Christianity of the days of the Apostles, untainted by the corruptions later imposed by Rome. These corruptions included suppressing belief in reincarnation, which according to the Cathars was a true and original tenet of Christianity.

In 1976, in *The Lake and the Castle*, the last of his Cathar trilogy, Guirdham unveiled a new, third phase to his extraordinary

saga. Not only did all the twentieth-century individuals whom we
have come across—mostly living within a twenty-mile radius of
Bristol—know each other as Cathars, but they experienced stir-
ring adventures together in other epochs as well. During the sev-
enth century Guirdham, Clare Mills, Jocelyn, Betty, and several
others had been members of the reincarnationist Celtic Church
before, like the Cathars, they met a sticky end at the hands of
those allegedly corrupted by Roman doctrines. The group had
also known each other in France during the Napoleonic era, and
in Roman Britain during the fourth century A.D.

But how much of the Guirdham saga can we accept as fact,
and how much can we attribute to individual or collective imagination, albeit innocent and well-meaning? Perhaps the biggest
enigma lies in the personality of Guirdham himself. He had a
long and successful career as a psychiatrist and today in retirement he is a well-established individual with a practical-minded,
no-nonsense wife and a sizable family of children and grandchildren. Furthermore, in contrast to the Rosemary saga, the historical details behind his writings are by no means easy to fault.
We can argue that his picture of the Cathars and the early Celtic
Church is romanticized and idealized beside that painted by history, but in fairness it has to be said that what has come down to
us has been written by the Celts' and Cathars' enemies, and just
conceivably Guirdham's version could be the more accurate.

There are, however, detectable weaknesses in his work. *The
Cathars and Reincarnation* contains some serious errors and inconsistencies. On page 67, for example, he says that Mrs. Smith
nearly died of peritonitis at the age of eleven; by page 101 this
had become the age of thirteen or fourteen, a puzzling discrepancy bearing in mind that Guirdham, as her psychiatrist, should
naturally have had full access to her medical records. A textual
comparison between this work, published in 1970 when he was
sixty-five, and *The Lake and the Castle* (1976), published when
he was seventy-one, is even more worrying. In the earlier work
Guirdham only quoted directly from written correspondence between himself and Mrs. Smith, for which he had the original
sources in front of him. Where he reported conversations he
outlined the mere substance of these, with no attempt to repro-

duce the actual words. Despite his use of pseudonyms, he confined accounts of events to the strictly factual throughout; his description of Miss Mills's birthmark, for instance, was clinical and objective. But in *The Lake and the Castle* he reported lengthy conversations verbatim, even though there is no evidence he was using a tape recorder at the time, and it would have been physically impossible for him to copy down the words as spoken. Previously he had annotated his work carefully, noting where events occurred and in what circumstances, but now many episodes were written up in the style of fiction even though they were supposed to have been real occurrences. At this point it is, perhaps, not irrelevant to note that one of Guirdham's sidelines for many years, quite separate from the Cathar writings, has been the writing of occasional works of fiction.

Given that Guirdham himself says he is known as a Doubting Thomas, it might be expected that on receiving a serious inquiry into his claims he would be prepared to offer some means of verifying that his cast of twentieth-century Cathar reincarnations, their identities all carefully concealed by pseudonyms, in his books, have been real people. This has not, however, proved to be the case. When I asked to be allowed to interview Mrs. Smith, and gave assurances that her anonymity would be fully respected if that was what she wished,[14] Guirdham's first reaction was perhaps a perfectly justifiable one: he was quite unable to release Mrs. Smith's identity because of the confidentiality of the psychiatrist-patient relationship. I then pointed out to him that it was quite obvious from his books that Mrs. Smith was now a personal friend. Surely, with appropriate assurances regarding the continued concealment of her identity, he might be prepared to ask her to release him of his professional obligations? Pressed on the matter, he said he had indeed asked Mrs. Smith, but she refused under any circumstances to be interviewed because she did not want the slightest risk of her neighbors thinking her an "odd woman."[15] I therefore diverted my efforts toward meeting the mysterious Miss Mills. It was clear from Guirdham's books that, unlike Mrs. Smith, she had never been a formal patient of his, so surely he could not claim difficulties on the grounds of medical ethics? Furthermore, unlike Mrs. Smith, Miss Mills seems positively to have thrived on her reincarnationist experiences. Again the promise was made that Miss Mills's identity would be kept confidential if this was necessary. Yet as before Guirdham politely but firmly blocked the suggestion, initially claiming that Miss Mills was unwilling to talk to anyone "not on the same wavelength" as herself, then later that she was suffering from cancer and was too ill to be interviewed.[16]

Balked of access to the two key living characters of Guirdham's books, I now turned my attention to others. Several of the main twentieth-century characters in Guirdham's Cathar books died between the years 1972 and 1976, among these Betty Butler and her mother Jane, Mr. Mills, Jocelyn, and others. Perhaps Guirdham would be prepared to release the identity of just one of these deceased, such as Betty Butler, so that some independent checking could be made of the details described? Guirdham ignored this request without explanation.[17] The final approach tried was in many ways the most telling of all. Guirdham had referred in *We Are One Another* to Miss Mills's "burning brand" birthmark. But he had published no photograph of it, a most regrettable omission, particularly because of the similar omission by Ian Stevenson and the importance both psychiatrists have attached to birthmarks as evidence for reincarnation. I therefore argued that as Miss Mills was undergoing hospital treatment surely Guirdham, with his medical connections, might even now be able to arrange for a medical photograph to be made of the birthmark, or even for its existence simply to be confirmed by a formal statement from some independent physician such as Miss Mills's own GP? Again Guirdham ignored this request.[18]

It should be emphasized that although Guirdham could offer me no help on these points, from every other point of view he behaved courteously and hospitably to me. Indeed, as some reassurance that his whole saga was not just a retired psychiatrist's pipe dream, he offered two items of potential corroboration. One was a torn-off cover of an old-fashioned school exercise book, printed on one side "English—Progress Test No. 12," with on the other in neat schoolgirl handwriting the words *Je vos ameroie Rogier*. This was said to have been written by Mrs. Smith during one of her schoolday reveries back to the time of the Cathars, and thoughtfully preserved by her father in an old trunk of personal effects. The other was a child's drawing book, somewhat yellowed with age, with drawings in crayon said to have been done by the seven-year-old Betty Butler when recovering from scarlet fever (see below). Guirdham has reproduced line versions of these drawings in his *We Are One Another* and there can certainly be no doubting their childish style of drawing and lettering, nor the occurrence of a succession of names of Cathar significance. But is it enough to justify the extraordinary claims of the whole Guirdham saga? It is perhaps not irrelevant to note at this point the incompatibility of the "rules" of the Guirdham claims—reincarnation in groups, and with centuries-long "limbo" periods—with the already-disparate yet quite dissimilar "rules" of Stevenson's material.

One of the "Cathar" drawings allegedly made by Betty Butler when she was seven years old. Guirdham interprets the two recumbent human figures as those of two inquisitors murdered during the Cathar troubles at Avignonet. The word AVIONEY is claimed by Guirdham to be "an exceptionally good attempt on the part of an English child of seven to render the pronunciation of Avignonet in her own language."

Because of such imponderables and the obstructions to any independent cross-checking, Arthur Guirdham's claims, for quite different reasons to those of Howard Hulme, have to be dismissed as similarly unacceptable. This is particularly sad because if only Guirdham could have been more open, and properly rigorous in his presentation, his might surely rank as among the most remarkable evidence for reincarnation ever produced, carrying all the more authority for coming, like Stevenson's, from a professional psychiatrist. As it is, although his material may be absolutely genuine (which he has assured me it is), he must be said to have thrown away every chance of being taken seriously. However, there are many further branches of the tree of past-life memory claims, and it is now overdue that we turn to what many would consider a particularly major one, that of past lives recalled via hypnotic regression.

Another of the Betty Butler drawings featuring, on Guirdham's interpretation, three names of Cathar significance: PIERE ROG refers to Pierre-Roger de Mirepoix, commander of the garrison at the Cathars' mountain fortress of Montségur; PONS is said to refer to Pons Narbona, a Cathar sergeant-at-arms; CONGOST is "indubitably" Gaillard de Congost, a Cathar participant in the massacre at Avignonet.

CHAPTER 4

The Bridey Murphy Case

As MOST PRACTICING hypnotists know to their cost, the history of hypnosis has been a long and not altogether happy one.[1] The Ancient Egyptians recorded their use of hypnosis at least as early as three thousand years ago; the Greeks, the Druids, and the Chaldeans are all said to have practiced it in various forms, and to this day the Seminole Indians of Florida use it as a protection against alligators. But it was given a bad name by the showman-like Anton Mesmer, who around the time of the French Revolution had hordes of neurotic Austrian women literally in convulsions with it. For some years after Mesmer's death the practice, which was named after him, carried with it the universal opprobrium of orthodox medical men. As an early issue of the British medical journal *Lancet* remarked:

> Mesmerism is too gross a humbug to admit of any further serious notice. We regard its abettors as quacks and impostors. They ought to be hooted out of professional society.[2]

Today renamed hypnosis (a mid-nineteenth-century piece of word coining, after Hypnos, the Greek god of sleep), the practice has at least progressed from the province of robed Svengalis working in darkened, incense-filled rooms and making esoteric hand-

passes in front of the eyes of their subjects. The modern hypnotist will often be an unassuming, casually dressed individual
practicing in an ordinary sitting room. He may aid the induction
of a hypnotic trance by asking the subject to stare at some bright
object, but it is increasingly common for him to use nothing more
than the rhythmic sound of his own voice, steadily, insistently
suggesting sleep. Among some 10 per cent of the population there
is simply no effect, but in around 80 per cent the steady suggestion of sleep will cause their eyes to roll back under their eyelids
and they will fall into a state of what is generally termed a light
hypnotic trance. On the suggestion that they cannot unclasp their
hands, for example, they will indeed find themselves unable to do
so, to their own astonishment. On appropriate suggestions they
may prove insensitive to pain and able to hold a limb immobile
for what would otherwise be impossible lengths of time. Among
some 10 per cent of the population the phenomena are even more
remarkable. These people are usually referred to as deep-trance
subjects, and they may be able to undergo major surgery without
conventional anesthetics, and with no sign of pain or discomfort.
Childbirth may also be painless. Should they be suffering from
some skin disorder, even something as severe as ichthyosis or
"fish-skin,"[3] such subjects may find that the disorder will disappear simply by repeated suggestions on the part of the hypnotist.
Nervous problems from bed-wetting to compulsive chain-smoking
may also be cleared by appropriate suggestions.

But although hypnosis has acquired a more respectable image
since Mesmer, medical men have not lost all their reservations
about it, and with some good reason. From many points of view
hypnosis remains unpredictable. The very procedure of inducing
the state requires a practitioner to go into what can only be
regarded as an act, alien to most doctors' whole methodology.
Many patients will not become hypnotized at all, or will go into
too light a trance, potentially ruinous to the confidence on which
the patient-doctor relationship depends. There is the added problem of the length of time induction of a hypnotic trance can take.
Most pertinent of all from the medical standpoint, to this day
there is no known method for determining whether the state of
hypnosis even exists, let alone what it is.[4] In what appear to be
states of the deepest trance, a hypnotized subject's brain waves,

measured on an electroencephalogram (EEG machine), show identical patterns to those of waking consciousness and are quite distinct from those for normal sleep. It is important to understand some of these complexities and anomalies of hypnosis as we turn our attention to the branch of the subject most central to our study—the mysterious phenomenon of hypnotic regression.

As has now been demonstrated on countless occasions, it is possible to suggest to a subject that he or she is back at an earlier time in their life, say at a birthday party. Even though consciously the events of that party may have been long forgotten, under hypnosis the subject seems to be back there once more; he may list the presents received, the friends attending, or the food eaten. Regressed to childhood, the subject may even write in an ostensibly childish hand and speak in a childlike voice. Interpretations differ as to exactly what is happening, but few deny that some significant heightening of memory takes place. No case illustrates this better than one in which hypnotic regression was used with undeniable effectiveness by the Scientific Interrogation Unit of the Israeli CID.[5]

Early on the morning of July 18, 1976, an Israeli Egged bus set out from the town of Kfar Sava, bound for Tel Aviv. In accordance with prevailing security regulations the driver had checked the vehicle thoroughly in advance for any suspicious packages, and found it completely clear. As was absolutely normal on the journey, numerous Israeli and Arab passengers on their way to work boarded and alighted at the frequent stopping points along the way. Then, as the bus was just outside a cinema, it was suddenly shattered from within by an explosion, injuring eleven passengers, one seriously. On-the-spot forensic tests established that someone had planted a homemade bomb, coupled to a wristwatch timing device, inside a food tin on the baggage rack. But who? And at what point on the journey?

The bus driver, Simha Wolf, who was unhurt, was immediately asked by the CID whether he could remember any suspicious-looking passenger among those who had boarded and alighted from his vehicle that day, particularly anyone carrying a package. To Wolf it seemed an impossible question to answer. At the time of the explosion the bus had been packed with at least forty people, and many more had got on and off earlier. Try as he might, and even though he was trying to remember events of only hours before, his conscious memory offered not the slightest clue that might pinpoint a particular individual. The Israeli detectives then asked Wolf if he was prepared to submit to hypnosis, explaining to him that regression was a technique sometimes helpful in these circumstances. To their satisfaction Wolf agreed, and proved a particularly good "revivification" subject, one of those who when regressed seem to literally see and live events again. He was told to go back in time to the start of his bus journey that morning, and to report every incident, however trivial, as it replayed before him. Although the Israeli detectives expected a long and tedious recital, to their astonishment what seemed to be a vital clue tumbled out almost immediately. As Wolf described his mental images of the passengers waiting at the Kfar Sava station, he found his attention drawn to a dark-skinned youth carrying a parcel. The youth was only going a short way, and as Wolf described handing him the change from the proffered fare money, an image of the palm of the youth's hand was replayed under the hypnotic memory. The skin glistened in a cold sweat, most unusual when it was still the cool of the early morning. Onward replay of the journey established that this particular youth alighted very soon at a stop just on the outskirts of Kfar Sava. Now that they had a Number One suspect, the Israeli detectives concentrated on playing in Wolf's mind the brief moment in which he had seen the youth face to face during the exchange of the fare money. When waked from hypnosis, Wolf was able to help construct a detailed Identikit picture from this, together with the information that the youth was slim, clean-shaven, about seventeen years old, with a dark complexion and black hair, and wearing a white shirt, light blue trousers, and a brown leather belt with copper studs. The details were immediately released to the Israeli news media, and the likeness together with accompanying description was so good that shortly afterward the young terrorist was identified and arrested, and subsequently confessed to the crime.

Since that particular case and others like it, hypnotic regression has been slowly and quietly becoming an increasingly useful tool for police forces around the world. By an ironic coincidence, the very same week the Israelis were questioning Simha Wolf, California police were using hypnosis to prod the memory of an American bus driver whose school bus, complete with twenty-six schoolchildren on board, was ambushed and ransomed by an armed gang near San Francisco.[6] Regressed to the moment he and the children were bundled into vans, the U.S. driver managed to see in his mind the last five letters and digits of the number plate of one of the vans, a vital clue leading to the gang's capture. In the last four years New York's Police Department Hypnosis Unit claims to have used the technique in some four hundred cases, 75 per cent of these providing significant new information.[7] And at the time of writing, Scotland Yard is said to be beginning its own trials with hypnotic regression, although its unofficial use over some years by British police forces appears to have been more extensive than has been publicly admitted.[8]

But any glib assumption that the individual under regression produces a totally accurate reproduction of his memories should be immediately countered by some words of caution. Even though speaking of recall of relatively recent incidents in their subjects' lives, the Israeli CID team have observed in a report on their work:

. . . it is believed that the information elicited by hypnotic techniques of memory improvement is generally reliable, but . . . [it] should be considered as a working hypothesis and not looked upon as fact.[9]

As they have also observed, stress, which may cause the repression of the memory of a particularly traumatic incident, may actually help its preservation once the repression is relieved by hypnosis. But conversely, where there is questioning on incidents that may have seemed trivial to the hypnotized subject at the time, fantasy or misleading information may be all that hypnosis achieves. No one has given more attention to this problem than Professor Martin T. Orne, a psychologist of Harvard University.

In one case[10] from studies made by Orne during the 1950s a hypnotized subject was asked the name of the teacher he had had when he was in his first year at school, aged six. Although initially he found himself unable to remember, when it was suggested that he might describe what she looked like this seemed to act as a spur to his memory, and he promptly announced that his teacher's name was Miss Curtis. Closely questioned, he gave repeated assurances that he was now confident that this was her name. He was then brought out of hypnosis, having been told that he would remember nothing of what had transpired in the hypnotic state, and asked who Miss Curtis might be. At this point he unhesitatingly identified her as a teacher not in his first school year but "near the end of my grammar school." He was quite sure she was not his teacher during his first year. What seems to have happened is that under hypnosis the subject seized upon the first available name of a teacher he knew, and having done so convinced himself, and the hypnotist, that Miss Curtis had indeed been his teacher at the age of six, even though this was total fantasy.

Another subject of Orne's was a young Harvard University student whom we will refer to as Harry.[11] When Harry was just six years old he had produced a series of drawings which his parents had carefully stored away as souvenirs of his childhood without ever showing them to him again. Discovering the existence of these from Harry's parents, Orne arranged for them to be sent to him in a sealed envelope, and found to his considerable satisfaction that they even carried the date on which Harry had drawn them, October 23, 1937 (a. page 52). After he had established that Harry was a particularly good deep-trance hypnotic subject, Orne regressed him under hypnosis to the very date of October 23, 1937 and asked him to draw again the same objects that, at the age of six, he had drawn that day—a tree, an Indian tepee, a map, a man, a balloon, and a house. Harry dutifully scribbled away, producing a series of drawings that could indeed, to the inexperienced eye, pass for those of a six-year-old (b. page 52). However, when Orne compared them with what Harry had actually drawn at the age of six he discovered to his surprise that they were quite different. As a check on the experiment he therefore repeated the procedure five days later, with the same result. After a further three weeks Orne decided to repeat the experiment yet again, but this time after showing Harry, just before hypnosis, the drawings he had originally produced at the age of six, which he had still not seen. To Orne's astonishment, Harry's hypnotic drawings still did not approximate those he had actually produced at the age of six, nor did they in subsequent repetitions of the experiment—until Orne began to show Harry his original drawings under hypnosis itself (c. page 52). In fact, as consultation with a children's-art expert confirmed, Harry's hypnotic drawings were not what a genuine six-year-old would have done, quite aside from the fact that they did not match Harry's originals. They were composed of a mingling of mature and immature features. Perhaps because the hypnotic state was not deep enough, or perhaps because the memory of the actual drawing done at the age of six was not meaningful enough to be preserved, Harry had produced no more than a clever and entirely involuntary fantasy of how he thought he had drawn at the age of six. Nevertheless, the fantasy was so strong that even repeated showings of the originals failed to shift this until the showings during the hypnotic state itself. Clearly, information produced under regression can be deceptive.

There is a steadily growing literature of cases of adults regressed to ages even earlier than six in which convincing and unconvincing elements intermingle to an extraordinary degree. Regressed to infancy, adults may suck their thumbs, cry, go into asthma attacks they have long grown out of, and even, amid considerable embarrassment, wet their pants. Yet asked the time, they may instinctively look for their wristwatch. Some hypnotists claim that if their subjects are regressed to pre-walking age they exhibit the so-called Babinski response, a flexing of the big toe upward when the sole of the foot is tickled, which normally disappears when the child begins to walk.[12] Rival hypnotists dispute this.[13] Some regressed subjects have been able to give a complete verbal commentary on the sensations of being regressed to an age before they could talk;[14] others similarly regressed have merely made gurgling and grunting noises and only put their thoughts into words after being brought out of hypnosis. Even birth and pre-birth memories have been described with extraordinary detail,[15] as, for instance, by the Irish playwright Bill Morrison when hypnotized for the BBC's *Spring of Memory* program.[16] According to the program's production team Morrison adopted a fetal position during his "in the womb" hypnotic reminiscences, and his facial features seemed to flatten out in a quite eerily embryonic manner. Yet some of his recorded verbalizations can only be regarded as unbelievable for what they purport to represent.

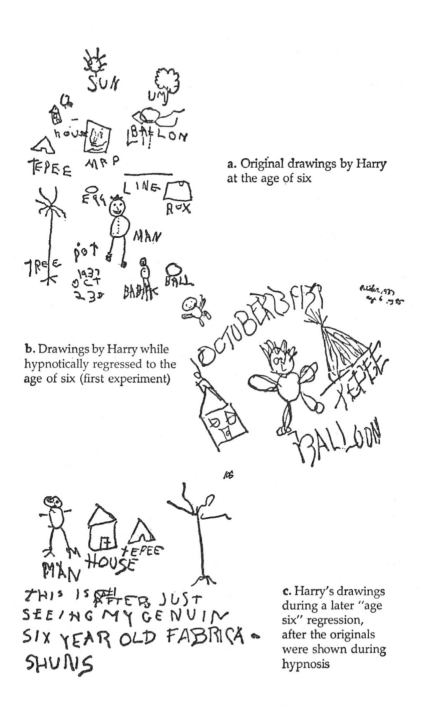

a. Original drawings by Harry at the age of six

b. Drawings by Harry while hypnotically regressed to the age of six (first experiment)

c. Harry's drawings during a later "age six" regression, after the originals were shown during hypnosis

1. Gillian and Jennifer Pollock today with *(insert)* a photograph of their dead sisters Joanna and Jacqueline.

2. The Egyptologist A. J. Howard Hulme, alias art teacher A. J. H. Howard.

3. The medium Rosemary, alias Ivy Carter Beaumont.

4. Dr. Frederic Wood, driven into spiritualism by the death of his brother Dennis, to whom he was very attached.

5. Joe Keeton, who has hypnotized some nine thousand subjects over the last twenty-five years.

6. Professor Hans Eysenck with Joe Keeton's subject Sue Atkins.

7. Carol Dow writing while under hypnosis during a regression with Derek Crüssell.

8. The real Eve of *The Three Faces of Eve*, Chris Sizemore.

10. Chris as the Purple Lady.

9. Chris as the Retrace Lady *(center)* with her sisters Tiny and Becky.

11. Billy Milligan at the time of his arrest; he has since been diagnosed as a case of multiple personality.

12. Billy Milligan's drawing as Christene, a personality with a mental age of three.

13. Milligan's lawyer displays some of the paintings by Billy Milligan's personalities.

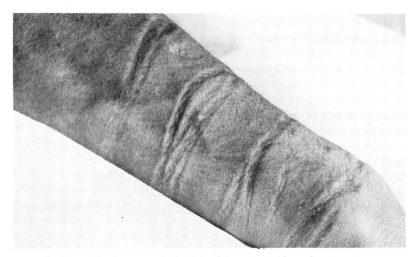

14. The right forearm of Dr. Moody's patient Alec, showing strong indentations resembling rope-marks. These appeared when, after a barbiturate injection, he relived an incident in India in which his arms had been bound with ropes.

15. The stigmatic Teresa Neumann.

16. Blood welling from the eyelids of Dr. Lechler's patient Elizabeth. This physical reaction was achieved purely by the power of suggestion.

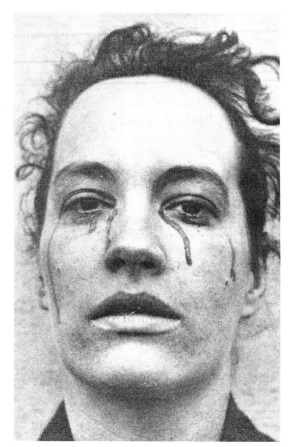

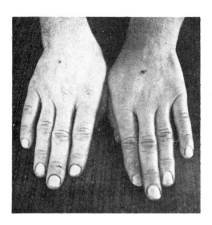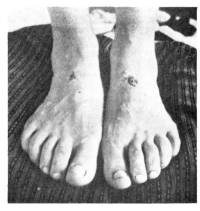

17. Phantom nail-wounds on Elizabeth's hands and feet. These also were produced entirely by hypnotic suggestion.

In the light of these examples, we must now turn our attention to past lives apparently remembered under hypnosis, and in particular to the famous case of Bridey Murphy.[17]

It is first important to understand something of the personalities of a case now more than twenty-five years old. The hypnotist, Morey Bernstein, was an amateur, being foremost a third-generation partner in the family business of Bernstein Brothers Equipment Company of Pueblo, Colorado. He took up hypnotism as a hobby after watching a demonstration and found himself naturally proficient at it. This spurred him to try his own experiments in regression. Virginia Tighe,[18] the subject of the Bridey Murphy regressions, was no die-hard enthusiast for hypnotic dabblings. Born in Madison, Wisconsin,[19] she was, because of her parents' broken marriage, taken to various U.S. cities, including Chicago and Denver, before she found at least temporary happiness in a marriage to Hugh Tighe, a Pueblo insurance salesman. She was vivacious and attractive, and her chief pleasure was accompanying her husband Hugh to the local bridge and cocktail parties that oiled the wheels of his business. It was at just such a gathering that she volunteered lightheartedly as a subject for Bernstein. She proved a deep-trance subject, capable of vivid recreations of childhood memories, even to the extent of assuming a convincingly childlike voice, and it was these which impelled Bernstein to plead that she should be his subject for the experiment he had long yearned to try—that of hypnotic regression to before birth, into possible past lives.

So it was that on the night of November 29, 1952, with his wife and a deeply distrustful Hugh Tighe looking on, Bernstein regressed the twenty-nine-year-old Virginia back through her early childhood, and then put to her the key suggestion that she was back at a time before she was born:

". . . One year old, one year old. See yourself when you were one year old. See some scene. Watch yourself. Be looking at yourself when you were one year old. Now go on even farther back. Oddly enough, you can go even farther back.

"I want you to keep on going back and back in your mind. And, surprising as it may seem, strange as it may seem, you will find that there are other scenes in your memory. There are other

All in the Mind

scenes from faraway lands and distant places in your memory. I
will talk to you again. I will talk to you again in a little while. I
will talk to you again in a little while. Meanwhile your mind will
be going back, back, back, and back until it picks up a scene,
until, oddly enough, you find yourself in some other scene, in
some other place, in some other time, and when I talk to you
again you will tell me about it . . .

"Now you're going to tell me, now you're going to tell me what
scenes come into your mind. What did you see? What did you
see?"[20]

There was a long pause, the Bernsteins and Hugh Tighe anx-
iously waiting for any response. Then suddenly, to their total astonishment, Virginia began talking in a soft Irish brogue:

". . . Uh . . . scratched the paint off all my bed. Jus' painted
it, 'n' made it pretty. It was a metal bed and I scratched the paint
off of it; dug my nails on every post and just ruined it. Was jus'
terrible."

Then Bernstein began to question her.

Q: Why did you do that?
A: Don't know. I was just mad. Got an awful spanking.
Q: What is your name?
A: . . . Uh . . . Bridey.[21]
Q: Your name is what?
A: Bridey.
Q: Don't you have any other name?
A: Uh . . . Bridey Murphy.
Q: And where do you live?
A: . . . I live in Cork . . . Cork.
Q: And what is the name of your mother?
A: Kathleen.
Q: And what is the name of your father?
A: Duncan . . . Duncan . . . Murphy.
Q: How old are you?
A: Uh . . . four . . . four years old.

So began to unroll the first of six carefully tape-recorded sessions, held at intervals during the course of the next year, in

which Virginia recounted in considerable detail the life of a Bridey Murphy living in Ireland during the first two-thirds of the nineteenth century. According to information she gave directly under hypnosis, in this past life Virginia was born Bridget Kathleen Murphy on December 20, 1798. With her father, a Protestant barrister Duncan Murphy, her mother Kathleen, and her elder brother Duncan Blaine Murphy, she lived just outside the "town and village" of Cork in an area she described as "The Meadows." The house had no immediate neighbors. At the age of fifteen she was schooled by a Mrs. Strayne (or possibly Strahan or Strange), in "house things and proper things," and at the age of twenty married Sean Brian Joseph MacCarthy, son of another Cork barrister. Brian MacCarthy and his father were Catholics, and after a Protestant marriage ceremony in Cork, Bridey went through a second, Catholic ceremony in Belfast, where their marriage was privately solemnized by Father John Joseph Gorman of St. Theresa's Church. The couple subsequently resided in Belfast for the rest of their lives, living in a cottage at the back of Brian's grandmother's house, described as being on Dooley Road. The couple were childless, and Brian, a barrister, was teaching at Queen's University in 1847 or later.

The end of Bridey seemed to come in 1864. She described dying in this year as a result of breaking her hip after a fall downstairs, and then seeing herself "ditched," or buried. Like a few of the Ian Stevenson subjects, she seemed to find herself in a form of astral world between her death in 1864 and her rebirth as Virginia in 1923. The long death-to-rebirth interval, compared to the general run of Stevenson's cases, is disquieting. But for Bernstein in 1952 any considerations of this kind were totally outweighed by the overwhelmingly convincing behavior exhibited by Virginia —her consistent Irish brogue, her use of strange Irish words, her wealth of factual information about nineteenth-century Ireland, and her totally plausible life histories of ordinary people of the period. From what Bernstein knew of Virginia she had not the slightest interest in any books, let alone books from which she might have derived the sort of information she was producing under hypnosis. It seemed quite obvious that Virginia's memories must be of a genuine past life, and Bernstein therefore set about publicizing this with a disarming ignorance of the furor he was about to cause.

The first, limited public disclosure came in September 1954 in the form of three articles by William J. Barker in Sunday editions of the Denver *Post*,[22] and these were well received in the State of Colorado in which the newspaper circulated. But even before Barker's articles appeared, Bernstein's activities had already come to the attention of Doubleday & Company, major American publishers, who provided the hypnotist with the necessary incentive to write a book on the Bridey Murphy case. Hugh Tighe had emphatically stopped his wife's involvement in any further hypnosis after the sixth session in 1953, so Bernstein was obliged in the book to cloak Virginia's real identity under the pseudonym Ruth Simmons. He was also advised that while as far as possible the details of Bridey's story should be checked out in Ireland, the fact that neither he nor Virginia had been out of the United States at that stage was too advantageous from the publicity point of view to be thrown away, at least until the book was in print. He was accordingly effectively stopped from going over to Ireland to check for himself.

Meanwhile, Doubleday approached a legal firm in Ireland to find out what they could of any Bridey Murphy and her husband Brian who might correspond to Virginia Tighe's hypnotic memories. But not only are there no formal birth, marriage, and death records for Ireland before the year 1864, but the Irish lawyers also performed with a slowness quite incompatible with the American publishers' eagerness to get into print. So although only minimal checks had been carried out, Doubleday went ahead with publication, which was in any case later than they had originally planned. From the publishing point of view they need not have worried. *The Search for Bridey Murphy* appeared on January 1, 1956, and caused an immediate sensation, being the first wide-circulation book seriously to vaunt the idea that hypnosis could uncover memories of past lives. It became a world best-seller.

What was particularly appealing about the Bridey Murphy story was its very ordinariness—Bridey Murphy had lived a completely obscure life, never touching on well-known events, and this made it all the more credible. But in this apparent source of strength also lay Bridey Murphy's weakness. Because the life *was* so obscure, it could not be checked against historical records. There was no way of proving it one way or another, and anyone, from whatever point of view, could do his own checking and twist the transcripts according to his own interpretation of their validity or otherwise.

The publication of such a book could scarcely go unnoticed by the great American newspaper empires, rich enough to finance expensive research, and eager to have things done quickly. The Chicago *Daily News*, which had paid a substantial sum for the syndication rights in *The Search for Bridey Murphy* in its circulation area, immediately sent its London man Ernie Hill to Ireland on what has been explicitly described as "a three-day pursuit of further verification" to accompany the syndication. Predictably, given that, once in Ireland, Hill had a 265-mile journey between the major cities in which investigations needed to be made, and was unfamiliar with both Ireland and the subtleties of historical research, the venture was virtually useless. Then it was the turn of the Denver *Post*, whose reporter William J. Barker had first brought the Bridey Murphy affair to press attention. Barker was sent to Ireland for three weeks. Before his arrival, information supplied by the Belfast Chief Librarian, John Bebbington, had established that two grocers from whom Bridey mentioned buying foodstuffs in Belfast, Farr and John Carrigan, were indeed listed in a Belfast city directory for 1865–66. To this intriguing but by no means conclusive piece of information Barker added the discovery of an 1801 map of Cork, drawn by William Beauford. On this he found marked, just outside the city, an area called Mardike Meadows, with a widely separated handful of houses which seemingly accorded well with "The Meadows," the area of Cork where Bridey described having lived with her parents before her marriage to Brian. There was also the information, although Barker did not learn it until his return to America, that a "tuppence," the first coin mentioned by Bridey as a unit of currency used at her time, was only in circulation between the years 1797 and 1850—the major part of Bridey's alleged lifetime. Barker found no evidence for the actual existence of Bridey, her husband, and her parents, nor of Father John Joseph Gorman, but all this could be explained by the absence of records of the time. It was troubling that there was no record of a Dooley Road in nineteenth-century Belfast, nor of a St. Theresa's Church (the present-day edifice was built in 1901). However, after having seen hypnotic regression demonstrated by Bernstein on his own wife, Barker felt confident that although the Bridey Murphy story might not be historically verifiable, its credibility could not be seriously shaken. His reasonable and objective nineteen-thousand-word article to this effect appeared in a special supplement in the Denver *Post* on March 11, 1956.

Two months later the bombshell struck. Ever since the Chicago *Daily News* coup in syndicating the Bridey Murphy story, the rival Chicago *American*, part of the Hearst newspaper empire, had been smarting from its wounds. The Chicago *American*, it seems, quickly decided that the *Daily News* Bridey story must be bunk and reporters were set to work to prove this. The Reverend Wally White of the Chicago Gospel Chapel came to their aid, concerned at the threat to established religious doctrines and anxious to destroy at any price the sudden fad for reincarnation which *The Search for Bridey Murphy* had engendered. For the publishers of the Chicago *American*, an exposé of the story was almost as good as an exclusive, and an exposé was certainly what their reporters produced. Somehow or other—the circumstances seem never to have been made clear—the protective cover provided by the pseudonym used in Bernstein's book was penetrated and the present-day Bridey Murphy publicly revealed as Virginia Tighe—to the intense annoyance of Virginia and her husband. Far worse, however, once the breakthrough had occurred, every crumb of information about Virginia's childhood was ferreted out in the hope that it might lead to some connection with Ireland by which Bridey Murphy might be explained. As Virginia had spent much of her childhood in Chicago, the hunting ground was an easy one for the *American* investigators, and they were not slow in finding just what they were looking for.

Discovery Number One, blazoned during May and June 1956 in articles in the Hearst newspapers, the San Francisco *Examiner* and New York *Journal American* as well as the Chicago *American*, was the revelation that Virginia had an aunt who was "as Irish as the lakes of Killarney" and had regaled the girl in childhood with stories of old Ireland. Discovery Number Two, the trump card, was the uncovering by the Chicago *American* investigators of what purported to be the real Bridey Murphy, a Mrs. Bridie Murphy Corkell from County Mayo in Ireland, who had lived in Chicago across the street from where Virginia once lived with her foster parents. Virginia knew this Mrs. Corkell, it was claimed, and—it was implied—had talked to her and been in her home many times. Virginia was also said to have had a "mad crush" on Mrs. Corkell's son John.

The handling of the Bridey Murphy affair by the Chicago *American* was a masterly piece of newspaper gamesmanship. The Bridey Murphy story, so prized by the Chicago *Daily News*, had been exposed as a hoax, and a powerful publishing coup scored. All around the world the story was picked up by the same newspapers who had become excited about the original revelations. Ecclesiastical publications, many of whom had not yet decided how they should play the Bridey Murphy affair, suddenly breathed easy again. As the story of the revelation was passed from one publication to another, inevitably embellishments were added. A Canadian newspaper published that Bernstein had explicitly confessed he had "hoaxed the world." Another newspaper claimed a similar admission from Virginia Tighe. On June 25, 1956, *Life* magazine, arguably the most respected popular publication in the United States, ran the headline "Bridey Search Ends At Last" and, accepting the Chicago *American*'s claims totally, printed a photograph of Mrs. Corkell with her grandchildren. Effectively the search for Bridey Murphy *had* ended. By the very power of the Hearst newspapers' blast, any case for the credibility of the Bridey Murphy story had been killed stone dead.

The irony is that amid all the hubbub the serious attempts that were made to answer the Chicago *American* charges and to set the record straight went unheeded. The Denver *Post*, mindful that Barker was too deeply implicated in the story to be objective, sent Bob Byers, an independent feature writer and no believer in reincarnation, to check out just what truth there was behind the Chicago *American* claims. Byers' findings were published on June 17 in the Denver *Post* under the headline "Chicago Newspaper Charges Unproved" and showed glaring inaccuracies in the hoax stories that had been so readily accepted around the world. For instance, although Virginia's Irish aunt was indeed a real person, a Mrs. Marie Burns, and certainly of Scots-Irish descent, she had, in fact, been born in New York and had spent most of her life in Chicago. Furthermore, this aunt only became really well known to Virginia when she came to live with Virginia's foster parents around the time of Virginia's eighteenth birthday. As Virginia subsequently remarked, "You'd think I would recall her having 'regaled' me with Irish tales, if she had, at that tender age, wouldn't you?"[23] Byers found that the story about Mrs. Corkell was also only half-true. Yes, Mrs. Corkell certainly existed and had originally come from County Mayo in Ireland—incidentally an area to the west of the country and far removed from the Cork and Belfast of Bridey's memories. Furthermore, Virginia readily admitted that she had lived opposite Mrs. Corkell, knew of her existence, and had known "Buddy" Corkell—Mrs. Corkell's son John. But there was no "mad crush" on Buddy Corkell. As Virginia explained in an interview, "Heavens, he was seven or eight years older than I was. He was married by the time I was old enough to have any romantic interest in boys." Nor had Virginia ever spoken to Mrs. Corkell, and she had no idea that her name was Bridie.

However, Byers' greatest difficulty was getting any information about Mrs. Corkell because she refused to answer any calls. Inquiries to her parish priest confirmed that her Christian name was Bridie (not Bridget, like the hypnotic Bridey's), but to this day there seems no evidence for the idea that her maiden name or any part of her name was Murphy. During Byers' vigorous pursuance of this particular point the reasons for Mrs. Corkell's coyness became clear. Her son Buddy (as Virginia had known him) was none other than the editor of the Sunday Chicago *American* at the time that the allegations were made. As William Barker of the Denver *Post* subsequently commented, "I won't hazard a guess what this proves!"[24]

If, therefore, nearly a quarter of a century after the event, we try to sum up the relative values of the claims, counter-claims, and counter-counter-claims made over the Bridey Murphy affair, they are perhaps more of an object lesson about the competitive methods of rival U.S. newspaper groups in the fifties than about the truth or otherwise of the phenomenon Bridey Murphy brought to public attention. Although many people now think that the Bridey Murphy affair has all been dismissed as a hoax, the real truth of the matter is far more complex. There can be little doubt that Bernstein himself acted in all good faith and was genuinely convinced by what his hypnosis produced. And Virginia Tighe, who was in any case amnesic for everything she said under hypnosis, can scarcely be accused of deliberately concocting her Bridey Murphy personality. When the controversy was at its height she resisted every financial inducement to become a public personality, steadfastly clinging to her greatly preferred role as an ordinary housewife devoted to the bringing up of three daughters. If it could be proved that there was a genuine historical Bridey Murphy from Cork who married a barrister called Brian and went to live in Belfast, then the Chicago *American* charges—already shown to be half-truths—could be even further devalued. But almost certainly, given the absence of formal Irish records before 1864, we will never know, and the fact that the grocers Farr and Carrigan actually existed can scarcely be said to be a compelling substitute.

But even if all Virginia's information as Bridey could be found to check out, would the case be evidence for reincarnation? The fact is that in common with Martin Orne's subjects, Bernstein's Virginia Tighe showed remarkable fluctuations in her Bridey Murphy state. Sometimes in the course of the regressions Virginia used words that are unquestionably modern Americanisms: "candy," "downtown," and "school" (in the American context of college or university), all quite foreign to nineteenth-century Ireland. Sometimes she used spontaneous and remarkably convincing Irishisms. For example, in the middle of routine questioning in the fourth session she suddenly sneezed violently, and with her eyes opened by the force of the sneeze, asked, "Could I have a linen?"—a request incomprehensible to her American listeners until they eventually realized she must mean a handkerchief. Features such as these convinced Bernstein that Virginia's Bridey Murphy memories had to be more than ordinary fantasies, and it is almost certainly because of the prevalence of such characteristics in subsequent cases that, despite all the hoax charges made in the late 1950s, the Bridey Murphy phenomenon has refused to die. All too often, like Morey Bernstein, people have uncritically interpreted them as evidence for reincarnation. And all too often the glaring inconsistencies to such an interpretation have been ignored. Yet the fact remains that while they may not be what they appear, they seem evidence for *something,* as yet unexplained, and when the dubious and the downright spurious have been discarded there remain signs of some not yet understood phenomenon at work.

CHAPTER 5

Hypnotic Regression Experiments—
Post Bridey Murphy

IN THE TWENTY-FIVE years since Morey Bernstein's Bridey Murphy experiments first hit the headlines, hypnotic regressions into past lives have become almost commonplace. There are many hypnotists practicing regression in the United States, some reputedly using it for therapeutic purposes, others for an esoteric form of ancestry tracing. One California psychologist claims to have regressed four thousand individuals back into past lives,[1] and in Britain, where at least eight hypnotherapists are currently practicing, Joe Keeton claims what is more than likely the world record—nine thousand past-life regressions.[2] Film stars, singers, and TV personalities have all got themselves in on the act, among these Glenn Ford, who remembers lives as a seventeenth-century French cavalryman and an eighteenth-century Scottish piano teacher;[3] singer Vince Hill, who recalls life as a farmhand at the time of Cromwell; television mimic Faith Brown, who seems to have been a nineteenth-century Englishwoman suspected of murder; singer Diane Solomon, whose lives range from one in Ancient Greece to one as an eighteenth-century Wild West pioneer called Jonathan Miller;[4] and authoress Taylor Caldwell, who claims that some of her historical novels are based on past-life reminiscences.[5]

Clearly, the phenomenon cannot be brushed aside out of hand. Although among any dozen individuals probably only one or two are likely to go into a trance sufficiently deep to produce past lives,[6] there is not the slightest need for these subjects to believe in reincarnation, or indeed any form of life after death. Given the suggestion that they are back before the time of their birth, in a different personality, even those hostile to the idea of reincarnation can produce some remarkably convincing past-life personalities, as I myself have observed. Nor can such individuals be dismissed as weak-minded, easily suggestible, or of low intelligence. Army officers, journalists, and research psychologists rank among those who have produced hypnotic past-life memories. But do these memories represent genuine evidence that the individuals have lived before?

The British edition of *The Search for Bridey Murphy* had hardly appeared in the bookshops when the *Daily Express*, which then had one of the largest circulations in the country, announced that it was offering £250 (worth some ten times that amount at today's prices) for the first one of its readers who, independently of the Bridey Murphy case, could provide conclusive evidence that reincarnation was real. As might be expected, the competition challenged the hypnotists of postwar Britain, and Henry Blythe of Torquay, then in his late fifties, immediately rose to this. On March 28, 1956, in the presence of *Daily Express* representatives, he conducted his first experiment in past-life regression on a thirty-two-year-old Devon housewife, Mrs. Naomi Henry. By what might seem a remarkable coincidence Naomi Henry, like Virginia Tighe before her, produced a past life set in late-eighteenth-century Cork as one Mary Cohen. In a soft Irish brogue she described herself as married to a certain Charles Gaul, and with two sons, Pat and Will. The whole demonstration seemed remarkably convincing, and Blythe arranged to rehypnotize Naomi Henry a week later in order to explore Mary Cohen's later years. At this session, each time Blythe suggested to Mary Cohen that she was a few years older, the woman seemed to age convincingly in voice and manner. Nothing had prepared Blythe, however, for her reaction when he suggested she was seventy years old. She failed to respond to two consecutive questions put to her. Then, to the hypnotist's horror and that of those observing, he began to realize the reason why. As he later recorded in his book *The Three Lives of Naomi Henry:*

> I was watching her closely, my fingers on the pulse of her left wrist. There was still no reply from Naomi and suddenly I felt her pulse die away, her breathing—clearly audible in the room during both sessions—stopped, every trace of colour left her face. She appeared to be dead. I bent closer to try to discover a trace of breath, but there was nothing. The atmosphere in the room was tense. I could feel the fear in my wife and the shorthand writer. Afterwards they confessed that they were terrified. Hurriedly I spoke urgently, whispering in Naomi's ear: "You are quite safe. I am with you. You are safe, safe, safe."[7]

Although Mrs. Henry was, in fact, brought round by Blythe's reassurances, the *Daily Express* considered the incident sufficiently alarming to abandon the whole countrywide competition. Nevertheless, the episode is interesting because Mrs. Henry's apparent death is an example of the "facial blank," the total loss of expression and other signs of life that sometimes occurs in deep-trance subjects when they switch from one apparent past life to another. This is just one of a whole series of eerie and disturbing facial changes which may be observed during regressions. If the subject is reliving a past-life old age, the whole countenance may take on a drawn and haggard expression. If he or she is reliving a past-life childhood, normal adult facial crease lines may smooth out. No one who has observed these changes can fail to be astonished by the sheer speed and subtlety with which they occur, as if at the press of a button, with none of the adjustment that even an experienced actor would normally require.

Perhaps not surprisingly Henry Blythe subsequently carried on very little further work in past-life hypnotic regression, but at much the same time, in a Hitchcock-style residence set high on Rhiwbina Hill just outside Cardiff in South Wales, a diminutive, bright-eyed, and birdlike Welsh hypnotherapist began exploring the regression phenomenon in an altogether more exhaustive manner. This was Arnall Bloxham, who, with his wife Dulcie, founded the Reincarnation Research Institute of Great Britain. Many people came to them with physical and emotional ailments which hypnosis seemed to cure, and over some twenty years the Bloxhams encouraged four hundred of these to be hypnotically regressed to what the couple believed were genuine past existences. Every such regression was carefully tape-recorded, but the Bloxhams' work was virtually unknown outside South Wales until the late 1970s—by which time Dulcie Bloxham was dead—when Jeffrey Iverson, an enterprising Cardiff TV producer, brought the tape collection to wider attention via a television program called *The Bloxham Tapes* which was shown on BBC Television in December 1976.[8]

It is difficult not to be impressed by the very range and diversity of the past lives recalled by Bloxham's subjects. One of his most fascinating cases involves a young South Wales housewife pseudonymously known as Jane Evans, whose repertoire included past lives as Livonia, a tutor's wife living in third-century Roman Britain; Rebecca, a Jewess of twelfth-century York; Alison, an Egyptian-born fifteenth-century French courtesan; Anna, a sixteenth-century Spanish maidservant; Anne, a late-seventeenth-century London sewing girl; and Sister Grace, a nun living in Maryland, U.S.A., in the late nineteenth century. But what gives these regressions their superior quality is the sheer wealth of detail. Names and descriptions of complicated events that might have occurred a thousand years ago pour out just as if they were happening again. Typical is this passage from her life as Livonia:

> We are on our way to Verulam [St. Albans], the *domina*, Constantine, Favonius, Hilary and me and Titus. We are on our way—it's dark. [Pause] I knew we shouldn't trust Allectus. When Constantius had sailed for Rome, Carausius brought the fleet over. He landed and has conquered Britain. Carausius has come over and he has taken over, and we have had to flee. Allectus came to our house—killed some of our servants—but Favonius managed to kill some of Allectus's men and we had to go by dark.[9]

Such fluency of handling so many obscure names must be considered astonishing—and this is no mere jumble of unknown characters. Constantius, who employed Livonia's husband, may be identified as Aurelius Valerius Constantius, nicknamed Chlorus (the Pale), who was the military governor of Roman Britain during the late third century A.D. Carausius and the untrustworthy Allectus are individuals known to history as having illicitly assumed power when Constantius left for Rome. The *domina,* elsewhere called "the Lady Helena" by Livonia, may be identified as Constantius' first wife, later to become St. Helena, the great patroness of Christianity. Constantine, son of Constantius and Helena, was the future Constantine the Great, the first Christian Roman emperor. The reference to Constantius' departure for Rome dates the year as 286 A.D.

Such past-life dramas are relived with great emotion. Graham Huxtable of Swansea, a normally soft-spoken swimming instructor, was another subject of Bloxham's. Under hypnosis he became Ben, a coarse and raucous master gunner on board a thirty-two-gun frigate at the time of Nelson. Early in the regression Bloxham was able to ask questions and receive answers in the normal manner, but soon Ben became so engrossed that he ignored Bloxham and began to give orders to his invisible gun crews, clearly in preparation for a sea battle:

Keep yer match ready, boy! Keep yer match ready! Cover it, ya fool. Ah, these boys. Swing it. Swing it. Don't let that spark go out, don't let it go. Swing that—you won't get another, not till the firepots come out.

Subsequently Ben became unstoppable, and launched into a spectacular recall of life belowdecks during an eighteenth-century naval gun battle:

Wait for the order, wait for it! Swing those matches. Aye Sirree! STAND CLEAR FROM BEHIND! NOW, YOU FOOL! NOW UP, FOOL, NOW.—NOW! [Screams in exaltation as the shot is fired] WELL DONE LADS! RUN 'EM UP! RUN 'EM UP! GET 'EM UP! GET 'EM UP THE FRONT! [Shrieks] Pull that man out! Pull 'im out! Send him in the cockpit. Now get in back! Get up there! Get up there! Get on the chocks there! Run 'em up again!

The shot in . . . ramrods! Swab it, swab it, you fool, swab

it first! The shot in, shot in! Come in Number Four, you
should be up by now! Shot in, ram it home! Prime! Swing
those matches! Aye, aye sir. Ready! And again lads! You had
him then! Hurry men! By God you bastard! Got him that
aim! That's the way to lay a gun. By Christ, they've got old
Pearce, they've got Pearce! [Sudden terrible screaming] MY
BLOODY LEG! [Screaming and moaning uncontrollably]
MY LEG! MY LEG![10]

By any standards this performance was extraordinary. It was so intense that Bloxham brought Huxtable out of hypnosis only with
considerable difficulty, yet after the regression the swimming instructor had not the slightest memory of anything he had said or
experienced while in the hypnotic state.[11] When the recording
was played back to him he could only listen, amazed that this tor-
rent of unfamiliar material had come from him. The only independent clue that it had occurred at all was a persistent pain in
his leg. This type of subject, who is completely unaware of anything he or she may say as a past-life personality, is usually called
"somnambulistic" (literally sleepwalking). Virginia Tighe, Naomi Henry, and—so far as can be determined—Jane Evans were
also somnambulistic.

Intriguingly, however, a substantial proportion of regression
subjects revivify as dramatically as Huxtable, and in addition retain clear visual and auditory impressions of everything they experience during the hypnotic state. The British hypnotist Joe Keeton of Hoylake near Liverpool, a genial, bearded man who used
to be a catering manager, can produce a whole string of subjects
of this type. One of these is Sue Atkins, a vivacious lexicographer
in her mid-forties.

Sue Atkins, a highly educated woman, was extremely skeptical
of the whole regression phenomenon when, at the request of a
friend, she first agreed to take part in a Joe Keeton hypnotic experiment. But when he suggested to her that she was back in the
early 1900s she became Charlie, an ebullient urchin hysterically
reliving the terrors of being burned to death in a Severnside
workhouse fire at around the age of twelve. When regressed to
earlier episodes in Charlie's life, Sue Atkins became so engrossed
—like Huxtable—in some of these that all communication with

Keeton was abandoned while she carried on an animated verbal exchange with invisible and inaudible companions:

> *I could so,* Robert Williams . . . D'yuh *all* think I couldn't? . . . That's got nothing to do with it . . . Well—*you* make it go up . . . Well . . . throw something at it . . . NOT TOO QUICKLY. I've got to be ready . . . No—well . . . it didn't go up far enough . . . you've got to make it go *right* high up . . . then I'll go under . . . Willie—well you go first . . . Yah—you're scared . . . I can do that . . . All right—*go on then . . . throw it . . .* Aaaagh![12]

Like Huxtable, Sue Atkins was brought out of her regression screaming in pain. But instead of recalling nothing, after returning to normal consciousness she was able to describe everything she had seen and heard during the regression in vivid detail. As Charlie she saw herself among a group of urchins gathered around a horse, and heard everything they said (represented by the gaps in her utterances). The urchins were going to throw something at the horse to make it rear up and they had dared Charlie to run under the beast's legs before it came crashing down again. Then she saw herself make the attempt and fail to clear the horse's hooves in time. Charlie seems to have been permanently disabled as a result of this incident. From Sue Atkins' own analysis of the phenomenon as she recalled it, two quite distinct elements of her mind seem to have been in play. One was the foolhardy guttersnipe personality of Charlie with his highly distinctive temperament and background, talking confidently of people and events foreign to the parent Sue, and speaking and behaving in a manner seemingly beyond her control. The other was the familiar twentieth-century Sue, conscious of her immediate surroundings but immobilized and detached, feeling, in her own words, "as if I were situated up in the back of my head, on the right, watching what was going on."[13] This variety of response may be labeled the "passive-observer" type, and it is extremely important from the investigative point of view.

Equally intriguing are the striking changes that occur on the apparent transition into a past life during hypnotic regression. There is, for instance, an often astonishing change of personality. Michael O'Mara, a subject of Joe Keeton's, is a very successful and well-educated publishing executive whose family, although of Irish origin, have lived in the United States for three generations. Michael has a restless energy for work and a strong aversion toward excessive drinking, both attributes in marked conflict with those of his past-life personality Stephen Garrett, a good-for-nothing nineteenth-century Dublin vagrant whose only interest seemed to be in porter (an early form of Guinness), poteen (an illegal and frequently lethal distillation from potatoes), and whiskey. The following, delivered in a consistent Irish accent, is typical:

A: I'm thirsty.

Q: Well here's a bar. [Keeton conveys to Garrett the suggestion of an imaginary pub bar] What would you like to drink?

A: Porter . . . Aaah. Porter. Aah. That's a nice [pauses and mimes drinking] drink . . .

Q: Would you like something short afterwards to chase it down?

A: You got it backwards.

Q: What would you like?

A: [very emphatically] Whiskey.

Q: Any particular brand? There are lots of brands here.

A: No . . . uh . . . jus' whiskey . . . Irish . . . That's whiskey.[14]

A similar contrast is to be observed between the soft-spoken present-day Graham Huxtable and his often foul-mouthed personality as Ben, the eighteenth-century gunner. The TV producer Jeffrey Iverson has remarked:

Comparing the present-day Huxtable to the earthy sailor, neither Graham nor I can find any point of contact or similarity. In experience and attitudes the sailor is a quite different sort of man . . .[15]

Again, there could scarcely be any greater contrast between the present-day highly literate personality of Sue Atkins and the gutter language of her past-life self, Charlie:

You can call people bleedin' bastards, but if you call them bleeding Jesuses, it comes down . . . that's what St. Mi-

chael's [a church] for . . . I once called somebody a bleeding
Jesus . . . an' the teacher took me out an' put my head in
the school bucket . . . right there . . . an' it was winter . . .
an' she put it in three times . . . an' then she said "Spit out
that word" . . . and I spat it out . . . *right back in the
bloody bucket*.[16]

The regressed subject will also experience a change of what we
may term "body image" by which, regardless of whether he is of
the somnambulistic or passive-observer type, he will see himself in
an appropriate past-life body. For instance, early on in Michael
O'Mara's regression as Stephen Garrett, Keeton asked him to
look down at himself to see how he was dressed. There was a
pause, then, in the distinctive Irish brogue so different from
Michael's normal East Coast American:

"My trousers are not very nice."
"What is the matter with them?"
"Ripped . . . they're comic."[17]

Joe Keeton's subject Edna Greenan, who under hypnosis assumes the personality of Charles II's mistress Nell Gwyn,[18] takes
on the mental image of Nell's body as well. Edna, a slight woman
in her mid-fifties, would not deny having modest chest propor-
tions but during one regression I attended she quite unembar-
rassedly loosened an invisible seventeenth-century bodice and
preened herself on an obviously pleasing pair of seventeenth-century breasts. When Graham Huxtable was regressed to Ben and
Arnall Bloxham asked him, "Have you been in any battle?" he
replied with the contemptuous "Where do you think I got these
marks?"[19] Ben obviously saw himself as badly scarred and was bel-
ligerently unable to comprehend Bloxham's inability to do the
same. The gender barrier is traversed in the same way, and without any suggestion of sexual deviation on the part of the real-life
subject a man may see himself in a past-life woman's body, and a
woman in a past-life man's. As we have already learned, Joe Keeton's Sue Atkins saw herself as Charlie, and she also exhibited another male past life in the form of a seventeenth-century Jesuit
priest, called Father Antony Bennet. Michael O'Mara, who became Stephen Garrett, also took on the past-life personality of
Emily, a six-year-old girl, and not only adopted appropriate ges-

tures and speech patterns but even lifted the hem of a little girl's dress he saw in his mind's eye to show off the edging.[20]

Such features as a change of body image cannot of course be examined by those watching, but others can be seen by anyone either during or after the regression. These include manifestations of past-life wounds and blemishes, and there are some examples among the subjects regressed by Joe Keeton. For instance, Ann Dowling, a forty-seven-year-old housewife, recalls the life of a nineteenth-century waif called Sarah Williams, and the morning after reliving Sarah's brutal beating-up and murder at the hands of an Irish navvy she invariably finds her body covered in bruises.[21] Pauline McKay of Ellesmere Port produces the past life of Kitty Jay, a Devon woman who hanged herself, and a livid red rope-mark has been reliably observed on her neck as she relives Kitty's suicide.[22] And when Edna Greenan, alias Nell Gwyn, regresses to another past-life personality called Charlotte Marriott, she invariably scratches herself vigorously and the next day finds her skin covered in a psoriasis-like rash.

Handwriting is another feature capable of outward observation and scrutiny. Just as age-regressed subjects have produced handwriting seemingly of their present-life childhood, so subjects regressed to a past life have produced ostensibly period scripts, although not always successfully, one Keeton subject, for instance, having thrown a twentieth-century pen across the room when asked to write with it in her past-life personality. Perhaps the most interesting specimens known to the author are ones from Carol Dow, a subject of Derek Crüssell, a former actor with a flourishing hypnotherapy practice in Bromley, Kent. As Zenia (or possibly Zellia), an allegedly late sixteenth-century, early seventeenth-century personality, Carol agreed to write down a rhyme she had learned at her past-life school (see page 73). The writing is fascinating from the point of view of its mixture of elements. There is, for instance, a childish element, the mirror reversal of the "d's" and "b's" (in "brought," "goods," and "and"), being typical of the early work of a child who is left-handed. There is also a historical element—the quaint period word "yea," the misspelled "contry," the old-fashioned "fayre," features if not genuinely period irrefutably intended to convey that impression. We might even note that Zenia has used a character shaped like a "3" (as in "was," "his," and "goods"), a letter form that does indeed frequently occur in period handwriting.

yea was a man from
fonky fayre

who drought his goobs
anb warez

you sine him ehy flay
you a tune

Carol Dow's handwriting when under hypnotic regression as the seventeenth-century Zenia, aged twelve.

Carol Dow's present-day writing.

As has previously been noted, past-life regression subjects sometimes display a marked change of accent, voice, and even language consistent with the personality adopted. During their regressions as Bridey Murphy and Mary Cohen the normal accents of Virginia Tighe and Naomi Henry, American and Devonian respectively, were replaced by reasonably consistent Irish accents, convincing at least to those who listened to them. At a hypnotic session conducted by Joe Keeton, Bristol research psychologist Dr. Tom Troscianko, who has not the slightest belief in reincarnation, became a nineteenth-century Polish past-life personality Armid, complete with a cultured and consistent Polish accent—even though Dr. Troscianko himself, although of Polish parentage, normally has not the slightest trace of any such accent.

Somewhat less convincingly those regressions purporting to describe lives in ancient Rome, ancient Egypt, etc., are all too frequently related in twentieth-century English, and there is a similar absence of appropriate period speech among lives allegedly remembered in pre-nineteenth-century England. Nevertheless, although extremely rare, there are cases of regression subjects speaking languages which, so far as can be determined, they have never learned in their twentieth-century existence. The crucial feature of such cases is whether the subject is able to utter sensible phrases in the language, and also to understand and respond intelligently to questions put in that language ("responsive xenoglossy"). The two instances most worthy of serious attention have both been studied and published by Dr. Ian Stevenson, the psychiatrist whose work on child past-life memories was discussed in Chapters 1 and 2.

The first involves a pseudonymous American doctor's wife who during regressions conducted in the late 1950s exhibited the personality of a somewhat crude seventeenth-century peasant called Jensen Jacoby, and spoke Swedish in a deep masculine voice. As Jensen, she proved capable of responding intelligently though somewhat monosyllabically in Swedish to questions put to her in English by her husband, and in Swedish by various Swedish nationals, who included the then Director of the American Swedish Historical Museum. A peculiarity of the language of the Jensen personality is a strong mixture of Norwegian to the Swedish. Dr. Ian Stevenson's published account, *Xenoglossy: a Review and Report of a Case*,[23] includes a 165-page transcript, and is undeniably impressive. The hypnotist involved was the subject's husband, now deceased, and although the identities have been concealed Dr. Stevenson claims that he went to great lengths to check the couple's credentials and the fact that she had no opportunity in her life ever to learn Swedish.

Stevenson's second xenoglossy case is that of a U.S. Methodist minister's wife, Dolores Jay,[24] also hypnotized by her husband. One day in May 1970 the Reverend Carroll Jay was using hypnosis on Dolores in an attempt to relieve her of backache when suddenly she began replying "*Nein*" and "*Ja*" to his questions. During further probing Dolores began speaking more German. On conducting proper regressions, aided by German-speaking friends, Jay discovered that his wife was producing a past-life personality as Gretchen Gottlieb, daughter of the Roman Catholic mayor of the German town of Eberswalde. Gretchen said that she was unable to read or write, and was in great fear of persecution from what she called the *Bundesrat*, a term which indicated that she was living during Bismarck's persecution of German Catholics in the 1870s. She could not be moved forward in time beyond her sixteenth year and would seem to have been murdered at that age by an angry mob who ambushed her in some woods as she tried to escape from Eberswalde on horseback. In a preliminary report on the case, Stevenson again claims that he has gone to great lengths to check on Dolores Jay and her husband, even to the extent of establishing that German was not even taught in the school the Jays attended. To all appearances both cases have seemed unassailable.

There are, then, in past-life regression a whole series of "mind out of time" phenomena that on the surface at least can only appear extraordinarily impressive. From the detail of the memories of Jane Evans it would seem impossible that she could have invented such material. From the highly emotional revivification occurring in regressions such as those of Graham Huxtable and Sue Atkins it would seem impossible that they too could have been doing anything other than seeing and experiencing in their minds scenes and events which actually happened. From phenomena such as the xenoglossy of Jensen and Gretchen all appears that they must be based on some form of transmission from the past. But is this truly the case? Is some form of reincarnation the only logical interpretation?

CHAPTER 6

Hypnotic Regression
Experiences Analyzed

WHEN CONSIDERING Dr. Ian Stevenson's past-life memory cases among children, it was illuminating to compare the death-to-rebirth intervals and the racial and geographical jumps of his subjects. These offered the potential for deducing hypothetical rules for reincarnation, but in the event they failed to exhibit such rules. Any attempt to apply the same principles to alleged cases of hypnotic past-life recall also faces difficulties. The fact is that most hypnotists involved in past-life regressions have failed to keep anything approaching proper records. Even when I provided suitable sheets by which they might keep such records in future there was little improvement in the situation, and it has to be acknowledged that most practicing hypnotists and hypnotherapists tend to be antipathetic to such paper work. This is a pity, since if hypnotic past-life regressions were genuine evidence for reincarnation, a master index of all such regressions, complete with place and date of past-life deaths and births and present-life birth, would be a most valuable aid to understanding how reincarnation worked.

Such difficulties did not, however, prevent me from gaining from a variety of sources quite enough information to make a general appraisal. For instance, the American psychologist Helen

Past Life Personalities	Sex	Period	Location	Characteristics
Woman merchant	F	400 BC	Egypt	Cold and material-istic personality
Cart driver	M	1300 BC	Egypt	Married, lived in adobe house
High priest	M	2000 BC	Egypt	Very commercial rather than religious

Helen Wambach hypnotic regression case of San Francisco businessman Robert Logg. (Based on material from Helen Wambach, *Reliving Past Lives*, Hutchinson, 1979.)

Wambach has published sufficient details of one of her subjects, a San Francisco businessman called Robert Logg,[1] for a chain of some fifteen of his alleged past lives to be reconstructed, stretching as far back as 2000 B.C. (see page 77 and above). It is to be noted that these lives do not suggest there is any kind of order to the reincarnation process in temporal, racial, or geographical terms. The lives flit from Ancient Greece to pre-Columbus America and Renaissance Europe, with widely varying gaps between lives in which the discarnate Robert was presumably in some form of limbo. Arnall Bloxham kindly lent me an unpublished book of transcripts of regressions he had conducted, which similarly exhibit no underlying logic, one subject lurching from a life in Ancient Egypt to another in China, another in Inca Peru, and another in Bavaria (see page 79), while others remember lives as far back as caveman days. Similar trends can be seen in regressions conducted by hypnotist Harry Hurst of Stockton, Cleveland, who also made available some transcripts of his cases.

Such an apparent lack of an underlying logic could in itself be considered a form of rule for reincarnation, but this idea must immediately be discounted by comparative observations of the work of Joe Keeton and Derek Crüssell. Both men are practical, down-to-earth, and genuinely open-minded on whether the past-life regressions they conduct are really evidence for reincarnation.

HYPNOTIC PAST LIFE REGRESSION CLAIM
Hypnotist: Helen Wambach of Martinez, California

Subject	Sex	Period	Location	Characteristics
Robert Logg *Past Life Personalities*	M	Present day, b. 1930	San Francisco, USA	Well-educated, well-read businessman
Child	F	1900–1902	Baltimore	Died in infancy
Urchin	M	1870	London	Cabin boy on ship called the *Dolphin*
Mill supervisor	M	1810–1870	Egypt	Cottonmill supervisor
Wool merchant	M	1715–1790	England	Successful in business, traveled abroad
Peasant	M	?	France	Only possession a wooden spoon
Unmarried mother	F	1590–1618	Wales	Pregnant by Spanish seaman
Nobleman	M	Early 1500s	Italy, S. of Naples	Unhappily married
Poor woman	F	1450	Portugal	Modest circumstances, short life
Native woman	F	1300	Central America	Died of fever aged 28
Unexplored period				
Orphan	M	AD 100	Greece	Ward of homosexual Greek governor
Cheese-maker & Cheese-vendor	M	?	W. Lebanon	A prosperous, happy individual of Jewish religion

Keeton dismisses outright a large proportion of his cases as what he calls "Walter Mittys" and the only preconceived notion that he has expressed is that "there is no limbo, no rest between one life and another. From death to conception is instantaneous."[2] Crüssell, highly successful as a conventional hypnotherapist, also has only one theory on the subject: that past-life memories might have an ancestral or genetic base.[3]

HYPNOTIC PAST LIFE REGRESSION CLAIM
Hypnotist: Arnall Bloxham of Cardiff, S. Wales

Subject	Sex	Period	Location	Characteristics
Unidentified	F	Present day	S. Wales?	Housewife of professional status
Past Life Personalities				
Pedro	M	Time of "Philip of Navarre"	Spain	Romantic young Spaniard
Arimon	M	16th c.	Peru	Inca priest
Enrique Reinhaldt	M	?	Bavaria	Son of Bavarian count
Alexis	F	Medieval	England	Gentle witch of gypsy birth
Van de Berg	M	?	Central Europe	Son of a steward
Um Sun	M	?	Chinese	?
Erastus	M	Roman era	Rome	Greek-born charioteer
Arema	F	Classical Greek period	Athens	Bored daughter of Greek governor
Onestes	F	Period of Ramses II	Egypt	Wife of Greek sea-trader

Arnall Bloxham hypnotic regression case of unidentified house-wife, showing wide historical and geographical diversity of past lives recalled.

HYPNOTIC PAST LIFE REGRESSION CLAIM
Hypnotist: Joe Keeton of Hoylake, nr Liverpool

Subject	Sex	Period	Location	Characteristics
Edna Greenan (née Stevenson)	F	Present day, b. 1927	Bispham, Lancs.	Wife of garden labourer, mother died when 6 months old
Past Life Personalities				
Sarah Henshaw	F	c.1850–1926	Ribble Valley, Lancs	Washer of pit clothes
Eleanor Thomson/ Smithson	F	c.1780–1850	Plymouth	Housewife
Charlotte Marriott	F	?–c.1779	Lincoln	Suffered from rash
Toby Matthews	M	c.1688–?	No fixed abode, England	Vagrant dwelling in woods
Nell Gwyn	F	1650–1687	London	Mistress of King Charles II
Margaret Fraser	F	1613?–1649?	London	?
Jenny (or Jennet) Preston	F	?–1612	Pendle, Lancs	One of the Lancashire Witches

Joe Keeton hypnotic regression case of a Lancashire housewife, Edna Greenan, illustrating the lack of interval between lives (Joe Keeton believes that from death to conception of the new personality is instantaneous), and the close geographical confines. (Based on material from regressions of Edna Greenan attended by the author.)

Intriguingly, once the cases of these two hypnotists are examined—and both have been most open to investigation—we can see that they not only deviate from the somewhat exotic nature of the Wambach, Bloxham, and Hurst variety, but also differ from each other precisely in accordance with the hypnotist's preconceived ideas. No subject of Keeton's lurches from caveman to Ancient Egyptian to Ancient Chinese. His British subjects usually remain British in past lives, trace back in time through relatively few generations—the sixteenth century is about the earliest —change accent more markedly than in the case of other hypnotists, but above all seem to reincarnate dutifully in a new body nine months after the death of the previous personality. Crüssell's subjects, mostly recruited from the English Home Counties, also exhibit English past lives going back through relatively few generations. Unlike Keeton's, however, they exhibit gaps, sometimes of several decades, between their lives, and on occasion have shown a definite hint of ancestral features, as in a case to be discussed later in this chapter. A generalization though it has to be, the observation can scarcely be escaped that the subjects of regression experiments, without any overt priming by the hypnotists, subtly and chameleon-like seem to reflect in their past lives the expectations held by the man who had hypnotized them.[4] At the very least, the suggestion is disquieting.

There are more disquieting factors to be discovered from a review of even the superficial features of the regressions. A typical case in point involves a subject of Harry Hurst who apparently claimed memories of a life in Thebes in Ancient Egypt during the reign of pharaoh Ramses III, and of using a sestertius coin. Even from this mere skeleton of information there has to be something wrong, for no genuine Ancient Egyptian, even assuming he was somehow able to communicate in English, would have known Thebes as "Thebes." He would have referred to it as "On"—Thebes was the name the Greeks gave to it. Nor would he have known Ramses or any other pharaoh by a number. This device of numbering pharaohs was only adopted for clarity by Victorian Egyptologists during the nineteenth century. Nor, in the reign of Ramses III, would he have known anything of a sestertius coin, since this did not appear until the Roman era a thousand years later. Even on the most superficial appraisal this regression (and it is typical of many) cannot be what it seems.

The same can be said of a Bloxham subject who remembered a past life as an "Iriqui" (presumably Iroquois) American Indian, and related stories he had heard from "the Coast Indians" of men with "horns," carrying "round shields which are good for battle," who "came in tall ships with huge blanket to drive it."[5] If one

tries to make a historical interpretation of this account, it is
difficult to regard it as other than an American Indian's description of Vikings making a landfall on the mainland of America, as
in all probability they did in the eleventh century. However, one
of the very features by which this deduction is made—that the
strangers had "horns"—is also one which argues against the account's credibility as a "mind out of time" memory. Up until the
most recent years almost every child's picture-book portrayal of
the Vikings has shown them with horns on their helmets, so
much so that this forms a prime feature of the mental image we
instinctively call up when asked to think of a Viking. Yet recent
scholarship teaches us that this image is false. The ordinary Viking helmet, from early Scandinavian art and from excavated
remains, is now known to have been a close-fitting, often conical
cap (see page 83), a much more practical proposition for battle
wear. Horned helmets seem to have been altogether more rare,[6]
worn mainly for the occasional religious ceremony, and then only
by individuals of rank. While on the available information any
categoric assessment would be unwise, there are good grounds for
inferring that Bloxham's subject saw Vikings not as they actually
were, but as he imagined them to be. This view finds further
confirmation in a remark of the same "Iriqui" Indian about deer-
hunting: "Wise men say, if you hit the part that pumps the
blood, deer will die straightaway." The very cadence of this
sounds more like the American Indian speech of films and popular fiction than that of any real "Iriqui." And it is particularly interesting to note the reference to "the part that pumps the
blood." Our poor ignorant savage apparently does not have a
word for "heart"—the existence of which he would certainly have
been aware—yet he knows not only that a pump exists, when it
was not introduced into North America until colonization proper
in the sixteenth century, but also that it works like the heart—
when the principle of blood circulation was not discovered even
in civilized Europe until the seventeenth century!

So it is becoming clear that in at least some past-life cases there
are major elements that cannot be based on fact. It is also
significant that in the Bloxham, Hurst, and Wambach past-life
cases there is a marked tendency to memories set in exotic cultures such as Ancient Egypt and Tibet and a distinct silence from

Viking head showing helmet with historically accurate absence of horns. From the top of a bone stick found at Sigtuna, Sweden.

less-fashionable civilizations such as the Hittites, the Assyrians, or the Scythians. Nuns and witches, Tibetan monks and Ancient Egyptian priests are particularly prevalent in past lives remembered by Bloxham subjects, and this suggests that historical stories of a glamorous or otherwise dramatic nature may have provided the fundamental inspiration for the material produced under hypnosis. In the case of the Tibetan monks, for instance, it is difficult to avoid speculating that the subjects (whose identities are unknown), might have been influenced by the early postwar vogue for Tibet created by Heinrich Harrer's *Seven Years in Tibet* and Lobsang Rampa's *The Third Eye*. One Bloxham subject's account of a past life as a mighty hunter and cave painter of prehistoric times, lured by his enemies to death in a stake-filled pit, has unmistakable echoes of a story I recall from a postwar *Commonwealth and Empire Youth Annual*. And while the settings of the regressions of a subject such as Bloxham's Jane Evans are altogether more sophisticated (see page 85), there are strong hints of sources in historical fiction. Although Livonia correctly used the Latin names for the cities of Roman Britain—*Eboracum* for York, *Verulam* for St. Albans, and *Aquae Sulis* for Bath, which is undeniably more convincing than the Hurst Ancient Egyptian's reference to Thebes—it has to be remarked that historical novelists often use such devices to suggest period. Furthermore, Livonia refers to her employer Helena as *domina*, Latin for mistress, using the word in dialogue just as a novelist would use, for instance, the words *monsieur* or *amigo* to remind the reader of the French or Spanish nationality of an individual speaking in a story.

If elements of some past-life regression are unconvincing and can possibly be ascribed to material the subject has once read, or seen on television or in a cinema, how may we distinguish cases that might be genuine? Jane Evans' regression as Rebecca, the wife of a wealthy Jew in twelfth-century York,[7] was featured on Jeffrey Iverson's television program *The Bloxham Tapes*, and has often been cited as particularly compelling evidence for reincarnation. Her hypnotic account of Rebecca and her family being pursued through the streets of York by an anti-Semitic mob, hiding in the crypt of a church, and then being discovered and put to death is vivid and compulsively credible. The massacre of Jews in York, a known historical event which took place in March 1190, is not the sort of episode readily found in popular history books, yet when the tape of the regression was played to Professor Barrie Dobson of York University, a leading expert on the Jewish massacre, he confirmed its general historical accuracy.[8] And it is Professor Dobson who has provided what many have regarded as one of the most tantalizing clues of all that the Rebecca memories could be genuine. Rebecca proved unable to name the church where she and her family hid, but she said it was small, outside the gates of York, close to the Coppergate and within sight and earshot of York Castle. After listening to the tape, Professor Dobson felt this had to be St. Mary's Castlegate. The one difficulty to this identification was that St. Mary's was not known to have a crypt. Then in September 1975, long after Jane Evans had recounted the Rebecca regression, a workman involved in converting St. Mary's to a museum discovered under the chancel what seemed to have been an original crypt, but it was hastily resealed before anyone could explore it.[9] This seemed remarkable, and re-

HYPNOTIC PAST LIFE REGRESSION CLAIM
Hypnotist: Arnall Bloxham of Cardiff, S. Wales

Subject	Sex	Period	Location	Characteristics
Jane Evans **(pseudonym)**	F	Present day, b. 1939	S. Wales	Housewife of ordinary high school education, then secretarial college. Suffered from rheumatoid arthritis in early life
Past Life *Personalities*				
Sister Grace	F	c.1850– 1920	Maryland	Roman Catholic nun, arthritic
Anne Tasker	F	c.1685– 1710?	London	Serving girl in large London house
Anna	F	c.1485– 1502?	Madrid	Handmaiden to Catherine of Aragon
Alison	F	c.1429– 1451	Bourges	Egyptian-born housekeeper to wealthy Frenchman Jacques Coeur
Rebecca	F	c.1150– 1190	York	Jewess, wife of rich financier
Livonia	F	c.260– 306	York ("Eboracum")	Wife of Romano-British tutor to future emperor, Constantine the Great

Arnall Bloxham hypnotic regression of Welsh housewife Jane Evans. (Based on material from Jeffrey Iverson, *More Lives Than One?*, Pan, 1977.)

incarnation exponents have argued that this is precisely the sort of evidence which provides proof of reincarnation—for how otherwise could Rebecca have displayed historical knowledge which not even experts possessed at the time?

Some strong words of caution are needed, however. At the time of the Jewish massacre York had more than forty churches, and Professor Dobson's identification of St. Mary's Castlegate, well reasoned though it is, can scarcely be regarded as more than a guess on the evidence available. There exists no proper confirmation that any crypt actually exists at St. Mary's, even Canon Basil Norris, the church's last rector, being unaware of the discovery. And since most people expect old churches to have crypts, even if one does exist at St. Mary's Castlegate it is scarcely sufficient to provide any sound basis for arguments for or against reincarnation. In any case, Rebecca made some actual historical slips in her regression account. She referred to Coppergate as an actual gate; even in the twelfth century this was a mere street (the word "gate" comes from Old Norse and means "road" or "path"). She spoke of "Coney Street" when in the twelfth century this was known as Cuninga Street.[10] And although at the time of her regressions Jane Evans had never even visited York, it should be stressed that we know this woman subject of Bloxham's only by a pseudonym. Although she concealed her identity to maintain her privacy, the fact is that we do not know enough about her personality and youthful reading habits to eliminate the possibility that she somehow, somewhere, read a story of the massacre that quite unconsciously provided the material for her Rebecca account. Furthermore, it has to be recognized that although it is altogether credible that a wealthy Jewess called Rebecca lived in twelfth-century York and died during the massacre in the circumstances described by Jane Evans, we have absolutely no independent proof that anyone of that name actually did so.

On this latter issue we come face to face with one of the awkward chicken-and-egg problems which investigation of past-life memory cases presents. If there is a historical record, however obscure, of an alleged past life, it is always possible to argue that the subject somehow managed to read it. From this point of view Joe Keeton's subject Edna Greenan (see page 80) and her Nell Gwyn memories are difficult to tackle seriously, for the historical Nell Gwyn has been featured so often in books, films, television plays, and the like that it is impossible to eliminate the influence of these on the twentieth-century Edna. It would be an easier matter if Edna's Nell memories were historically faultless, but this is by no means the case[11] for if cornered on matters that should be common knowledge to someone of the seventeenth century she has, under hypnosis, assumed a sudden attack of tipsiness or the like.[12] On the other hand, if the life remembered is one of an ordinary, obscure individual who would never have come to the attention of history books, problems of a different order arise. As in the case of Rebecca, while we might have no proof that the individual existed, equally we have no proof that she did not. These sorts of circumstances oblige us to consider subjects who have memories of individuals far too obscure for history books, but could conceivably be traced from records which no ordinary person would normally have seen.

Alfred Orriss, a subject of Derek Crüssell, is a case in point. He is a bank executive with no commitment to any belief in reincarnation, and when Crüssell appealed in a newspaper for volunteers early in 1979, he offered to be hypnotically regressed out of sheer curiosity. Orriss proved a good subject and under regression readily produced two lives. One was of a Trooper John Orriss, apparently in action with the Essex Regiment in France during the Napoleonic Wars.[13] This occurrence of a past-life entity of the same surname as the present-day subject was an event in itself, conceivably supportive of Derek Crüssell's hypothesis of an ancestral or genetic base for the past-life phenomenon. The fact that the name Orriss is rare in England[14] made it very likely that the two Orrisses would be related, assuming that we could establish that Trooper John Orriss did once exist and was not a figment of the present-day Alfred Orriss' imagination. The military records of the Napoleonic period were scoured, and at first all seemed to go well. Although it transpired that there was more than one Essex Regiment at that time, Trooper Orriss described one of his battle companions being dressed in "a tricorn hat with yellow facings on a red uniform," which provided important clarification. Yellow facings on red tunics are known to have been exclusive to the 44th East Essex Regiment during the Napoleonic period, and a battalion officer's jacket corresponding to Orriss' description is preserved to this day in Colchester Museum.[15] Then, although birth, marriage, and death registration was not compulsory in the United Kingdom before 1836 (and since Trooper Orriss could provide no information on his birthplace there was no opportu-

nity for checking parish registers), ever since 1795 the British
Army has kept regimental muster rolls listing every serving man
with notes of his place of birth, his age and trade on enlistment,
etc. Since the muster rolls for the 44th East Essex Regiment are
preserved to this day at the Public Record Office, Kew, it was theoretically a simple matter to consult the relevant rolls for the
Napoleonic period for any trooper by the name of Orriss.

Unfortunately, however, when this was done no Trooper John
Orriss came to light. Even Orriss' use of the term "trooper"
caused concern, since this suggested a cavalryman when, according to his regression description, Orriss was no more than a foot
soldier. Other details Orriss had provided under hypnosis proved
equally unsatisfactory. According to Trooper Orriss, the man to
whom he was directly responsible was a Sergeant Williams whose
immediate superior was a Lieutenant Darby, and the regimental
commander was a Colonel Wingfield. Patient searching of the
44th's muster rolls revealed neither a Sergeant Williams nor a
Lieutenant Darby. As for Colonel Wingfield, it became clear
from a comparative check on the annual *War Office List of all
the Officers of the Army and Royal Marines*[16] between 1800 and
1815 that there was no Colonel Wingfield in charge of the 44th
East Essex Regiment, and no Wingfield of any rank remotely
resembling that of a Colonel during the whole period in question.
In fact, the 44th's commander from 1800 to 1810 was a Colonel
Charles Rainsford, from 1811 to 1813 Colonel Thomas Trigge,
and after 1813 John, Earl of Suffolk. In short, despite the detail
produced by John Orriss under hypnosis, and even making allowances for Orriss' difficulty in pinpointing the exact dates he was
remembering, it is doubtful whether any Trooper Orriss of the
Essex Regiment ever existed. Since Alfred Orriss, who is open to
any explanation of his regression, has volunteered the information
that he lived for much of his early life in Essex and is interested
in the First World War and Napoleonic seafaring, his past-life
memory might have been some dreamlike amalgam of these, produced quite unconsciously.

A similar situation exists with Sue Atkins, whose Charlie regression was discussed in the last chapter. When regressed to the
seventeenth century, Sue assumes the personality of a somewhat
pedantic and humorless Jesuit priest, Father Antony Bennet. Al-

though the Father Bennet personality is of an entirely different
character to Charlie, he is in his own way every bit as credible. In
this regression extract the priest is reliving a moment of his "dark
night of the soul":

> My life of prayer is empty . . . every priest knows from his
> confessional . . . that into one's spiritual life can come bar-
> ren deserts, and a priest is God's help, [he] waters the desert
> of his people. But there is no one to water my desert. God
> has turned away [very tense] God . . . has . . . left . . . me
> [breaking down and crying in bitter, fearful sobs] God . . .
> has . . . left . . . me. [Several seconds of uncontrollable sob-
> bing, then hysteria, then a final agonizing cry] I fear the An-
> tichrist . . .[17]

Whereas Charlie, within the period of compulsory registration of
births, marriages, and deaths, provides all too little information
about himself, Father Bennet more than two centuries earlier is
much more informative. From his references to the reign of
Charles I and Oliver Cromwell's Protectorate his date of birth
can be gauged at around 1637. He described his father as a
wealthy Royalist Catholic wool merchant called Master Richard
Bennet who was "ennobled when the king came back" (i.e.,
knighted at the time of the restoration of the monarchy under
Charles II) and became Sir Richard Bennet. Although vague
about his birthplace, Father Bennet spoke of a Stapleford (of
which there are nine in England), Suffolk and East Anglia. And
he quite specifically said that he was at a Society of Jesus semi-
nary in Rome at the age of twenty-five, that he was in France as a
curé at the parish of Puissy-sur-Seine at the age of thirty-three,
and that at the age of thirty-eight he was back in England at a
house "in the South" where his companions were a Father Peter
Barnaby and a Father Bernard Reilly. But when we try to decide
whether all these details amount to a verifiable historical existence, we come, as in the Orriss case, to immediate problems. In
the Joe Keeton book *Encounters with the Past*, the author Peter
Moss points to a historically known seventeenth-century merchant called Sir Richard Bennet, knighted by Charles II and resident at Babraham Hall, a few miles southeast of Cambridge and
not far from a Stapleford, though not in Suffolk. Moss also argues

that the Bennets probably were Catholic, at least in secret, and there was a Thomas Bennet at the head of the secret Jesuit Order in England at the time.[18] Unfortunately, this attempt to associate the historical Thomas Bennet and the hypnotic Father Antony Bennet has to be dismissed. The simple fact is that the historical Thomas Bennet was not of any family of that name. The name Bennet was merely assumed as an alias for his real surname of Blackfan. Furthermore, his origins were in Sussex, nowhere near any of the possible locations mentioned by Father Antony.[19]

And the really serious problem relating to the Father Bennet regression is the fact that if any group of people in seventeenth-century England could be called well documented, that group is the Jesuits. Despite—or perhaps because of—persecution at that time, the names and movements of all the English Jesuits of that century were meticulously recorded, as is evident from the main source work for their history in England, Father H. Foley's monumental seven-volume *Records of the English Province of the Society of Jesus,* published between 1877 and 1883. Through this work it is possible to check the name of every Jesuit with the name Bennet active in England during the seventeenth century. Father Joseph Crehan, a present-day Jesuit, has done this, and has pointed out:

> There were five Bennets among the Jesuits between 1580 and 1800. Two belonged to the eighteenth century; two were Welshmen and were dead by 1625. One was an Irish lay-brother, not a priest. None was called Antony . . . Miss Atkins has identified with a man who never was.[20]

Furthermore, as recorded in Peter Moss's book, on one occasion when Sue Atkins was regressed to Father Bennet's youth, he was asked:

"If I said *amabam, amabas, amabat,* could you finish it?"

The reply was confident:

"*Amabam, amabas, amabat, amabamus, amabatis, amabant . . . amavi, amavisti, amavit, amavimus, amavitis.*" Then, very deliberately and proudly: "*Amaverunt.*"[21]

Clearly, Father Bennet was learning Latin during a period before his ordination. There was nothing particularly spectacular in this for, as Peter Moss already knew, Sue Atkins had herself learned Latin at school and, like everyone else, would have had to learn by rote the conjugations of the verb *amare,* to love. But what fascinated Moss, and very understandably, was Father Bennet's archaic Latin pronunciation. As he remarked:

> Sue was brought up on the Victorian pronunciation with "v's" sounded as "w's" and the "i's" short as in "hit." Antony spoke them in the older fashion with the "v" sounding as "v" and the "i's" long as in the French *vite.* Sue says that her conscious mind fought to say "amawit" but she was unable to prevent "amaveet" from coming out.

Again, however, there is a fatal flaw to Peter Moss's reasoning, for despite all the cunning pronunciation, the twentieth-century Sue knows the basic raw material of these Latin conjugations. But because Sue's upbringing has been Anglican, her twentieth-century mind has never learned the words of the Latin Mass and the great traditional prayers such as the *Credo,* the *Pater Noster,* and the *Ave Maria,* whereas a genuine Father Bennet would have said these every day of his life and would inevitably have known these even better than his Latin conjugations. So asking Father Bennet to say his Latin prayers would be a crucial test of whether or not the personality was real. This test was precisely the one that occurred to the well-known London University psychologist Professor Hans Eysenck, who in autumn 1979 was invited to study Sue Atkins' regressions for the magazine *Now!* He described the result as follows:

> Father Antony never got beyond the first two words of *"Pater noster."* The notion that a Jesuit priest who has been to Rome could not say a Latin prayer is of course preposterous, and that he would not know his Paternoster is beyond belief.[22]

Once submitted to closer scrutiny, the phenomenon of past-life regression suddenly appears less convincing, and we are obliged to look with renewed suspicion at some of the cases surveyed in the last chapter. What, for instance, of Crüssell subject Carol Dow's handwriting as Zenia (see page 73)? While at face value this does have a period look, there the illusion stops that it might be anything of a real past-life nature. In true period handwriting the "3" character remarked on normally denotes an initial "y" or a guttural "gh"; never, as in Carol's Zenia script, a final "s". Similarly, her use of the word "yea" within the "Contry fayre" poem is quite incorrect, the poem itself having no as yet identified historical provenance. As has, in fact, been verified from samples of Carol's hypnotic script studied by Mr. M. A. F. Borrie, Assistant Keeper of the Department of Manuscripts at the British Museum, the handwriting bears no real resemblance to any authentic sixteenth- or seventeenth-century hand he has come across, the letter forms being basically modern.[23] And when I submitted the Zenia poem to Dr. Vernon Harrison of Great Bookham, Surrey, a retired specialist in handwriting counterfeits, his view was that Carol had quite unconsciously adopted features from her own early handwriting, and that behind all appearances the twentieth-century Carol was still at work. Carol, a Crüssell volunteer with no commitment to any belief in reincarnation, has confirmed that she was born left-handed and taught to write with her right hand, and regards the Borrie and Harrison interpretations as acceptable as any. With Carol herself having absolutely no conscious intention to deceive, the intriguing feature has to be whatever it was that caused her while in the hypnotic state to write in the guise of a someone else, and with such flamboyance and inventiveness.

What of the accents? It cannot be ignored that those who exhibit these have invariably had friends or relations with similar accents. Whatever the source of Bridey Murphy, Virginia Tighe did have an Irish-accented aunt, just as Michael O'Mara had Irish relations—and, since he has lived in Britain for several years, has had the opportunity to pick up, albeit unconsciously, an Irish intonation. Tom Troscianko, the research psychologist who regressed to a Polish-accented Armid,[24] listened very carefully to everything he had said under hypnosis, and was confident that there was no feature, including the accent, which he could not have acquired through his upbringing with Polish-born parents. And what of the German of Gretchen? It is to be observed that although the Reverend Carroll Jay, the hypnotist involved in the case, has written his own lengthy account, *Gretchen I Am* (published in the United States in 1977), he has failed to make clear that Gretchen's German was, to say the least, of a very poor quality, a feature which Dr. Ian Stevenson has been at some pains to stress. As Stevenson reported:

> She rather often simply omitted words, especially auxiliary verbs. She showed no knowledge of the inverted word order used in German subsidiary clauses. And she seemed also to have no ability to use the past and future tenses of the German verbs.[25]

Most of what Gretchen said consisted of short phrases of only a few words, and the vocabulary this displayed was little more convincing. In nineteen tape-recorded sessions held over a period of four years she managed only 237 German words not perviously supplied to her by someone speaking to her in German, and since approximately half of these were cognates of English words, she produced on average a mere half-dozen "original" words per session—scarcely an impressive performance. She grossly mispronounced some words, and showed no signs of any convincing German regional accent. The first native-speaking German to whom Stevenson introduced the case, a Dr. Doris Wilsdorf, was so unimpressed that she declined to sign a statement saying that Gretchen could speak the language responsively.[26] Given that no one in the West can fail to acquire some German, albeit unconsciously, from snatches spoken in films, television plays, and the like, there really is little to commend Gretchen's German as compelling evidence for reincarnation. It is further to be noted that Mrs. Jay's ancestry was German, and although she claims that her parents did not speak the language, some early long-forgotten exposure to it, or perhaps even an inherited "dream" of the type hinted at in Chapter 2, cannot be ruled out.

The case of the Jensen personality and the Swedish xenoglossy is even more dubious once submitted to closer scrutiny. The American doctor and his wife who were hypnotist and subject in the case continually resisted publication or other publicity for reasons of privacy, hence Stevenson's obligatory adoption of pseudonyms. Although Stevenson has stressed that his own exhaustive checks on their integrity did not find anything untoward, he has also recorded circumstances relating to the subject's behavior which can only be regarded as disturbing. As Stevenson states in *Xenoglossy*, his report on the Jensen case:

> During the years 1960–61 . . . [the woman subject] developed a more conventional mediumship with a control and various communicators . . . [some of whom] delivered messages about scientific investigations in biology. On two occasions it was possible to trace these messages to sources earlier than their delivery by the subject in the mediumistic trances. Once notes closely resembling one of the "scientific messages" were found scribbled in a notebook she carried in her purse. And once a book she had borrowed from a public library was found to contain passages which were repeated almost verbatim in a message delivered during a trance. When she was told about the existence of the messages in her notebook and of the passages in the library book, she became extremely anxious and frightened. I was present during this scene. She insisted she had absolutely no recollection of having read the book in question or of having written the messages in her notebook (although she recognized her own handwriting) and concluded that she must have made these entries during an involuntary trance for which she was afterwards amnesic.[27]

Although Stevenson would argue otherwise, such circumstances (particularly given the concealment of the identities of the doctor and his wife involved) can scarcely do other than cause strong suspicions that the Jensen xenoglossy originated in the same manner. The identities of the doctor and his wife have become known to me and suffice it to say that the case does not merit the serious consideration which Stevenson has advanced for it.

It is now clear that some of the ostensibly compelling evidence for reincarnation as exhibited by past-life regression cases is fatally flawed. But I must also stress that in all cases discussed in this book, even that of Jensen, there is not the slightest cause for doubting the honesty of the subjects and hypnotists involved, for the integrity of those whose identities are known to me is absolutely beyond question.

This gives rise to a consideration which we cannot now overlook. However much we have explained away some of the material of past lives in this chapter—the inconsistencies, the anachronisms, the lack of depth—something must have fired a subject such as Jane Evans quite unconsciously to produce such fluent historical material in her regression as Livonia. Even if Graham Huxtable acquired his "memory" of the eighteenth-century gun battle from some long-forgotten historical novel, something very powerful must have caused him to relive the scene in his mind so vividly. Similarly, something must have inspired Sue Atkins to take on the extraordinarily contrasting personalities of Charlie and Father Bennet. Something must have worked so profoundly on Ann Dowling that it caused her to reproduce on her body bruises inflicted on the deceased and presumably illusory Sarah. Something has to have guided Carol Dow's hand in an albeit fake seventeenth-century script. And flawed though Gretchen's German may be, something has to have caused it to come so involuntarily from the lips of Dolores Jay, complete with a haunting tale of religious persecution. Indeed, the subjects of both the Gretchen and Jensen cases showed alarming signs of becoming "possessed" by their past-life personalities, suffering waking hallucinations and the like to such an extent that the hypnotists in each case were obliged to abandon further experiments. The question is: What can have brought about all these phenomena? We have some very profound questions to answer. If, as it might seem, it is all mere play-acting, where is the script coming from? What is making the actors perform the way they do? What is creating the special effects like handwriting, facial changes, and phantom wounds? What manner of producer is directing this extraordinary tableau if it is not coming from the subject's conscious mind? We now need to go backstage to examine the very machinery of a hypnotic past life.

CHAPTER 7

The Source of the Script

PSYCHOLOGISTS AND PSYCHIATRISTS have long recognized that in our day-to-day lives we receive through our senses far more than that of which we are consciously aware. As we walk down a city Main Street, our thoughts may seem to be totally preoccupied with some domestic problem. Everywhere we look there may be advertising signs, street names, shop numbers, traffic signs, car registration numbers, none of which we may be aware of reading—until the impinging of a single familiar car registration number tells us that a friend has just passed by. Unconsciously we have been taking in far more than that to which we were consciously directing our thoughts. A particularly powerful example of this is what advertising agencies refer to as "subliminal advertising."[1] Every second that a motion picture film runs before our eyes we actually see twenty-four separate and minutely different film frames, even though we are consciously aware only of the visual impression of motion. At every twenty-fourth frame or thereabouts subliminal advertising substitutes some simple sales message which is designed to pass before the eyes so rapidly that to the consciousness it is undetectable. As you might expect, the practice is universally banned, but from our point of view the important aspect is that the mind not only receives the message without being aware of it, but also may even feel an irrational compulsion to act upon it. We have been invaded by the back door.

On the same principle it is becoming increasingly clear that we record somehow and somewhere in our minds far more than that to which we have conscious access. Consider the almost embarrassing difficulty most of us will find if asked to describe exactly something we think we know really well—the face of our watch, the handle of our front door, the dial of the car speedometer. Consciously we will almost inevitably make mistakes, even with such familiar objects, yet if one of these was changed without our knowledge we would instantly recognize something was wrong. Unconsciously we really do know what they look like. Although research into such matters is in its infancy, theoretically there seems every probability that all our experiences, every book, newspaper, comic, or annual we have read or had read to us, every speech and sermon we may have nodded through, every snatch of conversation on which we might have eavesdropped, every magazine story we might have glanced at in a crowded waiting room, every radio program that might have blared at us unwanted from a neighbor's transistor as we dozed on a holiday beach, lie somewhere in the extraordinary repository we call the unconscious mind. And no man has contributed more to what we so far understand of this than a brilliant yet modest and publicly almost unknown Canadian neurosurgeon, Dr. Wilder Penfield.[2] From the late 1930s Penfield, who died in 1976, pioneered operations on epileptics during which, after only a local anesthetic, the surgeon removed a flap of the skull and explored with electrodes the conscious, working brain. Alarming as such techniques may sound, they are made possible by the brain's own insensitivity to pain, and enabled Penfield, from the patients' verbal responses, carefully to map which areas of cortex seemed to control which functions. But Penfield was quite unprepared for the response when one day he applied his electrode to a patient's temporal lobe. To his astonishment the patient suddenly began reliving a complete moment from earlier in his life just as if a moving picture was being rerun in front of him.

As Penfield was to discover, this was no mere freak of one patient in one operation. During his long and distinguished career at Montreal's Neurological Institute this extraordinary mechanism reappeared in operations on some forty different patients, each of whose "experiential responses," as Penfield called them, were carefully noted by attendant stenographers. A typical case in point was that of a twenty-six-year-old girl whom we will refer to as Mary[3] who, although of perfectly normal intelligence, had suffered intermittent epileptic seizures for years, these themselves being sometimes accompanied by strange flashbacks from her earlier life. Early on the morning of September 25, 1952, Penfield's nurses shaved her head completely, the surgeon opened up a large portion of her skull, and after preliminary explorations applied a three-volt electrical stimulation directly to the cortex of her temporal lobe. Mary was fully conscious and, although separated from Penfield by a surgical sheet, her response was immediate:

"I heard something. I do not know what it was."

Without warning Mary, Penfield restimulated.

"Yes, sir, I think I heard a mother calling her little boy somewhere. It seemed to be something that happened years ago."

Penfield asked Mary to be more specific.

"It was somebody in the neighborhood where I live," she explained, adding that she herself must be "somewhere close enough to hear."

Penfield moved the electrode an inch or so, to a neighboring point on the cortex.

"Yes. I heard voices down along the river somewhere—a man's voice and a woman's voice calling . . . I think I saw the river."

Penfield asked her what river.

"I do not know. It seems to be one I was visiting when I was a child."

Penfield reactivated the current in the same place, without telling Mary that he was doing so.

"Yes, I hear voices. It is late at night, around the carnival somewhere. Some sort of traveling circus . . . I just saw lots of big wagons that they use to haul animals in."

Penfield moved the electrode to a slightly different point and again restimulated.

"I seemed to hear little voices then. The voices of people calling from building to building somewhere. I do not know where it is, but it seems very familiar to me. I cannot see the buildings now, but they seemed to be run-down buildings."

Now Penfield took a needle that was insulated down to the tip and, after inserting this deep into the cleft of the brain known as the fissure of Sylvius, again reactivated the electric current.

"Oh! I had the same, very, very familiar memory, in an office somewhere. I could see the desks. I was there and someone was calling to me. A man leaning on a desk with a pencil in his hand."

Penfield, always sensitive to his prime objective of treating the patient's epileptic condition, nevertheless marveled each time he encountered this phenomenon. As his reports in the medical journal *Brain* make clear,[4] the type of incidents reactivated were almost invariably the trivia of life, the sort of material quickly and seemingly irretrievably lost to conscious memory: laughing with friends, listening for whether a baby is awake, grabbing a stick from a dog's mouth, watching a man crawl through a fence at a baseball game, even putting a hat on a hatstand. While ordinary memory seems to dart back and forth, the reexperiences of Penfield's patients moved forward and only forward, never back.[5] They always included moving pictures, never still. Reexperiences of music always followed the precise original tempo of the music, the full score of which the patient would be able to hum with total accuracy, something they would invariably claim themselves incapable of in normal consciousness. Like the tape on a video tape-recorder the reexperiences would run only while the current was applied and stop abruptly the moment the stimulation ceased. Most intriguingly of all, during the memories, Penfield's patients, just like passive-observer hypnotic regression subjects, would retain full consciousness of their immediate surroundings in the Montreal operating theater even while the sights and sounds of the past unrolled before them. At the same time, they would reexperience their original emotions. For example, one patient under stimulation shouted out: "There they go, yelling at me. Stop them!"

What Penfield seems to have found surgically is some kind of mental equivalent of an aircraft's "black box" flight recorder, a sort of recording track of all past experiences which can be reactivated under certain circumstances. The existence of this mechanism is independently attested to by a number of peculiar case histories from medical journals. One example is that of a well-bred elderly Englishwoman who in the year 1902, having been saved by her physician Dr. Henry Freeborn from a near-fatal bronchial attack, suddenly astounded him and the attendant nurse by beginning to declaim loudly in a language eventually identified by a visitor as perfect Hindustani.[6] The woman seemed to be asking to go to the bazaar to buy sweets and reciting complete Hindustani poems. When, after a week, she had sufficiently recovered from the delirium the woman was able to explain that while consciously she had no recollection of any Hindustani, and indeed had forgotten she had ever learned the language, she had spent the first three years of her life in India when she had been in the care of *ayahs* or nursemaids and had spoken nothing but Hindustani. During her delirium her recording track of this time, irretrievable to normal consciousness, seems somehow to have been reactivated. Later during her delirium she began speaking not only in normal English, but also in French and German, languages she had learned later in life. There was a detectable chronological sequence, just as if during the delirium her recording track was on some form of fast-forward wind (to use tape-recording terminology), to take her back to the present day.

The Freeborn case may today seem a little ancient, but it has been corroborated by reliable and recent research into the mind's retention of consciously long-forgotten language patterns. For instance, in 1970 the widely respected University of Chicago psychologist Professor Erika Fromm published the case of Don,[7] a twenty-six-year-old Californian whose parents, although racially Japanese, spoke at home only in English. Don grew up thinking he knew only a smattering of words of Japanese—no more than "grandmother," "good food," "Is it okay if I eat now?" and "Thank you," all learned from his bilingual grandmother. Hypnotically regressed to the age of three, however, Don spoke fluent Japanese, in a high-pitched child's voice, for some fifteen to twenty minutes. It transpired that at that age Don had been interned with his parents at an American "relocation center" for those of Japanese blood (a World War II security precaution), at which Japanese was the predominant language. When Don left the relocation center his parents reverted to being exclusively

English-speaking, and the child lost all conscious awareness that he had ever known the language. When the tape of his Japanese was played to him, Don was quite unable to understand most of what he said—just as Freeborn's patient would have been. Native Japanese-speakers, however, confirmed that his unconscious recording track had preserved the language perfectly.

Essentially what we are dealing with is a mental mechanism often called cryptomnesia, or memory of which we have no conscious awareness. It may come as a surprise that our first inquiries into the relevance of this to hypnotic past-life cases take us back three quarters of a century to one of the very earliest known examples. The case was thoroughly investigated by a member of the British Society for Psychical Research[8] and deserves recounting in some detail. The one unfortunate feature is that, in accordance with prevailing attitudes at the time, the actual identity of the subject was concealed. All that we know about her was that she was a clergyman's daughter of good general education, a moderately well-balanced personality, though perhaps with an unduly marked interest in paranormal phenomena. She is referred to in the case as Miss C., but for convenience we will call her Cynthia. The year was 1906, long before hypnotic past-life regression became fashionable, and Cynthia, purely for experimental purposes, agreed to be hypnotized by a doctor. At an early stage in these experiments she began producing remarkably detailed past-life material seeming to date from the time of King Richard II, who reigned at the end of the fourteenth century.

Going back in time (into what she called "the blue"), Cynthia found herself in conversation with a woman who gave her name as Blanche Poynings. Blanche told Cynthia that she was a great friend of Maud, Countess of Salisbury. She poured out detail after detail of the Countess' life: her maiden name, Maud Francis, the names of her first two husbands, John Aubrey and Sir Alan de Buxhull, the names of the Earl of Salisbury's children by Maud, the names of the Earl of Salisbury's brothers, the Earl's family name of Montacute, the Earl's title of Lord of the Isle of Man, his possession of the manor of Bisham, his religious affiliations with Lollardy, even the names of some of his retainers, such as Ralph Turval and his wife Ellen, one of the Countess' attendants. Blanche gave an equally complex set of names and personalities relating to her own domestic affairs, among these her maiden name, De Mowbray, and the varying fortunes of her four husbands: Lord Bertram, Lord Poynings, Sir John Worth, and Sir John Wilshire. She spoke warmly of a period she had spent at Court as one of the ladies in waiting to Richard II's Queen, and among various leading royal figures she mentioned with particular affection Richard II's mother Joan, "The Fair Maid of Kent," a memorably fat and jolly individual. Blanche was also full of information about the costume and social life of the period:

> She used to wear brocade and velvet, trimmed with ermine and a high-peaked cap of miniver. She wore blue velvet embroidered with gold. Men wore shoes with long points which were chained to their knees. They had long hair cut straight across the forehead.

She talked of three kinds of bread that used to be eaten: simnel, wastel, and cotchel, each eaten by different classes. She spoke of her own favorite food as being lampreys stewed in oil. She talked of the medicine of the time, when each major house had its own doctor whose invariable remedy was bleeding the patient:

> She used to have ague and they bled for that. When she had smallpox they bled her every third day, and put on cold water compresses and nearly starved her. They gave her bitter medicine. She thinks it was dandelion.

Blanche said her own time was chiefly taken up with conversation and needlework, punctuated by occasional journeys to Bisham and to "Stepany" to see the hawthorn hedges in the spring.

Cynthia's regression was as fluent and informative as that of Arnall Bloxham's Jane Evans. And when Mr. G. Lowes Dickinson began to check this out for the British Society for Psychical Research he was astonished to find that detail after detail about the lives and activities of the Earl and Countess of Salisbury in Richard II's time could actually be verified. What particularly impressed him was that so much of the material, especially that relating to the Earl and Countess, was not to be found in general history books, but had to be searched out in very obscure chronicles of the kind he felt sure that Cynthia could never have read. Lowes Dickinson even discovered that Blanche Poynings was herself a known historical character, although all he could find about her were the most meager references in a couple of chronicles, simply confirming that she was indeed one of the ladies in attendance on Richard II's Queen, Anne of Bohemia. When Lowes Dickinson questioned Cynthia, out of hypnosis, on what she knew of the reign of Richard II she claimed in all honesty never to have studied the period, and found herself quite unable to account for how she could have acquired such a wealth of accurate historical detail. She mentioned that she could remember reading one historical novel called *John Standish* about the period, but when Lowes Dickinson checked this it was quite clearly not the source of her story. Bearing in mind that Cynthia was a clergyman's daughter, a less diligent investigator might have left the matter there, but Lowes Dickinson was determined that there must be some rational explanation.

His breakthrough came one day when he went to tea with Cynthia and her aunt. The conversation turned to spiritualism, a subject in which the couple clearly had a keen interest, and Cynthia spoke with some enthusiasm of how with a planchette— a device similar to a Ouija board and used for spirit messages— she could draw faces which were faces whichever way you looked at them. Lowes Dickinson encouraged her to demonstrate this, applauding her for her skill, then switched the conversation to a more serious note. Would she be prepared to use the planchette for communications with Blanche Poynings? To his satisfaction, Cynthia agreed.

The emergence of Blanche Poynings via the planchette was almost immediate. Her first messages were critical of Cynthia for not having been in touch with her recently, then skillfully Lowes Dickinson directed questioning first to routine items on which he already knew the answers, Blanche responding in her familiarly factual and accurate way, then, obliquely yet insistently, to Blanche's sources:

Q: How can we confirm what you are telling us?
A: Read his will.
Q: Whose will?
A: Wilshire's [her fourth husband]. He died first.
Q: Where is it?

A: Museum.

Q: What part?

A: On a parchment.

Q: How can we get at it?

A: Ask the man.

Q: Any particular man?

A: No. Ask E. Holt.

Q: Who is E. Holt?

A: An antiquarian.

Q: Where is he?

A: Dead. There is a book.

Q: Where is it?

A: I don't know where it is. Mrs. Holt.

Q: What has she to do with it?

A: Ask her.

Q: Do you know where she lives?

A: No. Wrote a book.

Q: What about?

A: About all of them. All the people are in it.

Q: What else?

A: I am there.

Q: What else is it about?

A: Maud.

Q: Is what it says about you good?

A: Not interesting enough. *Countess Maud* by Emily Holt.

Q: Why didn't you tell me that before?

A: I would have told you but you went away.

By this totally unorthodox means Lowes Dickinson had obtained the vital information that the source of Blanche Poynings was a book of which he now knew the author and title. As soon as the planchette session was finished he began questioning Cynthia and her aunt on what they knew of Emily Holt and *Countess Maud*. Immediately a chord was struck in their memories. Cynthia said she thought there certainly was a novel of this title and that both

she and her aunt had read it some years ago. In all honesty, however, they had completely forgotten about it, and had no idea
whether Blanche Poynings was even mentioned. An inquiry at a
bookseller's revealed to Lowes Dickinson that an Emily Holt, a
prolific novelist with a scrupulous attention to historical detail
and accuracy, had indeed written *Countess Maud or The
Changes of the World, A Tale of the Fourteenth Century* back
in 1892. On obtaining a copy Lowes Dickinson immediately
confirmed that it was the source of the Blanche Poynings memories, for although Blanche was a relatively unimportant character
in the story itself, the people and events described were to all intents and purposes identical. The book even carried a historical
appendix in which everything known about the Earl of Salisbury's
family and Blanche Poynings and her husbands was carefully
listed.

Someone else might have left the discovery there, but Lowes
Dickinson decided to take it just one stage further. On November
10, 1906, he arranged one final hypnotic session with Cynthia, in
which the doctor-hypnotist regressed her to the moment in her
own childhood in which she had seen the book. In his report for
the Society of Psychical Research, Lowes Dickinson reproduced
the exact transcript of what followed:

Q: Can you see yourself young?
A: Yes.
Q: Can you see your aunt reading a book, *Countess Maud?*
A: Yes, blue book with gold line across name of it.
Q: What is it about?
A: Ellen Turval and the Earl and Countess of Salisbury.
Q: How old were you?
A: Twelve.
Q: Did you read it yourself?
A: I looked at it, and painted a picture in the beginning.
Q: Did you read the appendix?
A: No.
Q: Did your aunt?
A: No.

Q: What was it about?

A: The people in the book. I used to turn over the pages. I didn't read it, because it was dull. Blanche Poynings was in the book; not much about her.

Q: How much did you get from Blanche Poynings—how much from the book?

A: Nearly all the events from the book, but not her character . . . There was a real person called Blanche Poynings that I met, and I think her name started the memory, and I got the two mixed up.

Essentially the case was solved. The edition of *Countess Maud* that I obtained through the public library system was indeed in blue binding with gold lettering, and has a single illustration which happens to be of Blanche Poynings being presented to Richard II's Queen, with Joan "The Fair Maid of Kent" sitting to the left. It also has a very detailed appendix showing how meticulously Emily Holt assembled the novel from historically accurate material. In fact, Cynthia must have read this, despite her hypnotic denial, because some of Blanche Poynings' information was unquestionably derived from it. She must also have employed some degree of invention, albeit quite unconsciously, since in *Countess Maud* Blanche was delineated as pious and discreet, while Cynthia's regression portrayal of her was, in Lowes Dickinson's words, that of "a garrulous and flippant gossip." Clearly, *Countess Maud* had provided Cynthia's Blanche Poynings with a script, a source both historically factual and historically plausible, from which the whole basis of a past-life personality could be assembled. Given the fact that the mind really does seem to absorb every item of information which it comes across in its experience, a complete explanation of the content of past-life regressions has thereby emerged, an explanation that, ironically, was available nearly half a century before the Bridey Murphy case hit the headlines.

Jeffrey Iverson, Arnall Bloxham's author, has argued that, unlike the subjects of the hypnotic past-life regressions conducted since the 1950s, Cynthia never actually identified herself with Blanche Poynings; she merely spoke of her as a person she met "out in the blue," in very much the manner of a spiritualist guide.[9] Against this, however, it can be argued that Cynthia merely adopted the fashion of past-life communication of the time, which was based on spiritualism, and we have already noticed how the regressions can be prone to the expectations and dogmatic leanings of the hypnotist.

The real issue, however, is that Lowes Dickinson's findings are supported by recent work. Even in the 1950s, for instance, as a refutation of the Bridey Murphy case, the American psychologist Milton V. Kline produced a rather hastily assembled *Scientific Report on "The Search for Bridey Murphy,"*[10] strongly advocating the cryptomnesia or hidden-memory argument, and quoting a case which goes a long way to explain the Zenia handwriting referred to in Chapters 5 and 6. One of Milton Kline's contributors was a Dr. Harold Rosen of Toronto, who described how one of his patients under hypnosis wrote in an extraordinary script which at first baffled those who studied it until it was eventually identified as Oscan, a language spoken in western Italy only up to the first century B.C., when it was superseded by Latin. Few examples of written Oscan have survived, but one of these, the so-called "Curse of Vibia" (a fifth-century B.C. leaden scroll buried with a dead Oscan, to help him on his journey in the underworld), was found to match exactly with what Rosen's subject had written. Rosen thought that the patient must have seen a picture of this curse in a book, but the patient vigorously denied this, claiming that not only had he never heard of Oscan, but he had not even studied Latin. Eventually, however, Rosen traced the patient's memory to a source not unlike Cynthia's. Several years before, the patient had been sitting in a library while someone next to him was consulting a book open at a page on which the Oscan curse was reproduced. The patient had merely glanced at this page, retaining no conscious memory of ever having seen it. But the image of the printed letters imprinted itself so strongly on his unconscious mind that he was able to reproduce them under hypnosis with remarkable accuracy.

Another American researcher active in checking out past-life regression at this time was Edwin S. Zolik of Marquette University.[11] Zolik recruited undergraduate volunteers, replicated the Bridey Murphy experiment, and found one subject, a thirty-two-year-old of Irish descent, who readily produced a past life as Brian

O'Malley—an Irishman with the English Army, born in 1850 and killed in a fall from a horse in 1892. At a second hypnotic session, this time without regression, Zolik questioned the student on where he had first come across the name Brian O'Malley. It emerged that this was an individual about whom the student's grandfather had often told stories during his childhood. O'Malley was an Irish soldier with the English Army who had quarreled with his grandfather and had driven him out of Ireland. He was later killed in an accident with a horse. It was particularly interesting that the student associated the memory of the story with an incident in which, at the age of eight, he himself had earned his grandfather's wrath by taking out a particular horse which his grandfather had specifically instructed him not to ride. As Zolik suggested, the student could be argued to have identified himself with O'Malley because in association with a horse both were the subject of his grandfather's anger. However, the main principle is that again the source of a past-life regression has been identified, this time in a tale told by a grandfather.

But unquestionably the individual who has been foremost in recent years in demonstrating a cryptomnesic base to hypnotic past-life regression has been one whose work is largely unknown in the United States and Britain, simply because his studies have been in his native Finland. This is Dr. Reima Kampman,[12] a psychiatrist of the Department of Psychiatry at the University of Oulu, a Finnish town on the seacoast at the northern end of the Gulf of Bothnia. In the 1960s Dr. Reima Kampman obtained the cooperation of an Oulu secondary school in allowing large numbers of its older pupils, with parental permission, to take part in hypnotic regression experiments specifically aimed at uncovering the truth behind past-life regression. Finding a proportion of the students good deep-trance hypnotic subjects, Kampman gave several of these the suggestion that they were back in time in past lives, and early on uncovered some colorful personalities of this type, among these a seaman who allegedly sailed on the *Pinta*, one of the three vessels used by Christopher Columbus when he discovered America.[13] From such stories Kampman felt sure that they were based on items the subject had read, but actually proving

this and demonstrating the mechanisms involved was a task that
required years of patience and ingenuity.

Kampman found, for instance, one fifteen-year-old girl who produced a past life as a boy of seven living at the base of a big
mountain.[14] The "boy" said his father was Aitmatov, the captain
of a boat which sailed on Lake Issyjokul, and described a somewhat lonely existence, terminated by a dreamlike drowning in the
lake one day when he tried to swim to reach his father. This case
did not represent too great a difficulty to Kampman. Rehypnotiz-
ing the girl at a subsequent session, he suggested to her that she
could remember where she had first heard of the little boy, and
out tumbled the name of a book, *Valkoinen laiva* (*The White
Ship*). A check with the original revealed that it was unquestionably the source of the girl's story, for the circumstances of the
boy's drowning and the name of the lake were exactly the same.
Aitmatov was, in fact, the name of the book's author.

Far more interesting for Kampman were the past lives of a girl
whom we will call Niki.[15] Fond of music, painting, and writing,
Niki was a well-balanced student of average ability at the Oulu
secondary school, but as a hypnotic subject she was easily able to
enter a deep hypnotic state of the somnambulistic type—that is,
she was unable to remember anything that took place. Kampman
first regressed her to the age of fifteen, then to ten, then back a
year at a time to the age of one. He observed: "Her movements
became infantile, her speech was childish, and her vocabulary
consisted of only a few words." Kampman then suggested she go
back to a time fifty years before she was born, slowly repeating
the instruction several times, stressing that it would all be perfectly normal and that everything she experienced would happen
quite spontaneously. A past life was immediately produced. Niki
described herself as a twenty-year-old Karolina Prokojeff, only
daughter of a captain who had died in the Russian Revolution.
She had a fiancé, Vasili, who was a teacher at an elementary
school at Petrovski, near Petrograd. Asked if she too lived near
Petrograd, she became embarrassed and apologized for having
used this name. The name of the city had been changed to
Leningrad, she said, and it was forbidden to use the old name.
Age-regressed to earlier in her life as Karolina, she was orderly and

consistent in adhering to a chronological sequence of events, and
talked of being at home with her mother and her governess Helena while her father was at work on his duties as a captain.

Given the suggestion that she should go back in time to before
Karolina's birth, Niki immediately produced another personality,
this time as a ten-year-old Judith Martinson, living in Solby,
Skåne. She said she was friendly with a shopkeeper's son, Anders
Soldal. He went to school, but she did not. Brought forward to
the age of twenty in this personality, she said her name was now
Judith Ivarsson, for she had married a Johan Ivarsson, an alcoholic, who sometimes behaved violently toward her. Instructed to
go back in time to even before the birth of Judith Martinson,
Niki came up with an English personality, Emily Sunderland,
born in 1743. She described herself as wife to a member of the
House of Lords, and gave a detailed description of her travels,
talking of distances in miles, and adopting every air of a sophisticated and dignified English lady, although of course speaking
Finnish. Kampman decided to try to push Niki's memories even
further back, this time by the technique of suggesting that she
was free of them, and could, as it were, observe them at a distance, whereupon Niki then reeled off a list of lives yet earlier
than Emily Sunderland: one as Geneviève de Bonde, born in
Paris at the end of the seventeenth century; one as Dorothy, an
innkeeper's daughter living near Norwich, England, during the
Middle Ages; one as Gunhild, a fisherman's wife living in Stor-
viken, Norway, and born in 846; one as Ving Lei, a blind Chinese
girl from Nanking who died from falling off a steep cliff about
the year 100; and the earliest of all, one as Bessina, living in
Babylonia just before the beginning of the Christian era.

As will immediately be noted from the list on page 112, the dis-
parity of birthplaces and the relatively long gaps between lives has
much in common with some of Arnall Bloxham's cases, and this
is probably because, unguided by any reincarnation theory from
Kampman, the subject felt free to choose personalities across the
widest spectrum of time and space. But what primarily concerned
Kampman, fictitious as he believed Niki's past-life personalities to
be, was what lay behind the memories and whether, in fact, the
personalities changed over a period of years. He deliberately

waited some seven years before hypnotizing Niki again, to find, to his considerable interest, that while she had retained the memories of all the previous personalities (this memory retention being characteristic of Bloxham's and Keeton's subjects also), she had also acquired four new ones. One of the most interesting of these, because it was historically recent, was that of a girl whose name Niki gave as Karin Bergström.[16] Karin described herself as having died at the age of seven in a World War II air raid in 1939. She gave the exact day the bomb fell, the address where she was living at the time, together with the full names of her parents and her father's occupation. A case such as this could be directly checked against modern population records and could demonstrate the sort of material from which Niki derived her information. Kampman made his first check on Finland's national register of births, marriages, and deaths. Had a Karin Bergström, or any relatives of that name, died in an air raid on the date Niki had given under hypnosis? The answer was no. The source for Niki's material had therefore to be elsewhere. As in the case of the *White Ship* subject, Kampman rehypnotized Niki and, without regressing her to a past life, suggested that she was back in time in her present life at the moment when she first came across the information in the Karin Bergström memories. Niki immediately went back to when she was a little girl turning over the leaves of a book of souvenir pictures of Finland's history during World War II. One of the pictures showed the address Niki had given under hypnosis as that of Karin Bergström, and beside this was a picture of a seven-year-old girl of another name who had died with her mother during an air raid on the exact day Niki had quoted. Clearly Niki had assembled her Karin Bergström personality from all this information—the address and the date of the air raid—just as Cynthia had assembled Blanche Poynings.

Kampman now turned his attention to another of Niki's past-life personalities, Ving Lei, the blind Chinese girl who had fallen off the cliff. With Niki again hypnotized but regressed only in relation to her present life, Kampman asked her to relive any episode of this which was similar to the experience described by Ving Lei. Kampman immediately found Niki back in time at the age of four. As she recounted with great emotion, she had been

Subject	Sex	Period	Location	Characteristics
Niki (pseudonym)	F	Present day	Oulu, Finland	Well-balanced student of average ability, fond of music, painting and writing
Past Life Personalities				
Karin Bergström	F	1932–1939	Finland	Young girl, killed in World War II air-raid
Karolina Prokojeff	F	Early 1900's	Petrograd/ Leningrad	Daughter of White Russian captain
Judith Martinson/ Ivarsson	F	19th c.	Solby, Skåne	Did not go to school, married alcoholic
Emily Sunderland	F	1743–?	England	Wife of member of House of Lords
Geneviève de Bonde	F	c.1699	Paris	?
Dorothy	F	13th c.	England	Innkeeper's daughter
Gunhild	F	846–?	Storviken, Norway	Fisherman's wife
Ving Lei	F	c.100	Nanking, China	Blind Chinese girl who fell from cliff
Bessina	F	1st c. BC	Babylonia	?

Dr. Reima Kampman hypnotic regression case of Niki, a Finnish student. Dr. Kampman was able to discover twentieth-century cryptomnesia sources for the Karin Bergström, Dorothy, and Ving Lei memories. Note the similarity of the range of lives to those of the Bloxham and Wambach variety. (Based on Dr. Reima Kampman, *Hypnotically Induced Multiple Personality*, Oulu, 1973.)

left alone in a dark room, asleep on the upper level of a bunk bed. She had waked up terrified and, fumbling in the darkness, fell headlong onto the floor below. In the Ving Lei personality she seems to have recreated this actual moment of childhood terror, blending this with some "Chinese girl" storybook character which Kampman did not trace.[17]

Kampman's final choice for investigation, however, was unquestionably the most fascinating of all. On an occasion when he was exploring Niki's medieval English personality in further detail, she gave a strikingly detailed account of contemporary English happenings, then to his astonishment proceeded, while still in deep hypnosis, to sing in English what she called the "Summer Song." Kampman consulted English specialists at the University of Oulu and found that the language Niki, as Dorothy, was using for this song was not even ordinary English, but quite unmistakably Middle English, correct for the thirteenth-century period in which Dorothy claimed to live. When Kampman inquired of Niki, out of hypnosis, whether she had any recollection of how she might have come across such an unusual item, she was quite unable to account for it. So far as she was aware, she had never seen or heard it before. Kampman therefore tried yet again the procedure of suggesting to Niki, under hypnosis, that she was back in time to whatever moment she had seen or heard the "Summer Song." The results were more conclusive than he might have dared hope. This time Niki found herself back at the age of thirteen, browsing in a library. She saw herself picking up a book entitled *Musiikin vaiheet* (*The Phases of Music*), observing the authors of the book to be Benjamin Britten and Imogen Holst. She saw herself not reading the book, but simply flicking through the pages, one of these happening to fall open at the "Summer Song." Niki was even aware of the exact location of this page within the book. When Kampman checked with the original, everything was exactly as Niki described, the song even being in modernized Middle English, just as Niki had sung it.[18]

The work of Reima Kampman and the others that we have studied in this chapter suggest that the "script" for past-life regressions might be provided by present-life material so deeply buried in the subject's brain that he or she will not have the slightest awareness of it. We have learned of the very considerable emotion that people under hypnosis display: they see themselves in a different body, they assume a markedly different accent, their facial appearance changes, they take on a sometimes totally opposite personality, they display actual physical wounds, bruises, and rashes on the skin, they may even appear to die. We may now understand the source of the "script." But where can such "acting" come from—acting that every subject, without exception, has described as from something beyond their normal consciousness?

This question, a highly fundamental one, has hardly been considered by the psychologists. The clue lies in the descriptions of their experiences by those of the passive-observer type who have been in the regression state, both present life and past. The American student Don described his recollection of reproducing the childhood Japanese in this way:

> It was like my lips all of a sudden would move into these funny shapes. And then I would want to say something and wouldn't know what I was really saying. The words just came out and I wasn't sure whether they were real or not. The strangest thing is that my muscles without my volition would just take over. It was really like my mind wasn't involved in it.[19]

Michael O'Mara, describing his recollection of the Stephen Garrett personality, said:

> At first I assumed I was just making it up, and that it was just coming from my imagination. But I was just listening to these answers coming out of my mouth and not knowing what to expect next. It was like being inhabited by devils or something . . .[20]

"Inhabited by devils." The term sounds archaic, and is, but the meaning is there. Religious literature refers to the state as "possession." Modern psychiatrists prepared to acknowledge the existence of the condition sometimes prefer the term "multiple personality." Whatever we may like to call it, however, this state seems to lie at the root of the "acting" of past-life personalities. Dr. Reima Kampman is almost alone among psychologists and psychiatrists in recognizing this—he specifically entitled his Oulu University thesis "Hypnotically Induced Multiple Personality"— but even he has not made a full comparison between the manifestations of past-life personalities and what is known of the multiple personality condition.

CHAPTER 8

The Source of the Acting— the Phenomenon of Multiple Personality

"What is your name?" Jesus asked.
"My name is legion," he answered, "for there are many of us."
Mark 5:9

THIS CONVERSATION OF Jesus Christ with the Gerasene demoniac tells us in the simplest possible terms that the multiple personality condition—when many personalities seem to inhabit one body—was known even two thousand years ago. Throughout history people have thought multiple personality sufferers were "possessed" or "inhabited by devils," and the idea still persists today. Ignorance over the condition has been so great that it has frequently been confused with "demon possession" of the kind popularized by *The Exorcist*, and also with schizophrenia, the form of insanity characterized by irrational thinking, delusions, and disintegration of accepted interpretations of reality. The plain fact is that multiple personality is neither demon possession nor schizophrenia, but a quite distinct mental disturbance by no means understood yet by modern psychiatrists—though it has been observed frequently and reliably enough to receive proper recognition in medical literature. A sufferer from this condition may display twenty or more seemingly distinct personalities or subpersonalities collectively exhibiting the widest range of behavioral characteristics, not one of which need be "diabolic" in the accepted sense. Similarly, while an individual entity's characteristics may be quite untypical of the parent individual's "normal" self, they may in all other respects appear perfectly sane and rational. In 1887, for instance, one multiple personality case, an evangelical preacher called Ansel Bourne,[1] suddenly left his home in Providence, Rhode Island, and without a word to his family traveled to Norristown, Pennsylvania, where as Mr. A. J. Brown he very competently set up a confectionery shop, purchasing stock, and behaving in an entirely normal manner to those he dealt with. He was quiet and orderly in his habits, attended church regularly, and even gave a perfectly credible account of his earlier life as Mr. A. J. Brown. The shock came two months after having left home when he woke up one morning as the real Reverend Ansel Bourne to find himself in a strange bed, in a strange town, with two months totally missing from his life. Ansel Bourne the preacher knew nothing of Mr. A. J. Brown the shopkeeper, his other self.

The outward self's unconsciousness[2] of the possessing entity or entities is perhaps the single most consistent feature of the multiple personality condition. The subpersonalities will sometimes, but by no means always, be aware of the outward self, not infrequently despising it for qualities different from their own. Usually they, in their turn, will be unaware of their companion subpersonalities, but almost invariably there is one subpersonality who knows and observes the activities and even the thoughts of the rest. This personality will refer to the collection of personalities as "us"—like the Gerasene demoniac when addressing Jesus. The whole condition is an extraordinarily complex one, and it is only by reviewing a cross section of some of the actual cases that some proper understanding can be gained.

One of the classic examples, which emerged in 1898, twelve years after the Ansel Bourne case, was that of Claire Brenner,[3] a young student at Radcliffe College, Boston. After a long medical history of persistent and debilitating headaches, insomnia, fatigue, bodily pains, and weight loss, for which conventional treatments proved useless, in desperation she sought the help of the prominent Boston physician Dr. Morton Prince, a specialist in nervous diseases. The outward Claire who presented herself to Morton Prince was to all appearances a demure and sweet-natured twenty-three-year-old, very religious, fond of serious reading, fluent in French, adept in shorthand, a nonsmoker. Yet she felt something was draining and depleting her, and this was not helped by her tendency to punish herself by fasting and vigils if she felt she lapsed from the high standards of conduct she set for herself. Prince tried hypnotizing Claire, and found to his astonishment two personalities completely opposite to Claire's prim and proper exterior. One, whom Prince dubbed "B4", was impatient, vain, rude, bad-tempered, and irreligious, enjoying a healthy appetite, liking cream and sugar with her coffee, partial to strenuous exercise, and a heavy smoker. The other, "Sally Beauchamp," was a mischievous imp, flighty, free of the outward Claire's bodily ailments, but lacking her knowledge of French and shorthand. Claire's problem, Prince discovered, was that these personalities had a tendency to "come out" like a jack-in-the-box even outside hypnosis. One of Sally's pranks, for instance, was to pose herself stark naked on a pile of furniture in her room, adopting the precise position of a statue in an art book studied by Claire. She would then disappear, leaving the real Claire to wake up in a state of acute embarrassment. Sally would also make dates with a boyfriend the outward Claire had determined not to go out with again. The personalities would even write notes to each other, each in markedly different-looking handwriting.

Morton Prince, who managed to achieve a satisfactory cure for Claire Brenner, wrote up the whole story in *The Dissociation of a Personality*,[4] probably the classic work on a multiple personality case. But so bizarre is the whole condition that, despite Prince's unimpeachable credentials as a Professor of Nervous Diseases, his account went almost unheeded by the general run of the psychiatric profession until 1957, when a new case of multiple personality, even more dramatic than that of Claire Brenner, became of worldwide interest. This was the case of "Eve" of Thigpen and Cleckley's *The Three Faces of Eve*,[5] the best-selling book that became an equally successful film. Recently Eve has revealed her identity as Chris Sizemore,[6] today a happily integrated housewife in her mid-fifties living in Fairfax, Virginia. She has also told the full harrowing story of how it felt actually to experience multiple personality, and this forms the best introduction to the condition's myriad of astonishing features.

On April 4, 1927, Chris, the future Eve, was born two months prematurely to poor tenant farmers, Acie and Zueline Costner, of South Carolina. Because Chris weighed only two pounds at her birth she tended to be rather overzealously guarded by her mother, but what Zueline could not protect Chris from was a series of traumatic scenes in early childhood which seem to have been at least part of the reason for her later troubles. When Chris was barely two years old she saw at very close hand the floating corpse of a drunk being hauled from an irrigation ditch, a ditch which her mother had previously warned her not to go near because a "monster" lurked there. As she subsequently recalled, she seemed to switch consciousness at the sight, seeing herself as a tiny red-haired girl calmly surveying the scene from the bridge, as if it was someone else. A similar mental switch occurred on an occasion when her mother cut her arm badly on a glass jar, and far worse horror was to follow when, still aged two, she witnessed a sawmill accident in which a man was literally cut in two. Almost certainly because of such scenes, symptoms of Chris's disorder began to appear even in early childhood. Not long after the family had moved to Wallace, North Carolina, her mother gave birth to twin daughters and Chris was found one day tormenting these new sisters, only to protest that it was "the ugly little girl" (in reality, Chris as seen by herself), whom she had "seen" doing it. When Chris smashed her cousin's watch, or tore to pieces a dress lovingly made for her by her mother, she invariably explained that it was "the other girl." Understandably, her parents sorrowfully regarded their daughter as a wicked liar whenever an incident like this occurred.

Chris's disruptions of consciousness became more frequent as various deaths occurred within the family. After an uncle died, she had an attack of actual unconsciousness and woke up blind. The condition was clearly hysterical in origin, as it soon dissipated during her recovery from a simultaneous attack of pneumonia. Then there were more blackouts, violent headaches, renewed spells of blindness and periods of amnesia, mixed with incomprehensibly "wicked" behavior such as drowning cats or pushing a younger sister into the fire. All these ills hampered Chris's progress at school—particularly frustrating as she showed signs of high intelligence.

The girl who in childhood appeared so ugly grew into an attractive teenager, but this in its turn brought fresh problems. While still at school Chris was seduced by a racing driver who beat her and sexually abused her before she was rescued by her parents. At the age of twenty she entered into a lackluster marriage with Ralph White (a pseudonym), to whom she bore a daughter, Taffy, and it was in her deep unhappiness with this marriage that her multiple personality condition resurfaced in yet more alarming forms. For Chris, the first sign was that she heard voices. As an adult, her outward personality had become restrained and self-effacing, and she therefore found the violent tone of the voices that seemed to well from nowhere within her distinctly horrifying. The voices expressed real hate against Ralph White: "Knock his block off. He's just the son of a bitch." On one occasion, quite unprovoked, she was told to jerk the tablecloth from under a meal she had just served to her husband. To the latter's consternation she obeyed, spilling the meal onto the floor. On another occasion, without a word to Ralph White, she went to stay with her cousin Elen for a week. Like Ansel Bourne, she behaved entirely rationally during this time, yet when eventually traced by an angry husband, she had no recollection of the whole incident.

The crisis that finally brought about the identification of Chris's strange condition came when she involuntarily soiled herself during one heated argument with Ralph White, then involuntarily wet herself in similar circumstances a few days later. Convinced that his wife must be insane, Ralph White handed her back to her parents, who in turn had her referred to a psychiatrist in Augusta, Georgia, Dr. Corbett H. Thigpen. For Dr. Thigpen, there was initially nothing about this now twenty-five-year-old patient to suggest that her condition was in any way out of the psychiatric norm. As he noted of Mrs. Chris White during the first consultation, she seemed neat, quiet, formal, circumspect, somewhat colorless. He observed also that she was a nonsmoker.

He speedily established from physical examination, X rays, and laboratory studies that the headaches and blackouts of which she complained had no obvious organic cause. Nor were her marital troubles notably more traumatic than those he came across every day in the course of his practice.

Then, a few days after one of Chris White's visits, Thigpen received a strange letter. Although it was unsigned, the postmark, content, and handwriting all suggested Chris White was the sender, except that the letter had not been finished off, and someone else seemed to have scrawled a crude note at the bottom in different, far less mature, handwriting. Initially Thigpen speculated that Chris White must have addressed an envelope to him and started the letter, which had been tampered with by a child who sent it off without Chris's knowledge. Out of sheer curiosity Thigpen quite innocently asked Chris White about this letter when she next came to see him. He found himself totally unprepared for her response. Her first reaction was to deny ever having sent the letter, although she recalled having begun it. Then a look of extreme agitation and distress came across her face, a look Thigpen had never seen from her before. She asked him if the occasional impression of hearing an imaginary voice suggested that she might be insane? Thigpen had hardly begun to consider his reply to this question before he was shaken to the very roots of his psychiatric experience to see Chris's face change before his eyes, first to an eerie blank, then in a manner impossible to describe, into a quite new, mischievous cast of countenance. In a matter of seconds the previously demure, tightly constrained woman who had been before him relaxed, crossed her legs, took on a sudden attractiveness and buoyancy of posture quite untypical of anything previously, smiled, and in a voice that was unmistakably different, said breezily, "Hi there, Doc!" As Thigpen himself recorded:

Instead of that retiring and gently conventional figure there was in the newcomer a childishly daredevil air, an erotically mischievous glance, a face marvelously free from the habitual signs of care, seriousness, and underlying distress so long familiar in her predecessor . . . This new voice was different . . . the basic idiom of her language was plainly not that of

Chris White. A thousand minute alterations of manner, gesture, expression, posture, of nuances in reflex or instinctive reaction, of glance, of eyebrow tilting and eye movement, all argued that this could only be another woman . . .[7]

An immediate request for a cigarette reinforced this—Chris White was a nonsmoker. As Thigpen shakily lit a cigarette for the extraordinary newcomer, he found himself asking the most bizarre question of his psychiatric experience:

"Who are you?"

"I'm Chris Costner."

"Why are you using that name instead of Chris White?"

"Because Chris White is *her*, not me."[8]

The episode was the start of a fourteen-month period during which Corbett Thigpen and his associate Dr. Hervey Cleckley grappled to achieve some understanding of their most unusual case. Thigpen found, just like Morton Prince with Claire Brenner, that if he used hypnosis he had no need to wait for the chance coming out of Chris Costner. He could call her out like a past-life personality, and Chris White would literally change into Chris Costner on command. By this means he discovered that it was Chris Costner who had been out for the finishing-off of the mystery letter, just as it was Chris Costner who had been out during the week Chris had spent with her cousin Elen, and Chris Costner who on another occasion had been out and bought some extravagant low-cut dresses which Chris White, embarrassed at finding them in her wardrobe, had been quite unable to explain to her indignant husband.

It was the opposites in the Chris White/Chris Costner personalities which Thigpen found so striking.[9] The simple, neat, and conservative Chris White, for instance, would never have chosen the loud, revealing, yet by no means tasteless dresses chosen by Chris Costner. Knowing Chris White's invariably soft-spoken and restrained manner of speech, Thigpen found it extraordinary to hear Chris Costner's coarse wit and fluent vernacular vocabulary coming from the same lips. Having become familiar with Chris White's dignified, if somewhat oppressed posture, he found it remarkable to observe the same body take on an altogether more confident and sexually provocative appearance. So physical were

the differences that even nylon stockings, worn by Chris White
without the slightest discomfort, would on Chris Costner produce
an immediate itching followed by an angry *urticaria* rash which
would literally disappear before Thigpen's eyes when the Chris
White personality was restored.[10] Similarly, when Chris White
and Chris Costner were independently wired to an electroen-
cephalograph machine to register their brainwaves, the readings
for the two personalities turned out to have marked differences,
just as if they were in reality different people.[11] And, like Claire
Brenner's Sally Beauchamp, Chris Costner seemed not only to de-
spise her co-inhabitant Chris White, but even to observe her
from some undefined vantage point. After the dresses incident
she said, "You ought've seen the look on her silly face when he
[an angry Ralph White on whom the check had been drawn]
showed her what was in the cupboard." And on another occasion
when she managed to foil one of Chris White's suicide attempts
by coming out and knocking the razor to the floor, she said, "I
think she meant business, Doc."

Hardly had Thigpen become attuned to the idea of Chris
White having one companion personality than, quite unexpectedly, another popped out during an analysis session. This was
Jane, different again from the other two—cool, confident, with a
cultured, measured voice. As Thigpen recorded at the time, Jane
seemed to lack Chris Costner's obvious faults and inadequacies,
yet was "far more mature, more vivid, more boldly capable, and
more interesting" than the depleted Chris White. Although there
seemed to be deficiencies in her background memory (initially,
for instance, she had no idea who George Washington was), during the course of analysis she rapidly developed her knowledge,
managing to be intellectually objective about the other two personalities, and, above all from Thigpen's point of view, displaying
a detailed awareness of what both Chris White and Chris
Costner did and thought, which seemed to establish her as the
"us" or link personality.

In every way Jane seemed the ideal among the three and this,
plus his own emotional leanings toward the newcomer, gave Thigpen his idea for the cure. If the Jane personality could somehow
be amplified and the other two faded out, then a finally inte-

grated new Chris White, alias Jane, might emerge. Thigpen tried
to bring this about—at his own expense, as Ralph White had already abandoned financial responsibility for Chris, and rude comings out of Chris Costner invariably lost those few opportunities
for remunerative employment the demure Chris White managed
to acquire. For a while Thigpen's strategy seemed to work like a
dream. As Jane, Chris met up with a thirty-year-old electrician,
Don Sizemore, whose love for her was a match for her confession
of her strange mental plight. On December 29, 1953, the couple
married. Jane was out all the time and Taffy, Chris's daughter by
Ralph White who had been looked after by Chris's parents, accepted her enough to come and live with the couple when they
moved away from Augusta to Knoxville, Tennessee. Thigpen, believing he had a success story on his hands, wrote it all up in *The
Three Faces of Eve*, adopting the pseudonym to preserve Chris's
privacy. The book was adapted into the Twentieth Century-Fox
film of the same name, and when this had its world premiere in
Augusta in September 1957, Thigpen and his colleague Hervey
Cleckley were confident that, so far as they were aware, the real
Eve had indeed been cured.

What they had no way of knowing, and what Chris herself at
this stage hardly understood, was that the Jane personality which
Thigpen had so lovingly nurtured was a mere superficiality, a
sham. Just as Jane had rapidly remedied her ignorance about
George Washington, so too she had acquired, like Ansel Bourne,
a "memory," a credible past of her own that was not that of the
real Chris White. In her own mind she remembered having grad-
uated at Furman University, in such detail that not only she herself but anyone else might be convinced by it. According to
Chris's later autobiography:

> She knew the names of the dormitories, she had lived in
> Rosemary Hall, knew that it was located above the Fine Arts
> Building; she knew that the women's campus had recently
> been the Greenville Women's Academy and was affection-
> ately referred to by the townspeople as the "Zoo"; she knew
> the names of professors, what they looked like, what their
> much-touted mannerisms and quirks were; she had gone one

glorious summer to summer school, lived in Montague Hall, and missed the Dean's List because of too many dates with the lifeguard at the swimming pool.[12]

So confident was Jane of her memory that, seeking a teaching post, she unsuspectingly wrote off to Furman University for certificates of her exam grades. To her utter disbelief she received a reply from Furman telling her bluntly that, according to their records, no person of her name had ever attended the University. What had happened was that Chris had quite unconsciously modeled her Jane personality on her cousin Elen who *had* attended Furman University, and indeed did know all the "remembered" items. Just as Lowes Dickinson's Cynthia, as described in the last chapter, had absorbed *Countess Maud* in fine detail and personalized this for her Blanche Poynings memories, so too Chris had absorbed every crumb of information Elen had provided about life at Furman and personalized this for the background of Jane. Even the Jane voice, Chris was eventually to realize, was a perfect imitation of Elen's voice.

This quite shattering loss of identity—and with it all the benefits acquired from Thigpen's careful therapy—was a psychological blow from which, quite unknown to those who read and watched *The Three Faces of Eve*, it would take the real-life Chris more than twenty years to recover. She now suffered a recurrence of the blind spells, two suicide attempts, more voices. Thigpen was alerted by Chris to his mistake, and at the end of 1957 the psychiatrist tried his best to dismiss Jane, only partly succeeding. In fact, while Jane did indeed "die" not long after, she was followed, unknown to Thigpen, by a succession of new personalities far more bizarre than any encountered before (see pages 127–28).

Three were compulsive collectors, almost certainly expressions of the need for security on the part of the now itinerant Chris, constantly and not altogether willingly on the move due to her husband's job. One of these was the Bell Lady, born, already in her thirties (and therefore older than Chris's real age) in 1958, a generous, civic-minded, but—in Chris's mind's eye—ugly woman with an obsession for collecting bells. Another was the Turtle Lady, an introverted creature who collected anything in the form of a turtle. Yet another was the Card Girl, obsessed by astrology and fortune-telling, and a compulsive collector of all types of playing cards. Then there was the Blind Lady, shy and insecure, possibly the personality that lay behind the spells of hysterical blindness that occurred during Chris's teens. For Chris's poor long-suffering husband Don, most unfortunate of all was the Virgin, a woman mentally in her late fifties yet created when Chris was no older than thirty. The Virgin used to spray her hair white, dress in plain, unattractive clothes, and would flee in horror if ever she woke up to find herself in bed with Don.

As had been the case even before Thigpen's therapy, deaths in the family increased Chris's splinterings of personality. When Chris's mother Zueline died, there was born the Banana Split Girl, mentally a child of five, ill-mannered and bad-tempered, who would eat nothing but banana splits, sometimes amid squeals of delight, consuming so many at one sitting that the next personality to emerge would be immediately sick. At the death of Don's mother, there was born the Strawberry Girl, so named because she would eat only dishes containing strawberries. Although mentally the Strawberry Girl was in her twenties, she was as childish as the Banana Split Girl but had a body image of herself as "tall and slender as a wood nymph," whereas Chris was actually overweight at this time.

With Thigpen far away and no other psychiatrist at hand, poor Taffy had to act as the ever-necessary watchdog to her mother as these personalities, given their colorful names by Taffy herself, came and went. Taffy foiled the not infrequent suicide attempts, and when her mother was driving a car and suddenly changed to a nondriving personality, Taffy, herself a nondriver, had to keep her head and give calm instructions on how to bring the car safely to a halt. It took twenty years of such bizarre phenomena, and in all an estimated twenty-two personalities, before the last of them "died" and Chris found her real identity. Her cure was aided partly by the good sense of a quiet general practitioner, Dr. Ham, and a new psychiatrist, Dr. Tsitos; partly by taking up painting—in which her styles varied according to whichever personality was out at the time; and partly by "living out" her past through writing, in association with her cousin Elen Pittillo, a doctor of psychology, her complete and altogether remarkable autobiography.

MULTIPLE PERSONALITY CASE
Psychiatrists: Dr Corbett Thigpen of Augusta, Georgia; Dr Tony Tsitos
of Annandale, Virginia

Subject	Sex	Age	Characteristics
Chris Sizemore (née Costner)	F	Born 1927	A pleasant housewife with a soft, southern-tinged accent, today free of the multiple personality condition
Multiple Personalities			
An estimated 9 childhood personalities, including **The Poet, Freckle Girl, Singing Girl, Big-eyed Girl, Blind Girl**. All female, all the same age as parent personality at the time.			
Chris Costner	F	S*	Coarse speaking and sexually provocative. Cigarette smoker. Allergic to nylon stockings.
Chris White	F	S	Soft-spoken and restrained, a non-smoker. Self-effacing.
Jane Doe	F	S	Poised and cultured with an impressive voice.
Bell Lady	F	S	Obsessed with collecting bells. Very interested in politics.
Blind Lady	F	S	Shy, insecure, suffering total loss of vision for hours at a time.
The Virgin	F	Late 50s when Chris in 30s	Dressed very plainly, sprayed hair white. Unable to cook, drive or keep house.
Turtle Lady	F	S	Fascinated by turtles. Lived in fantasy world.
Card Girl	F	S	Obsessed with playing cards; also fortune telling and astrology.
Banana Split Girl	F	5 yrs old when Chris in 40s	A willful, spoiled child, who would eat only banana splits.
Purple Lady	F	58 when Chris 41	Obsessed with all things purple. Wore white wig.

*S = same age as parent personality at the time.

Multiple Personalities	Sex	Age	Characteristics
Strawberry Girl	F	Early 20s when Chris in 40s	Very childish and obsessed with strawberries. Body image tall and slender.
Retrace Lady	F	S	Mature and conscientious. Able to "see" other personalities.
Andréa de Cosná	F	33 when Chris 46	Had to write everything with left hand. Mute.

The personalities of Chris Sizemore, alias Eve of *The Three Faces of Eve*. Note the different mental ages, body images, and accents. (Based on information from Chris Sizemore, *Eve*, Victor Gollancz, 1978.)

Chris Sizemore's case is by no means unique. Some two hundred other cases have been reliably recorded in medical literature and several recent ones have proved similar in a variety of respects. One of these is the case of Sybil Dorsett[13] (a pseudonym), a patient of the very distinguished American psychiatrist Dr. Cornelia Wilbur. Unlike Chris Sizemore, Sybil was born into a relatively affluent home (her father was a wealthy building contractor in Willow Corners, Wisconsin) and of ostensibly the most strict puritan morals. For Sybil there were no external traumas, such as Chris's viewing of the sawmill tragedy. Sybil's source of stress was very much within the home, in the person of her musically talented and schizophrenic mother, Hattie Dorsett. Once husband Willard had gone to the office, Hattie Dorsett would lock the house doors, pull down the window blinds, stuff a towel down Sybil's throat to stop her crying, then submit the child to the most perverted forms of physical and sexual abuse, such as suspending her, legs forced apart, from the light cord, or filling her vagina with cold water, then tying her to a piano leg while she pounded out Bach, Beethoven, or Chopin. Compounding Sybil's troubles was the fact that she was an only child; that Willard Dorsett, with his strict fundamentalist beliefs, simply turned a blind eye to the more telltale signs of Hattie's atrocities; and that until the age of nine Sybil was forced to sleep in a cot in her parents' room, within sight and sound of lovemaking extraor-

dinarily exuberant for a couple who by day insisted that sex was
dirty and to be shunned.

Sybil endured these torments from before she could even walk
or talk. She was an intelligent child and before long she invented
an idealized imaginary companion called Victoria Antoinette
Scharleau, a sophisticated young lady with loving parents,
brothers, and sisters in faraway Paris. When at the age of three
and a half Sybil suffered her first personality split, it was this personality, Vicky, who emerged as an occupying entity. Not long
after, on an occasion when Sybil was unjustly blamed for breaking
a glass pickle dish, out popped Peggy Lou, a new "stand-up-and-
fight" personality clearly "designed" to receive her mother's
abuse. Years later Sybil was to learn that this personality had her
mother's exact voice. As in the case of Chris Sizemore, deaths in
the family exacerbated Sybil's condition, and when in 1932 at the
age of nine the girl lost her grandmother, the one member of the
family in whom she placed most trust and affection, Peggy Lou
took over again. She was followed briefly by a new personality carrying her grandmother's name, Mary Lucinda Dorsett, and—as
subsequent analysis revealed—closely modeled on her grandmother. Between them Peggy Lou and Mary Lucinda Dorsett literally lost Sybil for two years of schooling, for Sybil could not
remember anything between attending her grandmother's funeral
as a nine-year-old and "waking up" as an eleven-year-old in a class-
room that seemed for children two years older than she. During
the missing two years she had performed competently at school,
receiving "A" grades, but this waking up caused severe difficulties
for, to the incomprehension of those around her, she proved totally amnesic for everything she had so successfully learned during
the intervening period. By the age of twelve Sybil was exhibiting
classic warning signs of the multiple personality condition—
headaches, twitches, spells of hysterical blindness, and further episodes of memory loss. Nevertheless, she managed somehow to
struggle through to art college, where she was continually aware
that she was suffering from some serious mental disturbance. The
medical writer Flora Rheta Schreiber described this in her biography of Sybil:

> People she had never seen before would insist they knew her.
> She would go on a picnic and have a vague sense of having

been there before. A dress that she had not bought would be hanging in her closet. She would begin a painting and return to the studio to find that it had been completed by someone else—in a style not hers. Sleep was a nightmare. She just couldn't be sure about sleep. Often it seemed as if she was sleeping by day as well as by night. Often too there was no dividing line between the time of going to bed at night and waking up in the morning. Many were the occasions of waking up without going to sleep, of going to sleep to wake up not the next morning, but at some unrecognizable time.[14]

By the age of twenty-two Sybil was sensible enough to realize that she had to seek the help of a psychiatrist and, despite outright sabotage attempts by Hattie Dorsett, eventually found her equivalent of Dr. Thigpen in Dr. Cornelia Wilbur, a sympathetic woman then in private practice in New York, where Sybil was taking her Master's Degree. In an almost carbon-copy repeat of the letter incident by which Chris Sizemore's multiple personality condition became recognized, Cornelia Wilbur one day found herself listening to Sybil as Peggy Lou insisting in an angry child's voice and uncharacteristic bad grammar, "Jist everyone knows I live in Willow Corners." Peggy was swiftly followed by Vicky. Cornelia Wilbur soon found that, like Chris Sizemore's Jane, Vicky knew everything the other personalities did, and referred to the collection of personalities as "us." Further investigation revealed that "us" was a collection of personalities almost as extensive and bizarre as those of Chris Sizemore—sixteen in all, each with their different characteristics and body images (see pages 131–32).

Besides the sophisticated Vicky (who saw herself as blond and highly attractive) and Peggy Lou (who saw herself as brunette and pug-nosed), there were Marcia Lynn Dorsett, a painter and writer, who saw herself with brown, side-parted hair and a shield-shaped face, Vanessa, the only personality able to play the piano, who saw herself as a tall and willowy redhead, and Mary Lucinda Saunders Dorsett, the personality representative of Sybil's dead grandmother, who saw herself as small, plump, middle-aged, and with long dark-brown hair parted at the side. Then, as a counterpart to Chris Sizemore's Banana Split Girl, there was a baby,

MULTIPLE PERSONALITY CASE
Psychiatrist: Dr Cornelia Wilbur, today Professor of Psychiatry,
University of Kentucky

Subject	Sex	Age	Characteristics
Sybil Isabel Dorsett (pseudonym)	F	Born 1923	American art graduate, born Willow Corners, Wisconsin. Remote and constrained during multiple personality condition, but today cured.
Multiple Personalities			
Victoria Antoinette Scharleau	F	Born 1926	A self-assured, sophisticated, attractive blonde. Able to "see" other personalities.
Peggy Lou Baldwin	F	Born 1926	An assertive, enthusiastic pixie with pug nose and Dutch haircut.
Peggy Ann Baldwin	F	Born 1926	Similar to Peggy Lou, but not sharing the latter's angry tendencies.
Mary Lucinda Saunders Dorsett	F	Little old lady	Thoughtful, plump, home-loving, maternal. Long, dark brown hair. Mid-western accent.
Marcia Lynn Dorsett	F	Born 1927	A writer and painter. Very emotional. Shield-shaped face, gray eyes, brown side-parted hair.
Vanessa Gail Dorsett	F	Born 1935	Intensely dramatic and very attractive. A tall red-head with willowy figure. English accent.
Mike Dorsett	M	Born 1928	A builder and carpenter. Olive skin, dark hair, brown eyes.
Sid Dorsett	M	Born 1928	Carpenter and general handyman. Fair skin, dark hair, blue eyes.
Nancy Lou Ann Baldwin	F	?	Interested in politics. Afraid of Roman Catholics. Physically like the Peggys.
Sybil Ann Dorsett	F	Born 1928	Very listless. Pale and timid. Ash-blond hair, oval face, straight nose.

Multiple Personalities	Sex	Age	Characteristics
Ruthie Dorsett	F	a baby	Little developed.
Clara Dorsett	F	?	Very religious and critical of waking Sybil.
Helen Dorsett	F	Born 1929	Very afraid. Light brown hair, hazel eyes, thin lips.
Marjorie Dorsett	F	Born 1928	Serene, vivacious, a tease. Willowy brunette with fair skin and pug nose.
The Blonde	F	Born 1946	A perpetual nameless teenager. Blond, curly hair, lilting voice.

The personalities of Cornelia Wilbur's patient Sybil. Note the very different body images, mental ages, and even sex changes. (Based on information from Flora Rheta Schreiber, *Sybil*, Penguin, 1975.)

Ruthie, who talked like a three-year-old. And two of Sybil's personalities, Mike Dorsett and Sid Dorsett, were male, both talented in carpentry, and unmistakably deriving this characteristic from Sybil's father, a master builder. Each different personality exhibited such distinct nuances of facial expression, body posture, gait, and accent that in time Cornelia Wilbur could tell from these which personality was out. Cornelia Wilbur did not make Thigpen's mistake of trying to suppress all other personalities in favor of one. Instead, she employed lengthy psychoanalysis, culminating in hypnotic progression of all personalities to the same age as the parent Sybil, a process which, although eventually successful, took all of eleven years.

We have begun to build up a picture of multiple personality—of the consistent causative stresses, of the persistent amnesia, of the extraordinary diversity of the personalities exhibited. The cases we have observed so far have been highly traumatic and have frequently brought the subjects to the point of suicide, but fortunately they have been resolved happily and without serious harm to others. Not all, however, fall into this category, and one of the most recent, that of William Stanley Milligan[15] of Columbus, Ohio, has also been one of the most tragic.

Billy Milligan's problems also seem to have arisen through stress in childhood, although at a later stage. Born illegitimate in Miami, Florida, in 1955, Billy's first three years would seem to have been relatively happy ones, a happiness punctuated in 1958 when his natural father, a Jewish comedian by the name of John Morrison, committed suicide. Billy's mother, a club singer, who had borne Morrison no less than three children but had never been able to marry him because of his difficulties obtaining a divorce, now lurched first into one unhappy marriage, which lasted two years, and then into a second, to an intensely devout Methodist called Chalmers Milligan, who became young Billy's third father in eight years of life.

Religious fanaticism recurs frequently in multiple personality cases, and at this point Billy's troubles began in earnest. Chalmers Milligan proceeded to try to expunge from Morrison's children both the Roman Catholic prayers and the Jewish traditions that had formed earlier parts of their upbringing. Just as Sybil suffered at the hands of Hattie Dorsett, so young Billy Milligan was locked in cupboards and boxes, and subjected to merciless thrashings and attacks of a sexual nature, including anal intercourse. Whenever Chalmers Milligan had the opportunity to be alone with his stepson he would try to make the child fear for his life, on one occasion threatening to "bury him in the barn and tell the mother that he had run away."[16]

By the age of twelve or thirteen Billy began to slip into what were described at the time as trances, wandering about his school in a distracted state, and sometimes straying, as if in a daze, into the town of Lancaster. He suffered spells of being unable to speak, an equivalent of Chris Sizemore's hysterical blindness, and in the spring of 1970 was admitted for observation to the Children's Unit of the Columbus State Hospital, Ohio. After a few months he was discharged, apparently because he had become a nuisance to the hospital authorities, and without his condition being properly diagnosed. In the spring of 1972, aged seventeen, he enlisted in the U. S. Navy, but was discharged within a month because "he did not possess the necessary degree of adaptability for naval life." In July 1972, still only seventeen, he was arrested and convicted on his first charge of rape and assault. After a year in prison he returned to Lancaster, losing a series of jobs and unable to establish a proper relationship with a potential girlfriend. He then committed two robberies, one on a drugstore, the other on two transvestites, and served a further prison spell. His condition was still not identified and on release he proved yet more incapable of controlling himself than before. Moving to Columbus, Ohio, he gained and as quickly lost a job as a maintenance man at an apartment block in the Livingston Avenue area of Columbus. Jobless and needing money, he proceeded to fortify himself with Biphetamine tablets and alcohol, and between August and October 1977 carried out a series of rapes with robbery. As was to be discovered later, behind these lay a series of strange personalities haunting Milligan's mind.

The planner of Milligan's rapes was Arthur, just a year younger than Milligan himself, intelligent, in accent and manner "English" to the core, and, like Sybil's Vicky, the memory trace for all Milligan's personalities. But once the plan was set into action it was an altogether more sinister individual who took over; Ragen, "keeper of hate," aggressive and violent, with a heavy Slavic accent, and protector of all the other personalities since Billy had been sixteen. As Ragen, Milligan would walk from his apartment to the Ohio State University area and accost the first lone woman that he saw, demanding at gunpoint that she drive him in her own car to the nearest lonely spot. At this stage Milligan's nineteen-year-old female personality Adalana would take over. Adalana, a lesbian desperately in need of love and affection, would then proceed to carry out the rape, a particularly twisted piece of body image logic, as the victim's testimony left no doubt as to the rape's physically masculine character. Finally the victim, still threatened by a gun, would be forced to cash a check for Milligan using a banker's card, after which Arthur would take over again to decide what bills should be paid. As Ragen never actually saw the money he had set out to get he felt cheated and was impelled to set out on a further robbery. And so the extraordinary process was repeated.

It took four episodes of this kind, spreading considerable alarm in the Columbus University quarter, before Milligan was finally caught on October 27, 1977. Psychiatrists were called in, and his

MULTIPLE PERSONALITY CASE
Psychiatrist: Dr George T. Harding, Harding Hospital, Worthington, Ohio

Subject	Sex	Age	Characteristics
William Stanley Milligan *Multiple Personalities*	M	Born 1955	A convicted robber and rapist. Depressed, guilt-ridden and suicidal.
Ragen	M	Same	"The keeper of hate"—aggressive, violent, with a heavy Slavic accent.
Arthur	M	22	Intellectual and a planner. By far the most intelligent, and with an English accent. Able to "see" all the other personalities.
Adalana	F	19	A lesbian in great need of affection.
Allen	M	18	Talented artist and drum player. Smokes cigarettes (only personality to do so). Sociable.
Tommy	M	16	Quiet, frightened by drumsticks. Clever, but did not like school.
Danny	M	14	Extremely timid and shy, and concerned for David.
Christopher	M	13	Quiet and rarely "out".
David	M	9	Frightened, withdrawn, and subject to depression. Semi-autistic.
Christene	F	3	Loves drawing and painting butterflies.

The personalities of Billy Milligan. The different ages shown relate to Milligan's age of twenty-three at the time of his arrest and psychiatric analysis. Note the sex and accent changes. (Based on information from a psychiatric report prepared by Dr. George Harding for legal proceedings, and published in the Columbus *Dispatch*, 1978.)

whole complex condition was gradually identified. As it turned out, Arthur, Adalana, and Ragen were by no means alone in the Milligan repertoire (see page 135). There were no fewer than six other subsidiary personalities: Allen, eighteen years old, a talented artist and drum player, the only personality to smoke; Tommy, a quiet sixteen-year-old who was the front man for Milligan's enlistment in the U. S. Navy; Danny, a timid and shy fourteen-year-old; Christopher, a quiet thirteen-year-old; David, a very sick and depressed nine-year-old, semiautistic and with all the memories of Milligan's early sexual abuse; and Christene, a rarely communicative three-year-old, expressing herself in drawings and watercolor paintings and, like Milligan's other female personality Adalana, in great need of being "held and loved." As in the Chris Sizemore and Sybil cases, there were different accents, tastes, and body languages of stance and gesture for each personality. The only common factor in Milligan's "human zoo" was that the girls were starved of affection, and the males anti-sex.

Not unexpectedly, Billy Milligan's case caused some legal wrangles. Charged with the rapes and robberies, he was eventually found not guilty on the grounds of insanity and at the time of writing is still in the maximum-security State Hospital for the Criminally Insane, Lima, Ohio, although some psychiatrists have declared that his multiple personality condition has now been satisfactorily resolved. While in prison Milligan has exhibited a remarkable artistic talent, with each personality adopting a different and quite distinctive style, just like Chris Sizemore.

We have seen, then, that multiple personality is a psychiatric condition, hitherto underdiagnosed. The personalities do not have an extraterrestrial origin, but can be traced back to the characteristics of real-life persons who have formed a strong impression upon the sufferer, who has then personalized them and unconsciously developed them into a character of his own. In short, each personality is nothing more than a satellite, a superficial fragment split off from the parent individual as a result of extreme stress—yet from our point of view the equally important aspect is that each is extraordinarily convincing.

CHAPTER 9

Hypnotic
Regression Experiences
and Multiple Personality

WE NOW KNOW that the multiple personality acting phenomena —changes of accent, handwriting, facial expression, body image, and the like—are caused by some extremely powerful and unconscious acting mechanism within the mind. The reader can scarcely have failed to notice the similarity between these and the past-life hypnotic regression state. So might the very same mechanism be responsible for the "acting" aspects of past-life hypnotic regression, and, if so, to what extent might it be possible to demonstrate this?

As can be gauged from even a casual glance at a typical list of past-life personalities alongside those of a multiple personality subject, once the historical trappings are set aside there are fundamental similarities. We come across the same variety of personalities within any one individual, some very convincing, some much less so. We see the same sort of incidence of changes of sex, a preponderance of personalities being of the same sex as the parent individual, with approximately one in ten of the opposite gender. We find each personality possessing its own memory, having its own ways of behaving, its own characteristics of speaking, even its own allergies and skin complaints not shared by the others. We even see in multiple personality cases something of the same somnambulistic and passive-observer states we observed of past-life regressions. Chris White's amnesia for Chris Costner's dress-buying expeditions and the like may be regarded as somnambulistic, just as Chris Sizemore's Jane, Sybil's Vicky, and Billy Milligan's Arthur, each of whom said they could perceive all that the other personalities did and thought, may be defined as passive observers.

Though much further research is needed, it might be argued that a multiple personality sufferer, while gripped by any one individual entity, is, in a sense, locked in a form of self-hypnosis. It can certainly be said that just as past-life personalities of the same subject (such as Sue Atkins' Charlie and Father Antony Bennet and Michael O'Mara's Stephen Garrett and Emily) can exhibit marked differences from each other, a classic feature of the multiple personality condition is the strong contrasts evident, for instance, between Chris Costner and Chris Sizemore, between Peggy Lou and Sybil, and between Sally Beauchamp and Claire Brenner. No better example can be cited than the following extracts of letters by Dr. Morton Prince's Claire Brenner, one as herself, the other as the willful and flighty Sally Beauchamp. This is Claire Brenner as herself:

Dear Dr. Prince,
I am so anxious to see you and talk with you a little—if you are not utterly exasperated with me. And I do want you, please, please, to hypnotize me again. You know that it is the only thing that has ever helped me, and I am sure it is the only way, save by fasting and vigil—which you know I am not up to . . .[1]

Claire Brenner as Sally:

My Dear Dr. Prince,
You are most absurd and idiotic to waste your time and sympathy on such a perfect chump as our friend is. I do not like it at all, and I won't have you doing it. And moreover I won't have you trying hypnotism again on any account. Do you understand? . . . You make me so angry talking a lot of absurd nonsense that you know isn't one bit true. Goose![2]

The behavioral similarities between past-life regression cases and those of multiple personality are particularly strong. There is the facial blank frequently observed at the moment when a hypnotized subject changes to a past-life personality, which author Peter Moss refers to as "some light state of death." This same feature occurs in multiple personality. It made such a strong impression on Chris Sizemore's psychiatrist Dr. Thigpen that he arranged for it to be carefully built into Joanne Woodward's performance as Eve in *The Three Faces of Eve*. When a friend of Sybil's observed it in this film it convinced her that Sybil was a case of multiple personality.[3] And one writer said of Billy Milligan:

> Those witnessing the moment of personality change find the process eerie and unforgettable. Milligan stops talking in midsentence and freezes. His eyelids flutter uncontrollably, his face smooths out for an instant, turning strangely ageless.[4]

Facial expression is as significant as the facial blank. In past-life cases we noted how the whole set of the face seemed to change according to the nature and age of the personality adopted—and a strikingly altered facial expression is commonly referred to in multiple personality literature. Besides Thigpen's observations on Chris Sizemore's change to Chris Costner, quoted on pages 121–22, Sybil's psychiatrist Dr. Cornelia Wilbur even claimed to be able to recognize which of Sybil's personalities was out merely by the expression on her face as she sat in the waiting room. These changes may happen in a matter of moments, as Dr. Morton Prince observed in his study of Claire Brenner:

> One of the most curious of these automatisms was the flashing of Sally's facial expression—revealing her presence and amusement—through Claire Brenner's sadness. This is the way it would happen: I would be talking with Claire Brenner when she was in a state of depression, her face weary and sad. Suddenly the gleeful expression of Sally would flash over it momentarily, as if Sally's joy at the scene was too intense to be hidden.[5]

Both past-life regression subjects and multiple personality sufferers often acquire a new body image of themselves. In Joe

Keeton's regressions, for example, a slight individual such as Edna Greenan saw herself as the amply bosomed Nell Gwyn and a well-groomed Michael O'Mara saw himself in the filthy rags of the down-and-out Stephen Garrett. Likewise, each of Sybil's personalities had a markedly different appearance, which she went so far as to draw both visually and verbally for Cornelia Wilbur. She saw Vicky as an attractive, ringletted blonde, Peggy Lou and Marcia Lynn Dorsett as brunettes, Vanessa Dorsett as a tall redhead with light-brown eyes and an oval face, Sid Dorsett as a fair-skinned male with blue eyes, and so on.

Then we can observe the same unconscious, seemingly natural handwriting changes in past-life regressions and multiple personality cases. This was Chris Sizemore's writing, as herself at the time she was married to Ralph White:

on top. It has ever since
the day I was down there
to see you. I think it must
be my eyes. I see little red
& green specks. and I'm covered
with some kind of rash.

This was her scrawl as Chris Costner:

baby please be quite dear lord
don't let me lose patience with her
she's ___ sweet and innocent and
my self-control

And this was her writing as the sophisticated Jane:

It is against the law to use letters without permission!

Jane

As these specimens show, the multiple personality mechanism somehow imprints a totally different style on the subject's handwriting, without the subject having the slightest conscious intent to deceive. It is as though a quite different mental attitude, of which the handwriting is but one expression, has been "switched on" in the mind. Even so, the handwriting expert can see telltale characteristics of the parent individual. For instance, the U. S. Army handwriting specialist Ward S. Atherton looked at Chris Sizemore's specimens and concluded that "extensive examination of these handwriting materials establishes beyond any doubt that they have been written by one and the same individual."[6] It so happens that several notable multiple personality cases have been artistic, and no doubt if a special study were made of the apparently widely different artistic styles exhibited by the different personalities of each sufferer, very similar conclusions would be reached. It is interesting to observe that in Billy Milligan's "child" art as the little girl Christene (plate 12), the cat and the table are very clearly sophisticated simplifications, just like the tepee drawn by Professor Martin T. Orne's subject Harry when hypnotically regressed to the age of six (see pages 50–51, 52).

Yet another aspect of the past-life regression cases that multiple personality seems to account for is that of changed accents and voice characteristics. Joe Keeton has frequently remarked of those cases of his which feature a change of accent, "If this is acting, then the wrong people are being employed as actors." Although no one who has attended a Joe Keeton regression can fail to acknowledge a certain respect for this point of view—Dr. Tom Troscianko's Polish accent and Michael O'Mara's Irish accent both being remarkable for their fluency and consistency—the counterparts in multiple personality cases are all too obvious. Chris Sizemore flawlessly took on her cousin Elen's more cultured tones for Jane, her sophisticated personality, just as she took on, from an undetermined source, an uncultured tone for her Chris Costner. Sybil took on her grandmother's Midwestern accent for her Mary Lucinda Saunders Dorsett personality, and an English accent for Vanessa; Billy Milligan adopted a Slavic accent for Ragen and an English accent for Arthur.

Even the adoption of a different language by a past-life personality, as exemplified by Gretchen, can be explained from the mechanisms of multiple personality. Subpersonalities do not necessarily have the same linguistic knowledge as the outward self; thus in Morton Prince's Claire Brenner case, Claire's knowledge of French was peculiar to her outward self and not shared by the subpersonality Sally Beauchamp. Only under hypnosis as his childhood self[7] could Professor Fromm's subject Don speak and understand Japanese. Had Don's childhood background not been known, and had he assembled his unconscious knowledge of Japanese into an exclusively Japanese-speaking past-life personality, his case could have been presented as a particularly striking example of a past-life unlearned language—with Don as convinced as anyone that he was producing material of which he had no conscious knowledge. As it is, the known mental mechanisms are more than sufficient explanation.

There remains one characteristic of past-life regression yet to be discussed, which would seem beyond the capabilities even of a Sir Laurence Olivier. This is the phenomenon by which Ann Dowling exhibited on her body the bruises of the murdered Sarah Williams, Pauline McKay's neck showed the rope-mark of her hanging as Kitty Jay, and Edna Greenan's skin exhibited the rash which afflicted an earlier incarnation, Charlotte Marriott. No one, with the possible exception of a yoga adept, is able consciously to affect their skin in this way. The question is, can this too be within the capabilities of the multiple personality mechanism?

The answer is yes, and by way of demonstration in her autobiography *Eve* Chris Sizemore has described a particularly traumatic evening shortly before her fiftieth birthday during which, quite spontaneously and unexpectedly, she began to relive a childhood accident in which her clothes had been set alight by the fire heating the family washtub. In a shrill voice typical of a three-year-old she began calling out, "Mummy, I'm burning! Mummy, I'm burning!" at one and the same time rolling on the floor and tearing at her dress. Those who rushed to her aid were astonished to find that the skin of her right arm and shoulder had turned a livid red color, and that an old puckered scar from the original injury had become dramatically reinflamed. A wet towel applied to cool the area literally steamed from the heat of the arm.[8]

By the spontaneous power of the multiple personality condition Chris had effectively suffered what is known medically as an abreaction (a "reliving" of a repressed trauma)[9] of a variety undeniably rare but nevertheless known to us quite independently from reliably recorded examples. A typical case was published in the *Lancet* in December 1946 by London psychiatrist Dr. Robert Moody.[10] Four years before the outbreak of World War II, a then twenty-six-year-old Army officer, whom we will call Alec, repeatedly walked in his sleep during hospitalization in India for a minor infection. In order to prevent him from injuring himself, the nurses sometimes tied Alec's hands behind his back while he was asleep, but nevertheless one night he managed to slip away and wander the countryside for some hours. By 1944 Alec's sleepwalking had become a matter of serious concern, and was sometimes accompanied by aggressive behavior for which he had no memory in the waking state. Admitted to the Woodside Hospital, London, he was observed one night thrashing for an hour, as if trying to untie imaginary bonds, then creeping out into the hospital grounds with his hands still "tied" behind his back. Although it was not recognized at the time, he was reliving the occasion of the sleepwalking in India. The nurses, who had been given orders not to interfere with his sleepwalking, were shocked at the sight of Alec's arms on his return. Both bore deep weals as if real ropes had tied him, even though nothing of this kind had been used. The matter was reported to Dr. Moody, the consultant in charge, and two nights later he administered a barbiturate to Alec, and stayed up to see if the phenomena would be repeated. They were, and in the course of the strange thrashing movements Moody turned the light full on and saw with his own eyes clearly defined weals appearing in both Alec's forearms, these becoming visibly indented and finally oozing small quantities of fresh blood. Even the next morning, after a further spell of sleep-walking, the marks were still sufficiently clear to show up in photographs (plate 14).

But striking though these examples are, there is one respect in which they cannot be likened to the wounds of Ann Dowling, Edna Greenan, and Pauline McKay, for Chris Sizemore's burns and Alec's rope-marks stemmed from memories of real injuries. Unless our thinking so far has been entirely wrong, however, no real hanging memory can have produced the rope-mark on Pauline McKay's neck, nor the wounds of the other past-life subjects. To argue for the multiple personality condition producing wounds of this latter kind, we have therefore to believe that it can produce complete *fantasy* skin injuries as well as real ones. The question is, can it?

Since the time of St. Francis of Assisi there have been those who, at times of intense spiritual excitement, have exhibited on their bodies stigmata or wounds seeming to be those of the actual Passion of Jesus Christ. Mysterious as these manifestations are, even the most hardened skeptic has had to acknowledge that far too many cases have been scrupulously investigated, reliably recorded, and attested to by doctors for them to be attributed to mere physical self-mutilation. But are the stigmata actual reproductions of the wounds of the Passion as they once existed on the body of the historical Jesus? Simple comparisons of the shapes and locations of each stigmatic's wounds one against the other reveal not the slightest master pattern. Some stigmatics have manifested the *coup de grâce* spear-wound on their left side, others on their right; some have exhibited it as a round puncture, others as a straight cut, others as a diamond shape, yet others as a crescent shape. The nail-wounds in the hands have varied from simple red spots in some to complete penetrations of the flesh in others, again taking every conceivable shape—oval, round, square, oblong, etc. There is no way, therefore, that these can be argued to reproduce those of Jesus himself. A particularly telltale feature is the fact that in cases such as those of St. Gemma Galgani and Anne Catherine Emmerich the wounds have been found to correspond in appearance to those featured on the particular crucifix before which the stigmatic most frequently worshipped.[11]

If the stigmata are fantasy wounds, mere mental imaginings by the stigmatic of what and where Christ's wounds might have been, how are such extraordinary manifestations formed? Can the mind, albeit unconsciously, be capable of such dramatic phenomena? And if this is the case, what sort of psychological or psychiatric state might be responsible? Astonishingly, when we ask these questions we find ourselves back on familiar ground. Even as early as the 1930s a leading Roman Catholic theologian, the Reverend Herbert Thurston, S.J., suggested the strongest connection between stigmatics and the multiple personality condition.[12] If we consider, for instance, what is known of the psychological history of one of the most recent and best recorded of twentieth-century stigmatics, Teresa Neumann of Konnersreuth[13] in West Germany, who died in 1962, we find alongside lavish descriptions of her bloodstained tears and highly realistic nail-wounds, reference to visionary trances when she spoke in different voices, one that of a child of five,[14] another that of a well-spoken male personality with a deep voice. We find the male personality referring to Teresa in the third person—"She will have a vision this evening at eight"[15]—in a manner similar to the way multiple personalities such as Chris Costner have referred to their parent selves. We find also that Teresa, exactly like multiple personalities and the somnambulistic type of hypnotic regression subject, was amnesic for everything she said in her trances. We even find that her medical history includes side symptoms typical of many multiple personality cases.

So does the multiple personality mechanism lie behind the phenomena of stigmatics as well as past-life regressions? The answer seems to be yes, and although a far deeper study of this question is called for, there is one little-known medical case that is so relevant to past-life regression that it deserves recounting in some detail. This is the case of a girl whom we know from the point of view of medical anonymity only as Elizabeth K., born of peasant parentage in southern Germany in the year 1902.[16] Elizabeth was a sensitive, intelligent child with a lively imagination, and her problems seem to have begun at the age of six when her mother died and she came into the care of an overly strict stepmother. By her early teens she was suffering from now-familiar symptoms —headaches, nausea, paralyses, bouts of unconsciousness, bladder and bowel disorders—but her doctors, seemingly unfamiliar with multiple personality, treated her only with brain surgery and electric shocks, both to no avail. Elizabeth's multiple personality condition is, however, quite evident from some of her recorded third-person comments regarding the electric shock treatment: "Miss K. will walk properly all by herself without being electrified by you," and "Miss K. will be happy again as soon as she won't have to do such heavy work anymore."

It was only in 1928, after persistent insomnia and some suicide attempts, that Elizabeth came to the attention of Dr. Alfred Lechler, a psychiatric specialist and practitioner in hypnosis, who early on detected that at least some of Elizabeth's troubles were of a psychological nature. Partly so that he could observe her problems better, Lechler suggested that Elizabeth might be happier employed within his own home as a domestic servant, and, aided by Lechler's periodic use of hypnotherapy, the girl's physical and mental well-being certainly seemed to improve. Despite this, however, Lechler could not avoid observing from time to time a strange tendency of the girl to take upon herself any medical symptoms that happened to be talked about. When one day she heard of a hernia case, a fall prompted her to assume all the symptoms she had heard about in connection with a hernia, even though she was actually quite unharmed. On another occasion, when she was supposed to make a duty call on her family home, she began coughing blood as if she had contracted tuberculosis, even though, as tests proved, her lungs were in reality perfectly clear.

Then came the denouement of her strange condition on Good Friday, 1932. On this day Elizabeth attended a religious talk, illustrated with slides showing the various sufferings of Jesus prior to and during the Crucifixion. When she returned to Lechler's home she complained of severe pains in her hands and feet, and, finding no organic cause, Lechler immediately suspected the psychological effect of the slide show. Knowing of the Teresa Neumann case, Lechler theorized that both Teresa and Elizabeth might share an unconscious susceptibility to act out in their bodies sufferings of which they had merely read, or seen pictures, and what he needed was the opportunity to prove it. Faced with Elizabeth's embryo stigmata, he decided on a unique method of experiment. He rehypnotized Elizabeth and, instead of suggesting to her that the pains in her hands and feet would get better, he instructed her to concentrate on the idea of their getting worse, on "real" nails being forced into her hands and feet. As a somnambulistic subject, when Elizabeth was brought out of the hypnosis she had no idea of anything she had been told, but her condition the next morning spoke for itself. She was clearly in considerable distress and pain. On her hands and feet, at points exactly appropriate to crucifixion nails, there were red and swollen marks the size of a medium-sized coin, the skin around them torn and weeping (plate 17).

Lechler now took Elizabeth fully into his confidence. He explained to her that the marks were purely because of his hypnotic suggestion of the night before, and that he would be able to make them go away by the same form of verbal suggestion by which they had been created. But first, in order for him to be able to understand her condition more fully, he hoped she would be prepared to cooperate with him in further experiments. Given Elizabeth's consent, Lechler asked her, during ordinary consciousness, to try thinking of the bloodstained tears he knew she had seen in press photographs of the stigmatic Teresa Neumann. While she did her housework she was told to hold such mental images in her mind and concentrate on Teresa's sufferings as her own. The effect was dramatic. Within hours Elizabeth once more presented herself to Lechler, a by now pitiful spectacle. Blood was welling up from inside her eyelids and pouring down her cheeks, a sight he immediately photographed (plate 16). Lechler was as alarmed as he was astonished at the sheer power of his suggestion and instructed the blood-flows to cease, which they did as he watched. He gave separate instructions for the healing of the nail-wounds, which similarly disappeared during the course of the next two days.

Later Lechler repeated the experiment with Elizabeth in a variety of ways. As one variant, while she was hypnotized he gave her the suggestion that a crown of thorns was being placed on her head. Although he merely brushed her forehead with his fingers, she immediately jerked in severe pain, and the next morning showed him her forehead covered with irregular-shaped puncture-type wounds which, on Lechler's suggestion, oozed blood within an hour. As another variation Lechler suggested to Elizabeth she was Jesus carrying the cross. Although, because the suggestion was given under hypnosis, she had no conscious memory of it when awake, the next day she duly complained of severe pains in her left shoulder, which was found on examination to be red and swollen. Invariably on the appropriate suggestion these injuries and the pain that went with them disappeared far more quickly than their real equivalents would have done.

What Lechler had established beyond doubt was that stigmata-type wounds, given a subject such as Elizabeth of the multiple personality type, could be replicated and as readily dismissed, purely by the power of suggestion. From the point of view of past-life regression, however, perhaps the most significant of all Lechler's experiments was that which he conducted in May 1932. Giving Elizabeth a copy of the Bible, he asked her to read carefully through the gospel of St. John, studying the accompanying pictures and really thinking herself into the New Testament scene. As Lechler himself described it in his careful report:

> After fifteen minutes she slowly closed her eyes, put the Bible aside, took deep breaths and groaned frequently while I watched her. I asked her, "Do you see anything?" She didn't answer. Soon her groaning became louder. She opened her eyes for a time and cried. After asking her again whether she saw anything she answered with several pauses: "They want to crucify our Saviour . . . crucify, crucify him. Pilate cannot find him guilty. Jesus is quite calm. They are putting the red cloak on him."
>
> She was crying loudly now.
>
> "One is particularly angry . . . He is hitting him in the

face. Our Saviour is carrying a cross . . . the cross himself
. . . three crosses . . ."

Suddenly she stretched out her arms and got into the position of a crucified person. Her breathing nearly stopped and she said quietly: "Now it's finished."

I asked her what was happening. She didn't answer for several minutes. At last, after demanding to be answered, her breathing became normal again and she replied between sobs: "I have seen the Saviour on the cross. And then I was hanged there myself. There were the thieves hanging. I am a sinner and I belong to the thieves. Our Saviour was on the cross beside me. And then I didn't see any more."[17]

No one reading such an account can fail to be struck by the powerful similarities to a past-life regression—the scene unfolding before the eyes, and therefore being described in the present tense; the intense emotional involvement, complete with weeping, groaning, and even apparent cessation of breath; the subject's identification with the scene even to the extent of Elizabeth, unprompted by Lechler, seeing herself as one of the two thieves crucified with Jesus, and all this alongside her actual production of crucifixion wounds. As Lechler went on to describe:

During the time following these events I hypnotized her several times suggesting to her to concentrate on the suffering of Jesus, but to imagine herself being among the crowd and not on the cross. The results were always the same. After being put under hypnosis she soon "saw" the events taking place and her facial expression and movements of the body told of the inner turmoil she was going through. Even when suggesting some other event to her she would soon see herself in that role and her face would take on a different expression. Especially touching was the experience of her being a child and Jesus as the friend of the children. Her face took on a childish expression, she would wave exuberantly with both arms and speak in a childish voice, and make caressing movements.[18]

There can therefore be very little doubt that every single element of the acting displayed in past-life regressions can be explained within the mechanisms of multiple personality. Of course, this does not take account of the birthmark scars of the Pollock twins and the Dr. Ian Stevenson subjects, but it seems by no means implausible that they could be transmitted to the unborn infant by the mother's unconscious traumas during pregnancy. There remains one enigma yet. For an individual quite unconsciously to exhibit personalities of the complex nature displayed in past-life regressions something more is needed: something to select and assemble the "script," decide on the "casting" of personalities, organize the body phenomena such as the wounds, all this somehow without the slightest conscious control on the part of the individual in whose body this extraordinary performance is being carried out. In other words, somewhere, somehow, the show must have a "director." It is like watching a puppet show; we can see the puppets, see some of the strings by which they are made to work, but cannot see the puppet master. Our next step will be a search for this hidden director.

CHAPTER 10

The "Hidden Observer" Mechanism

WHEN THE BRITISH Society for Psychical Research investigator Lowes Dickinson concluded his report on Cynthia and the Countess Maud case, described in Chapter 7, he remarked:

> Though Miss C. [Cynthia] got her facts from the novel, she made up . . . a quite new setting. She selected as her interviewer in this imaginary world a subordinate character, not the heroine of the book (who is Countess Maud). And she introduced the data, not in the order or connection in which they occur in the book, but most naturally and skillfully, as they might actually come out haphazard in a conversation. Her subconscious self showed in fact *remarkable invention and dramatic power* . . .[1]

Writing back in 1906, Lowes Dickinson used the term "subconscious" where today we might substitute "unconscious," but otherwise these comments could have been made about any recent past-life regression. If we abandon the idea of real dead people speaking behind past-life utterances we are forced into an almost equally remarkable alternative—to the mind possessing not only extraordinary memory and acting capabilities but also inventive processes independent of and beyond the awareness of any con-

scious control. The question is: What are these and how can they
be better understood? Are we really far more active unconsciously
than we give ourselves credit for? Just as our ancestors once
thought of the earth as the center of the universe, might we not
have a similarly inflated idea of the importance of our conscious
"I"?

One man who has recently given a refreshingly original twist to
this question is the American psychologist Julian Jaynes, lecturer
at Princeton University, New Jersey, who has commented:

> Consciousness is a much smaller part of our mental life than
> we are conscious of, because we cannot be conscious of what
> we are not conscious of. How simple that is to say, how
> difficult to appreciate! It is like asking a flashlight in a dark
> room to search around for something that does not have any
> light shining upon it. The flashlight, since there is light in
> whatever direction it turns, would have to conclude that
> there is light everywhere. And so consciousness can seem to
> pervade all mentality when actually it does not.[2]

Jaynes has gone on to demonstrate numerous examples of how
frequently we think we are conscious, in the sense of self-aware,
when really we are to all intents and purposes unconscious, not
imposing our "selves" on our thoughts and actions. Thus if a pi-
anist in the midst of playing a furious set of arpeggios became
properly conscious of himself and his fingers, he would almost certainly ruin his performance. If a motorist in a traffic emergency became properly conscious of what he had to do to stop the car, he
would most likely react too late to avoid an accident. If you the
reader, in the midst of this sentence, became properly conscious
of the process of reading, then the assemblage of letters into
words, words into sentences, sentences into thought patterns
would at the very least interrupt your natural assimilation of the
ideas just presented. Once we begin to think in this way we may
justifiably become a little uncertain about our assumption that we
are conscious all the time. We may become even more uncertain
when we begin to consider the singularity of that "I" which each
of us fondly imagines for ourselves perched in our brain space,
controlling every thought and action. For us to drive a car

through a busy city center, with a talkative passenger sitting alongside, may seem mundane enough. But consider the number of simultaneous processes of "consciousness" involved—listening to what the passenger has to say, planning a reply, thinking how boring the passenger's remarks are, observing the slowing down of a vehicle ahead and carrying out the appropriate braking and changing of gears, not to mention at the same time noting the shapely legs of a girl walking along the pavement. In which particular process was the conscious "I"? Consider too how different our behavior might have been in almost every respect depending on whether the talkative passenger was our wife, managing director, five-year-old daughter, mother-in-law, or an extravert colleague from the office. Which was the conscious "I"—the one who in the presence of the five-year-old daughter hardly noticed the shapely legs and slowed the car gently? Or the one who in the presence of the office colleague wolf-whistled loudly and braked violently? Suddenly the experiences of individuals such as Chris Sizemore and Sybil begin to seem not quite so far removed from our everyday lives as we may have thought. Do we all have a little of the multiple personality about us?

One of the most persistent factors in past-life regressions is that the subjects do not recognize what has come from within themselves, and this has been fundamental in persuading so many participants in past-live regression experiments that what they have seen must have been real. This has been true even of the most hard-headed journalists, as in the case of *Now!* magazine assistant editor Brian Hitchen who, after being regressed by Joe Keeton to a life in the reign of King James II, remarked:

> When the recording of my regression was played back to me I found myself listening to a man I had never known. The voice was mine but the sentiments belonged to somebody else. Answers that I would have given consciously if I had tried to cheat were not coming out right. It was as if another part of me had taken over almost completely.[3]

This factor is so central to our study that it is important to demonstrate it in a variety of ways.

In the winter of 1976 at the BBC Television studios in Bristol, the experiment of inducing a volunteer subject to see a ghost of her own mental fabrication was tried. It is well known to hypnotists that while a subject is hypnotized it is possible to implant what is called a post-hypnotic suggestion: that is, a suggestion which the subject will feel impelled to act on, according to a pre-arranged cue, long after he or she has been brought out of the hypnotic state. The author Colin Wilson described the experiment:

> A volunteer—a housewife who was known to be a good hypnotic subject—was placed under hypnosis by a doctor. She was told that when she awakened she would be taken to another place, where I [Colin Wilson] would approach her (followed by a television camera). As I spoke to her she would "see" the sinister figure of a seventeenth-century clergyman standing nearby; the man's appearance was described in detail. She was awakened and taken to the Bristol Docks, where I was waiting. As I walked towards her she smiled at me, then her eyes strayed across the water to an abandoned wharf. Her smile vanished and she asked me with amazement "Where did he go?"
>
> "Who?"
>
> "That man." She pointed to the dock and described the unpleasant, sallow-looking man dressed in old-fashioned clothes, who had been standing on the wharf then vanished. Even when the hypnotist explained that she had been responding to a suggestion made under hypnosis she was obviously only half convinced. Several times during the rest of the afternoon she tried to persuade us to admit that it had been a joke and she had seen a real man. She said there was nothing "ghostly" about him; he looked quite solid and normal.[4]

The fascinating aspect of this particular experiment is that although the woman subject was given only verbal information about what she would see, quite unconsciously she invented a pictorial image so convincing that the conscious part of her not only failed to recognize it as her own creation, but even when given a clear logical explanation she remained convinced that the ghost was real.

There are numerous further examples. Joe Keeton has related one early experience in which, purely as a party trick, he suggested to a hypnotized girl subject that she was walking on a tightrope. What he did not know was that the girl suffered from vertigo. Although the drop the girl saw below her was purely an invention of her own mind, it was so convincing to the observing part of her that she broke into all too real hysteria which proved difficult to control. Keeton will never forget the incident, which persuaded him to abandon hypnotic party tricks. Similar devices continue to be used by stage hypnotists for their acts, taking the form of what psychologists refer to as positive and negative hallucinations. Positive hallucinations involve subjects under hypnosis being induced to see people or objects that are not, in fact, there. Negative hallucinations involve the same subjects not seeing people or objects that are, in fact, there. One of the most intriguing as well as illuminating variations is regularly employed by the hypnotist Martin St. James in a stage act. He offers the subject a pair of perfectly plain glass spectacles which, he says, will make everyone he looks at appear stark naked. To universal amusement the recipient of these spectacles, as he looks around at what may be a large studio audience, blushes and giggles in ever-increasing embarrassment. It has to be emphasized that this is not mere play-acting. He really is seeing everyone without their clothes, but not of course their real naked bodies, merely invented ones of his own—below every real face is a mentally stitched, appropriately detailed yet illusory naked body, with light and shade all perfectly natural.

The relevance of all this to past-life hypnotic regression is profound, and no case illustrates this better than one described by the very eminent American psychologist Professor Ernest Hilgard of Stanford University in his book *Divided Consciousness*.[5] One evening during the early 1970s one of Hilgard's brightest students, of Mexican ancestry, happened to attend a California party where some very convincing past-life regressions of the Joe Keeton type were being demonstrated. Because of his professional interest in hypnosis the student volunteered to be regressed, and proved an excellent subject, falling easily into a deep-trance state of the passive-observer type. To his astonishment he literally saw himself back in Victorian England during the middle part of the nineteenth century. The experience was so extraordinarily vivid that he found himself speaking in contemporary terms about the family of Victoria and Albert, and familiar with the names of the princes and princesses of the royal court. The next day in Hilgard's laboratory the student explained to the Professor what had transpired, and expressed his own belief that it was a genuine reincarnation experience. He was so convinced he was right that he offered Hilgard the fullest cooperation in any investigation of the phenomenon. Hilgard, very astutely, did not scoff, but carefully interviewed the student about events which might have provided the memories that the student had evoked during hypnosis. He was not disappointed, and eventually established that the student had many years earlier made an intensive study of the British royal family, but then, with a shift of interest from the literary to the scientific, had quite genuinely forgotten about the study until Hilgard's skillful questioning awoke the memories of it.

Like Martin St. James's and Colin Wilson's subjects, the student remained unable to come to terms with how he had been able to see it all so convincingly. Hilgard recognized that he had a highly active visual imagination (a factor present consistently in both past-life regression and multiple personality cases), and judged that the only manner of convincing the student that it really was all coming from his imagination was to stage a proper, informal laboratory exercise, hypnotizing him, selecting a totally fictitious event, and then getting the student to relive it in precisely the manner he had done for the past-life regression. Hilgard therefore hypnotized the student himself and, when satisfied that a deep-trance state had been achieved, made the following suggestion:

> Just transport yourself to the scene I am about to describe. This is a place where you and some friends are exploring a newly discovered cave. You have already found the cave so you've come back to it with all the necessary equipment and you're prepared to explore it. Just describe what the scene is around you now . . .[6]

To the astonishment of those observing, the student launched into seventeen minutes of the most sustained, fluent narrative. I have quoted the following excerpts simply to convey the considerable detail and wealth of visual imagery:

> The cave that several friends of mine and I are about to explore, we stumbled upon just a week ago when we were having a day off and taking a picnic. We just came to this spot that had been a favorite spot of one of my friends, we saw this huge rock, just a mammoth rock, several of them, sort of juxtaposed upon each other and covered with all sorts of vegetation.
>
> We climbed up and had our lunch. As we climbed down we realized that there was a sort of little tunnel that was formed by the series of rocks not quite touching each other. We climbed down about fifteen feet which was as far as the light filtered into it, and we were afraid to go any further. We had no means of artificial light so we couldn't see. I yelled, however, down in the cavern and the echoing of my voice made us believe that this would be quite a large cavern.[7]

At this point the student related in great detail how they used ropes to ease themselves into the cavern, flashlights to guide them, what they saw, stalactites, stalagmites, a reflecting lake, fanciful shapes, and exciting colors. One of the friends found another opening and then they crawled through on hands and knees to discover a veritable Shangri-La.

> To our amazement we found ourselves in a beautiful small valley with vines growing down the sides and hills going sharply up in all directions, and at the back of the valley a waterfall falling down, cascading over rocks, forming a little river that went down along the base of the valley, formed one pool, and trickled onward underneath the rocks. Flowers of every variety grew in abundance in this valley so that one saw just as much yellows and reds and blues and all other types of colors as one saw of the green vegetation. Again there was no sign of mankind having been there, although we were sure that we could not have been the only people to have ever enjoyed the beauty of this sight. Some of the flowers we

see are huge flowers like none I have ever seen before. The blossoms would be as large as a basketball, thick with pollen, beautiful bright colors.[8]

As the student described afterward, in all this he felt a complete spectator as everything unfolded before him, without, seemingly, any conscious effort from himself—just like Sue Atkins in her passive-observer viewing of the activities of Charlie. Although the story was entirely fictitious, he stressed that he actually saw it all happening. Afterward, for comparison, Hilgard asked the student to tell a story without hypnosis, and although he did so with a not dissimilar inventiveness, there was a vital distinction which he himself appreciated:

> In hypnosis, once I create the pattern, I don't have to take any more initiative; the story just unfolds. In fact, once I start talking I know the main outlines of what is happening. For instance, I knew ahead of time that there would be another room outside of the cavern, and I knew I would go outside but I didn't know what it would look like until I walked through and was describing it. In the waking state it seems more fabricated. I don't see things that I describe in waking in the way I actually see them in hypnosis. I really saw everything today that I described.[9]

The real enigma lay in who or what was the hidden planner, the mechanism that seemed to be directing everything, dipping into unconscious memory stores for the visual scenes and, where necessary, inventing new ones, selecting in past-life and multiple personality cases appropriate personalities as actors. As it happens, it is Hilgard's research that has, more than any other up to the present time, thrown a fascinating light on this "hidden observer," as he defines it, cautiously stressing it to be a mechanism rather than some wonder-working genie lurking in the hidden recesses of the mind.

According to Hilgard, the student's experience exemplifies something he has been studying for some while which he called "divided consciousness," of which he recognizes multiple personality as an example. He has pointed out that the student's mind was literally operating in two parts, one part which he called the hidden part doing the planning like a stage director providing the moves for an actor, and the other part both watching what the first part provided, and acting upon it as if it was real:

> The hidden part knew, for example, that the cavern was to have a beautiful room, and that there would be a garden beyond. The hypnotized part did not know their *qualities* until *seeing* them . . . The two parts worked together to form a story.[10]

The process is an extraordinary one, and no one, least of all Professor Hilgard, claims it is properly understood yet, but it is certain that it cannot be regarded as a mere quirk of hypnosis and nothing more. As we have said, there are varying degrees of unconsciousness with which we perform even the most everyday tasks, and this hypnotic type of imagery may well be closer to the surface in ordinary waking life more often than we think. For instance, innumerable novelists, when asked how they create their stories, talk of a point after what may be a long and very conscious period of building up characters, when these characters come to life and assume vivid interrelationships of their own. This particular characteristic has fascinated the New Zealand psychologist Professor Peter McKellar of the University of Otago, and during the 1950s he entered into a lengthy correspondence with the famous children's story writer Enid Blyton on this very point. She told him: "I shut my eyes for a few minutes with my portable typewriter on my knee . . . My characters stand before me in my mind's eye . . . as if I had a private cinema screen there."[11]

Exactly like Hilgard's hypnotized student, Enid Blyton described how she could act as a spectator to the stories of her books as they unfolded in her mind, and so create situations which time and again seemed beyond what she would consciously have expected herself to think of:

> To write book after book without knowing what is to be said or done sounds silly, and yet it happens. Sometimes a character makes a joke, a really funny one that makes me laugh as I type it out on my paper—and I think, "Well, I couldn't have

thought of that myself in a hundred years!" And then I think, "Well, *who* did think of it then?"[12]

Nor is this situation peculiar to the literary world. However hard-headed scientists may seem, most of their inventions have come into being with precisely the same mysterious floating into consciousness as Enid Blyton's Noddy and Big Ears. Many of Einstein's greatest ideas are said to have come to him during his morning shave, so suddenly that he had to train himself to hold the blade carefully lest he cut himself with surprise.

What we have to acknowledge, then, is a still not yet understood state behind normal consciousness, a state with seemingly boundless reserves of memory to which it seems to be able to gain instant access; a state with extraordinary creative abilities of its own, able to construct stories and visual images of striking originality (Martin St. James's subjects are scarcely likely to have ever seen an all-nude studio audience); a state with physical resources (hence the abreaction-type wounds, etc.), and above all a state so independent of consciousness that what it projects into the consciousness fails to be recognized by the consciousness as coming from itself. What has to be emphasized is that this state, for all its mystery, is not one of mere make-believe psychological theory. The concept is being taken increasingly seriously in psychological circles, and nowhere more so than by Professor Hilgard and his team at Stanford. Hilgard's name for it, "hidden observer," is probably an inadequate title, but he has been at pains to avoid too outlandish or exaggerated claims that might alienate serious scientific opinion.

The hidden-observer part of the mind can be scientifically demonstrated, and what has been learned so far begins to set to rights some long-cherished misconceptions about hypnosis. For instance, one considerable body of psychological opinion has long argued that hypnosis is mere play-acting or role-playing—that while in a state of acute suggestibility the hypnotized subject will do anything to please the hypnotist. Having observed entire surgical operations performed with hypnosis as the only pain-killer, Hilgard has for many years felt strongly that no amount of wanting to please the hypnotist could account for this. He felt quite sure that during hypnosis the consciousness was in some way being switched off or dissociated. But he also felt quite sure that while the conscious "I" was quite genuinely receiving no sensation of pain, something somewhere else in the mind was—hypothetically, the hidden observer, whatever it might be. The difficulty of proving this lay in producing and maintaining a genuine hypnotic pain-killer in the conscious "I" while at one and the same time demonstrating some form of contact with whatever part of the mind might genuinely be feeling the pain.

The first breakthrough came in 1960 when E. A. Kaplan[13] hypnotized a twenty-year-old student, and suggested to him that his left hand was insensitive to pain. There was nothing new in this, but Kaplan also told the student that while his left hand remained insensitive, his right hand would be free to write automatically, without conscious awareness of what it was communicating. With the student in deep hypnosis, Kaplan then vigorously pricked his left hand three times using a hypodermic needle. The student's desensitized left hand showed not the slightest reaction. But the right hand was immediately provoked into vigorous activity, scrawling frantically, "Ouch, damn it, you're hurting me!" A few moments later the student asked Kaplan in all innocence when the experiment was going to begin, clearly consciously unaware of anything that had transpired. But an important discovery had been made—something had felt the pain, and something with sufficient resources to commit the feeling to writing.

At Stanford, Hilgard became fascinated by the possibilities raised by this experiment and carefully devised a way of taking it a stage further.[14] Knowing that one of the most unbearable forms of pain is submersion in circulating iced water, Hilgard set a scale of zero to ten for the degrees of such pain, then proceeded to ask subjects in their normal waking consciousness to immerse one hand in the iced water, reporting numerically on the increasing intensity of the pain until they were able to keep the hand in the water no longer. Normally they reached the unbearable level—ten —within less than a minute. Hilgard then hypnotized a young woman volunteer and suggested, as in Kaplan's experiment, that while she should feel no pain in the hand immersed in the water, the other would record, without control of the consciousness, any degrees of discomfort she might be experiencing according to exactly the same scale adopted during normal consciousness. Her hand was plunged in the iced water, and verbally she consistently reported zero discomfort even though she was being asked this every five seconds. But while she was saying this, her writing hand was vigorously recording values for the increasing degrees of pain that something that was within her was experiencing: 2, 5, 7, 8, 9, and beyond. The woman could be described as literally in two minds, one part—the outward hypnotized part—feeling nothing, the other hidden "seeing" part experiencing everything. Communication with the hidden observer had been achieved.

And that, in the present light of psychological knowledge, seems about as far as the whole phenomenon is understood, but at last we have, albeit imperfectly, a theoretical structure for the complex processes behind the exhibition of past-life personalities. Once the subject is in the hypnotized state the will of the hypnotist is paramount and the subject's hidden observer, like an Aladdin genie, is largely—though not completely—at the mercy of the hypnotist's own commands and predisposed thinking. If commanded to produce a past-life story and if it is within his mental resources to do so, then the subject must provide something suitable and appropriate to what he has come to understand of the expectations of the hypnotist, hence the fluctuations in the "rules" of reincarnation between different hypnotists. Dr. Tom Troscianko, who was hypnotized by Joe Keeton, described the strongest feeling of compulsion to produce a past life, despite the total antipathy of his observing passive-observer consciousness to the whole idea. Precisely similar sensations were described by *Now!* journalist Thomson Prentice during a regression for which he volunteered. Anxiety and embarrassment were the sensations he experienced as he listened to Keeton's relentless "Who are you?", "Where are you?" after being told he was back in time before his birth.[15] Stress seems to be an important element in activating the hidden observer and the result becomes believable despite every expectation to the contrary.

Nevertheless, it is important to recognize that quite outside hypnosis other powerful emotional forces may well have precisely similar illusion-creating properties, particularly in childhood and old age when consciousness is arguably weaker.

It is also particularly significant to note that, while we have had to argue for some extraordinary mental states involved, we have not found the slightest need to believe that the material produced in past-life regressions has come from anything other than what the individual has acquired during his life by perfectly normal means. In all fairness, however, we do have to acknowledge that the hidden observer is so spectacular in its properties, and as yet so little understood, that some past-life factor, perhaps genetic, cannot be entirely ruled out.

CHAPTER 11

Two False
Seventeenth-Century Trails—
Philip Gaston and John Fletcher

As REMARKED IN an earlier chapter, trying to check the validity of any past-life claim, hypnotic or otherwise, presents a chicken-and-egg problem. If the past life remembered does not appear in contemporary records, there can be no guarantee that an individual of that description did not exist. We have expressed strong doubts relating to cases such as Trooper John Orriss and Father Antony Bennet, but were the records of the time conceivably not all that has been claimed for them? Or might the subject have fantasized the names while reliving real past-life situations? Even glaring mistakes and anachronisms in past-life memories are no absolute guarantee that the fundamental material is not authentic. Our twentieth-century memories are often all too fallible. Why should we expect a memory of, say, a seventeenth-century life to be any better? Conversely, if a subject appears to remember a past life that has been historically recorded, it represents no proof that the present-day subject is necessarily his reincarnation. Even if the documentation regarding that individual is obscure or difficult to come by, it is virtually impossible to eliminate some opportunity the present-day subject might have had to gain access to it.

It is against the background of these difficulties and all that we have so far learned in the course of this book that in the ensuing chapters we will be checking in far more detail than hitherto cases of past lives remembered, both recorded and unrecorded, with the maximum emphasis on the former. Ideally, I would have wished myself to have been suitable as a deep-trance subject, but I fall into the 10 per cent or so who are unresponsive to any hypnosis, and in the event it was a colleague, filmmaker David Rolfe, who proved far more suitable. At the end of 1978, Rolfe submitted to a trial hypnosis session with Leonard Wilder of Stanmore, a former dentist. Wilder, who had some twenty years of spare-time experience in past-life hypnotic regressions,[1] succeeded in inducing a deep-trance state in Rolfe, and the glimmerings of a regression into what appeared to be a seventeenth-century life. As Rolfe himself had no predisposition either for or against a belief in reincarnation and as Wilder was a man of professional status, the circumstances seemed ideal for a carefully controlled and objective past-life experiment. For psychological observation and advice we sought the help of the Bristol University Medical School Brain and Perception Unit, and Professor Richard Gregory, the Unit's head, very kindly made available the services of one of his researchers, an Oxford University graduate psychologist Jon Beer.

The outcome was a very carefully observed and recorded past-life regression with myself and Jon Beer as unobtrusive observers. When Wilder judged Rolfe to be in a deep enough trance, he began the regression, taking him first to childhood and then to before birth until Rolfe again claimed he was back in the seventeenth century. With no change in his twentieth-century voice, Rolfe described being in a hallway which had a heavy, brass-knobbed door and a black-and-white tiled floor with one or two of the tiles cracked. Standing at attention in the hallway was a footman in a dark-green shiny coat, with a gray waistcoat, frilly collared shirt, black leggings, and gold-buckled black shoes. Rolfe was able to describe the footman's natural hair as black, showing under a white wig, and he observed that he was in need of a shave. Rolfe spoke of himself as Philip Gaston. He gave the year as 1694, and his age at the time as thirty-four. Under close questioning from Wilder he disclosed that he was a farmer, specializing mainly in pigs and living in Esher, Surrey. The location in which he found himself, although identical to the setting of his

166 *All in the Mind*

first regression, was not his home. It was the hallway of the house of a Sir Robert Morton, and Gaston was waiting there impatiently because he had asked Morton for the hand of his daughter Angela in marriage, and now Sir Robert and his son William were conferring on his suitability. Gaston did not rate his chances too highly as Morton seemed to be set on marrying Angela to a cousin of the reigning king, William III. On this occasion, Gaston's offer had apparently been refused, but with progression to a few years later a happy outcome was revealed. He married Angela Morton about the year 1700, and five years later this union produced a son, Tim, followed after another two to three years by a daughter, Pegatha. General questioning of Gaston brought to light a comfortable and seemingly uneventful life, the main highlights being his enjoyment of a one-and-sixpenny spit roast at the local inn, the Dog and Bottle, and drinks with neighbors.

It was a notably unspectacular account to have come from a man with a high creative flair, and this was perhaps the feature which more than any other gave Rolfe's hypnotic story an air of credibility. From every other point of view, however, there were serious flaws. Some of these were immediately obvious. For instance, when Gaston was asked in the year 1710 whether he had heard any recent news of the royal family, he replied, "We have a new king now, King Charles." The year 1710 was, of course, in the middle of the reign of Queen Anne, and England's last King Charles had died back at the time that Gaston was theoretically a young man of twenty-five, in 1685. Similar ignorance was displayed over William III's Queen, Mary, who Gaston said was still alive in the autumn of 1695—even though she had died, to great national sorrow, nearly a year before.

Gaston might just have been forgiven for such ignorance of national affairs, but there was cause for similar doubts over his local information. Although it would have been useful to have more information about Sir Robert Morton than Gaston was able to provide—for instance, exactly where he lived—no family answering Rolfe's description has proved traceable, the only prominent Morton in William III's reign being Richard Morton, the king's physician, whose daughters were named Sarah and Marcia. Additionally, inquiries made with Surrey local historians concerning the existence in or around Esher of any seventeenth-century inn called the Dog and Bottle have met with a negative answer, despite an appeal made in the *Surrey Comet* by June Tims, a journalist and local-history enthusiast. Most telltale of all, there is not the slightest trace of any Philip Gaston and his family farming in Esher during the late seventeenth century. Under regression, Gaston specifically described himself as owning "a lot of land" and having "a house full of servants," both items suggesting a man of considerable substance and therefore likely to be well recorded. The parish records for Esher in the late seventeenth century are extant and well preserved in the Muniment Room of Guildford Museum. All baptisms, marriages, and deaths since the year 1678 have been carefully entered by successive local vicars, and even when the unidentifiable body of a vagrant was discovered, its burial as such was noted down. But although I searched thoroughly in Guildford,[2] entries for the baptisms of the Gaston children Timothy and Pegatha were nowhere to be found. Nor was there any record of the deaths of Gaston and his wife, even though every entry was checked up to the year 1750. In short, David Rolfe's Philip Gaston, like Sue Atkins' Father Antony Bennet, was a man who never was, an invention of David Rolfe's imagination, or, as we might now put it, his hidden observer.

For David Rolfe himself, uncommitted to any belief in reincarnation, this explanation is as satisfactory as any. A subject of the passive-observer type like Sue Atkins, Rolfe retained the memory of what he had seen under hypnosis, and was able to recall particularly vividly the warmth and savory smells of the Dog and Bottle —evidence, as supported by other cases, that even the senses of touch and smell are fully in play in the past-life experience. Rolfe was also able to describe how, in what seemed to be the later life of Gaston, he saw himself from outside himself, in precisely the way in which Chris Sizemore described many of her early multiple personality experiences. But even from the very outset, after his first trial regression with Leonard Wilder and long before either of us knew anything of the hidden-observer mechanism, Rolfe remarked that he simply could not be sure it was not all coming from his own imagination.

By coincidence, the second case to be studied in this chapter also involves a prosperous seventeenth-century farmer, although this time the memories were received in waking consciousness. The twentieth-century subject of the case, who died recently, was an Englishman, Edward Ryall of Benfleet, Essex. In May 1970 he wrote a letter to the *Daily Express*, claiming clear and orderly memories of a past life as a West Country farmer called John Fletcher living in Weston Zoyland, Somerset, during the reigns of Charles II and James II. Ryall had the satisfaction of seeing his letter published in the *Daily Express*,[3] and this brought his case to the attention of Dr. Ian Stevenson, whose work on cases of waking memories of past lives was discussed in Chapter 3. Stevenson corresponded with Ryall, became convinced that he was genuine, and in due course encouraged him to write a full-length book of his John Fletcher memories. This was published as *Second Time Round*, with an introduction and notes by Ian Stevenson, in 1974.[4]

John Fletcher's story, as set out in Ryall's book, is an undeniably vivid tale of a seventeenth-century yeoman farmer born in Taunton in the year 1645 and brought up from the age of two at his grandfather's farmhouse in Weston Zoyland. According to his account, he was but three years old when his mother died, and a mere lad of fifteen when with the death of his father, gored by the farm bull, responsibility for the family's farm fell to him. Fletcher's subsequent career was both amorous and industrious. After a brief romantic encounter with the lovely Melanie Poulett, one of the seven daughters of the historically known John, second Baron Poulett, in 1674 Fletcher settled down to a marriage with a local fuller's daughter, twenty-one-year-old Cecily Fuller from Dunwear. Fletcher had two sons by Cecily in 1675 and 1677 and lived out a relatively comfortable and prosperous life until 1685, when he happened to find his farm in a dangerous no-man's-land between the opposing armies of the rebel Duke of Monmouth and the royalist forces of King James II. It might be supposed that in such circumstances Fletcher would think his overriding responsibility was to stay at home to protect his wife and young family. Instead, he accepted a rash entreaty from a lifelong friend, Jeremy Bragg, to help guide Monmouth's troops during their ill-fated night attack on the royalist forces before the battle of Sedgemoor. Fletcher was even careless enough not to equip himself with proper weapons and armor for such a dangerous exploit.

Ryall's final memory of his life as Fletcher was of being cut down and killed by a royalist trooper very soon after the attack was discovered.

Throughout Ryall's account there are persistent items of detailed information relating to seventeenth-century Somerset personalities, some of them relatively obscure, that are historically accurate. The Reverend Thomas Holt, who buried Fletcher's father in 1660, the Reverend Joseph Alleine, a fugitive priest, whom Fletcher hid in a priest-hole in the house in 1666, the Reverend Thomas Perrott who officiated at Fletcher's marriage in Weston Zoyland in 1674, can all be shown to have had a definite historical existence. It would have been difficult to acquire this information in ordinary casual reading, and because of these features Dr. Ian Stevenson has vigorously upheld the authenticity of the case and even after Edward Ryall's death has stoutly defended it against historical skepticism.

Yet even at a superficial level there are well-founded grounds for such skepticism. The whole account is peppered with examples of reported speech, which the author employs like a historical novelist trying to create a period effect, rather than in the manner of a genuine seventeenth-century writer. In one passage, for instance, "leman" is used as a synonym for "lover," even though this late medieval word had died out long before the seventeenth century. In another episode, Fletcher remarks how at a time of particular stress his wife used the Latin invocation to the Virgin Mary, *Ave Maria, piena di pietà,* a somewhat unfortunate slip as the words happen to be not Latin, but modern Italian, more than likely originating from Ryall's known war service in Italy, rather than from any genuine seventeenth-century material.[5] Ryall also describes suspiciously idealized sexual adventures with one Susannah, married to "a miserable Shaker"—again a little disturbing, as the Shakers, a branch of the Quakers, or Society of Friends, were not founded until more than sixty years after Fletcher's supposed death.[6]

Such anachronisms might be forgiven were it not for historical difficulties of an altogether deeper nature. One of these relates to Ryall's claim that Fletcher helped guide Monmouth's army on the fatal night of the battle of Sedgemoor. According to the well-documented contemporary descriptions of the battle,[7] Monmouth's guide was no Fletcher, but a farm laborer named Godfrey. Ryall tries to explain this by saying that Monmouth's men did not trust Godfrey and so he, as Fletcher, with his detailed knowledge of Sedgemoor's terrain, was called upon to see that Godfrey made no mistake. The objection here is that had Monmouth's men in reality been guided by any such allegedly well-known local landowner, historical attention would have inevitably been focused on him rather than on any doubtful farm laborer. The further difficulty is that Godfrey did indeed lose his way. There was a thick mist the night of Sedgemoor and he spent some time walking up and down the rhines (or drainage ditches) which crisscrossed Sedgemoor at that time, desperately trying to find the great Langmoor Stone that marked the army's easiest crossing place. There is not the slightest historical evidence that any local landowner named Fletcher came to his aid.

If these difficulties are serious enough, far more so are the issues of the historicity or otherwise of a Fletcher family in Weston Zoyland during the seventeenth century, and what evidence exists for there having been any appropriate Fletcher farmstead at the location Ryall has indicated. Fletcher specifically states that in 1660 the Reverend Thomas Holt buried his father after the goring by the bull. As already mentioned, there certainly was a Reverend Thomas Holt as vicar of Weston Zoyland in 1660, but it also happens that the Reverend Holt's records of all the baptisms, marriages, and burials he performed throughout his period of office in Weston Zoyland (along with those of all other vicars of Weston Zoyland since 1558) have been preserved, and are available for inspection at the Somerset County Record Office, Obridge Road, Taunton. Unfortunately for Fletcher's story, Holt's list of burials shows no entry for anyone by the name of Fletcher being interred in 1660. Nor, among the list of marriages performed by the Reverend Thomas Perrott (Holt's successor), do we find any entry for the marriage of any John Fletcher with a Cecily Fuller, despite the fact that Fletcher specifically tells us that Thomas Perrott conducted this service. Nor, among the lists of baptisms performed by Perrott, faithfully kept until his death in 1708, is there the slightest trace of a reference to the baptisms of Fletcher's two sons John and Jeremy, allegedly born in 1675 and 1677. We might also expect to find some reference to the death of Fletcher's mother in 1647, and the death of Fletcher himself at Sedgemoor in 1685. Yet so far as Weston Zoyland's parish records are concerned, no Fletcher family can be found in existence at the period, even though the comings and goings of numerous other families can be followed with fascinating regularity, generation by generation. It should be stressed that at the time there was no legal compulsion to register births, marriages, and deaths, such as has been in force since 1836. Nevertheless, many local vicars were punctilious in keeping careful parish records, and Holt and Perrott appear to have been no exceptions.

All this is damning enough to the credibility of Ryall's account, but any remaining uncertainties may be dispelled by investigation into the case for the existence of any farmhouse answering Ryall's description in the area of Weston Zoyland he suggested. Not long after the publication of *Second Time Round*, Ryall's claims came to the attention of Michael Green, by profession an architectural historian and archaeologist, and an Inspector of Ancient Monuments and Historic Buildings for the Department of the Environment in London. Green carefully noted the details of Fletcher's Weston Zoyland house as described by Ryall.[8] The house was said to have been built in 1530, constructed in the Tudor style of timber and plasterwork, and was, in Fletcher's description, of "fair size," including on the lower floor a "Great Hall," a buttery, a dining room, a kitchen, a drawing room, and a private sanctum for Fletcher, with on the upper floor a seating area (which Fletcher called the "old Solar") and six bedrooms. But although *Second Time Round* included a map[9] showing Weston Zoyland at the time of Sedgemoor and the route Fletcher took to join Monmouth's army (thereby, by implication, showing the site of Fletcher's house), it was not quite specific enough. Since Ryall claimed in his book that his memories as Fletcher had continued to become ever clearer, Green decided to write to him at his Benfleet home to try to persuade him to pinpoint the site exactly.

Even in its own right the correspondence that followed between Green and Ryall is highly illuminating. While it would almost certainly be unfair to suggest that *Second Time Round* was written as a deliberate deception by Ryall, his uneasiness at having his memories submitted to highly professional scrutiny is unmistakable from the very outset. Despite Green's never more than gentle probing, Ryall responded with prevarication upon prevarication. In fairness, it has to be acknowledged that he had some justification. Since the seventeenth century, the countryside around Weston Zoyland has changed almost beyond recognition. At the time of the battle, for instance, Sedgemoor was segmented by the drainage ditches known locally as rhines. One was the Langmoor Rhine, its easiest crossing-place marked by the great Langmoor Stone; another, closer to Weston Zoyland, was the Bussex Rhine, which half-encircled the village. During the eighteenth century these and other landmarks of the seventeenth century disappeared following the construction of the great King's Sedgemoor Drain. However, their positions are still known and certain key features of Weston Zoyland, such as the Reverend Thomas Perrott's church (where hundreds of Monmouth's rebels were temporarily incarcerated after the battle), remain to this day. It was therefore not an altogether difficult matter for Michael Green to provide Ryall with a detailed Ordnance Survey map of the late nineteenth century showing enough of the seventeenth-century landmarks for the site of the Fletcher farmhouse to be accurately identified. Green asked Ryall to indicate on this the approximate extent of the lands he had owned as Fletcher, and to provide a separate layout of the farmhouse's main features. Eventually, after over a year of letters, Michael Green managed to persuade Ryall to show the farm's position in relation to seventeenth-century topography, and to draw an elevation of the farmhouse with accompanying plans of the ground and first floors. He refused to identify the location of the farmlands, even though as a farmer Fletcher might have been expected to remember these clearly.

Even the material which Ryall did provide seems to justify the disquiet already raised by the suspect details in *Second Time Round*, and by the absence of any Fletcher family in the Weston Zoyland parish registers. Michael Green was able to establish from old maps and topographical records not only that the farm location indicated by Ryall had been open moor until the late eighteenth century, but also that Ryall's allegedly seventeenth-century droveways were not in fact created until the enclosure of the parish common lands in 1795. A fuller appraisal by Michael Green is awaited of Ryall's elevation and plans of the farmhouse, but suffice it to say that the house depicted by Ryall was neither of the type nor built of the material to be expected in Somerset in the early sixteenth century. Not only is Ryall's plan more reminiscent of the cross-winged farmhouses with which Ryall would have been familiar in his native Essex, but his elevation bears some striking resemblances to Figure 15 of Marjorie and C. H. B. Quennell's *Everyday Things in England, 1500 to 1799*.[10]

So how are we to account for Ryall? Was he a deliberate hoaxer, or bemused by fantasies of his own unconscious creation? He died early in 1978 at the age of seventy-six, and unfortunately not a great deal is known of his life. It does so happen that, like Fletcher in his book, his mother died at the age of three; he was cared for by a grandmother until he was six, but for most of his formative years his sole parental figure was a stern and silent father who immersed himself in hard work and, in addition to his daily occupation, worked two ten-rod allotments. In Ryall's own introduction to *Second Time Round* he claimed: "I have never been a great reader, and the amount of research I have done is negligible," but this seems to have been true only of his life after the age of fifteen. After interviewing Ryall, Ian Stevenson stated without hesitation that Edward Ryall read extensively up to the age of fifteen, and noted, "Edward Ryall showed a most creditable knowledge of such subjects as Hindu religious customs and Provençal poetry."[11] Elsewhere Ryall himself spoke familiarly of works such as the *Rubáiyát* of Omar Khayyám and Boccaccio's *Decameron*[12]—scarcely the choices of the barely literate. While Ryall denied that he had ever visited the Weston Zoyland area properly before 1970, he admitted reading in his schooldays a textbook summary of the Monmouth rebellion and the battle of Sedgemoor. He also admitted having read at least part of R. D. Blackmore's novel *Lorna Doone*, set in the same historical period as the life of Fletcher, in much the same Exmoor countryside, and also with a yeoman farmer hero. Given his lonely, motherless early youth, Ryall, much against his other inclinations, may well have buried himself in the romantic historical novels prolific in the period before World War I. When, after the age of fifteen, he thrust himself into the activity of an everyday occupation, he may well, so far as his ordinary waking consciousness was concerned, have forgotten his early reading proclivities. In these almost classic circumstances, a private romantic fantasy about Fletcher may well have been born, quite unconsciously, to emerge, much later in life, in unrecognized hidden-observer style.

Ryall made no mention of any past-life memories until comparatively late in life, and when he did this was much to the surprise of his wife and family, especially since he claimed always to have had them. But the real key to the nature of his memories seems to lie in his own words. In the introduction to *Second Time Round*, he described the memories as "remarkably easy and free from effort," "present in my waking consciousness," and "bright and interesting, almost like watching a TV play in which one was an actor"[13]—all classic descriptions of the hidden-observer state as identified in the last chapter.

In the light of all these factors, the explanation of Edward Ryall's case would seem utterly straightforward but for the attitude of Dr. Ian Stevenson. Stevenson adopted the Ryall case at an early stage and since Ryall's death has defended its authenticity tenaciously. Yet Ryall's cannot be considered a classic Stevenson case. Most of his subjects have been children who lost their past-life memories after the age of six, but Ryall has claimed that age only made his memories more "vivid and animated." In most Ian Stevenson cases the interval between the past and the present life has been a matter of a few years, but in Ryall's case the span is more than two centuries from his death as John Fletcher in 1685 to his rebirth as Edward Ryall in 1902. Stevenson, who visited Ryall's home on two occasions and indulged in a lengthy correspondence with him, is, of course, entitled to his opinions. But there are now several historians who have voiced well-reasoned doubts about the validity of the evidence for Fletcher's historical existence—including some whom Stevenson has himself contacted, Renée Haynes, editor for the British Society for Psychical Research (herself an Oxford history graduate), Michael Green, and myself. Within all the mechanisms we have encountered—cryptomnesia, multiple personality, and the hidden observer—it is perfectly possible for Ryall to have believed implicitly in his Fletcher memories, just as Colin Wilson's woman subject believed in the seventeenth-century ghost clergyman she saw. Ideally, of course, historians should be able to identify exactly how Ryall assembled his detailed knowledge of Weston Zoyland's seventeenth-century vicars and the like. But Stevenson's almost impassioned stance against consistent and well-grounded historical opinion is scarcely that of a totally objective scientist, and the Ryall case serves to reinforce the doubts about many of Stevenson's Asian and other child memory cases discussed in Chapter 3.

Of course, had the Fletcher family shown up in Weston Zoyland's parish records even as one-line entries, attitudes might have been different. Had the 1530s farmhouse shown up on the right site in land registers, allowances might have been made for some of Ryall's other errors, which brings us to the real, final test of a hypnotic past-life memory case. This has to be a case, unlike those of the Philip Gaston or John Fletcher type, in which the individual's existence can be identified in the pages of history, and can be checked against the best available contemporary sources. Such cases are rare but they do exist.

CHAPTER 12

Joan,
the Chelmsford Witch

IN 1977, MILLIONS of television viewers throughout the Granada Television region of England, serving the major cities of Liverpool and Manchester, heard an appeal from Joe Keeton for volunteers for past-life hypnotic regressions. One of those who responded was Jan, an attractive twenty-three-year-old from Merseyside. Well read, with a grammar school education, she had no strong views on reincarnation—her boyfriend had prompted her to respond to Keeton's appeal—and lightheartedly imagined that if any past life emerged, it might be that of some romantic female historical figure such as Boadicea or the Empress Josephine. A preliminary hypnosis test by Joe Keeton proved that Jan was a good subject and, thus encouraged, she readily agreed to be taken back in time to a past life. As those attending this particular group session watched, her face assumed the facial blank typical of the between-personality state. Then almost immediately she began screaming, "Not me! Not me!", behaving so uncontrollably that Joe Keeton saw no alternative but to abandon the regression.

With some difficulty, Keeton persuaded Jan to be hypnotized again, and the regression which followed must rank as one of the most emotionally charged in Joe Keeton's collection. For just a few opening moments there was bewilderment and disorientation:

Q: What can you see?

A: [whispered] P-persons.

Then on Keeton's question "What is your name?" which went unanswered, Jan suddenly broke into hysterical breathing, sustained for almost the entire remainder of the regression:

A: I am . . . nigh on . . . my eighteenth year.

Q: What is your first name? How shall I call you?

A: I'm the daughter, sire, of Mother Waterhouse.

Q: Where do you live?

A: Hadfald.

Q: What is your first name? How shall I call you?

A: My name's Joan.[1]

No one could have prepared Keeton for Jan's reaction to his next gambit:

Q: Are you married, Joan?

A: No.

Q: Are many boys paying court to you?

To Keeton's astonishment she burst into a bitter and cynical laugh.

Q: Why do you laugh?

[No answer]

Q: What are you doing right at this moment?

A: I'm at the Assizes.

Herein lay the reason for Joan's reaction to the word "court." But what was this girl doing at the Assizes? When Keeton asked this question, at first Joan's response was more nervous breathing. Then, with sudden inspiration, he tried volunteering to aid her in her distress: "We will help you if we can. We will bring some people to defend you."

A: It's too late.

Q: Why is it too late? Why are you there?

A: 'Tis my mother, sire.

Q: Yes, and what about your mother?

A: *Pah!*

To the shocked surprise of those watching, Joan spat venomously into the room. Amid the hubbub of spectator comment only Keeton remained composed.

Q: What about your mother, Joan? Why are you at the Assizes?

A: [in a seething, scarcely audible whisper] 'Tis because of her I'm here.

Q: Pardon?

A: It's because of her . . . I'm in . . .

Q: What did she do? And of what are you accused?

A: *Witchery!*

Joan tossed the word savagely into the air and the crescendo of heavy breathing that followed carried with it all the horror of an age in which witchcraft meant death for those caught practicing it.

Q: Are you a witch?

A: No . . . ! No . . . !

Joan was now literally breathless with terror.

Q: Does your mother practice witchcraft?

A: Sire . . . she's all . . . of the old religion, sire . . . But I am not . . .

Q: What religion are you?

A: [scarcely audible] I'm not of hers . . .

Q: What year is it, Joan? What year is it we are in?

A: It is the year of our Lord . . . fifteen hundred and . . .

Q: And?

A: Fifty . . .

Keeton, thinking Joan had finished giving the date, turned his questioning to identifying the Assizes, only to hear Joan mutter the word "six," then repeat clearly and emphatically, "Fifty-six."

Q: Which Assizes is it, Joan?

A: Chelmsford.

Q: Chelmsford? And who is the presiding Judge?

A: Southcote.

Q: If we know him we'll try and get to him.

A: *Bastard!*

The name Chelmsford in association with witchcraft struck a chord in Joe Keeton's memory. Vaguely he remembered that he had heard of the case of the Chelmsford witches during research on another subject who claimed a past life as a witch. On the bookshelves of the very studio room in which he was conducting the regression he knew he had an *Encyclopaedia of Witchcraft and Demonology*,[2] and, after asking for this to be handed to him, he deftly flicked through the pages for the entry "Chelmsford Witches." As he scanned this, with a quiver of astonishment he noticed the name Waterhouse, and he realized immediately that the Joan Waterhouse on the couch before him was known to the pages of history. The *Encyclopaedia* said eighteen-year-old Joan Waterhouse and her mother Agnes had been tried for witchcraft at Chelmsford Assizes during the sixteenth century. They were from the Essex village of Hatfield Peverell, clearly corresponding to the "Hadfald" mentioned by Joan. The presiding judge at the Chelmsford trial, so contemptuously spoken of by Joan, was John Southcote (1511–1585), Justice of the Queen's Bench.

Armed with the *Encyclopaedia*, Keeton now found himself in a position where he could put questions to Joan with the correct answers set out before him:

Q: There is one more person in the dock with you. What is the name of that person?

A: Francis.

This was quite correct. Elizabeth Francis, most likely Agnes Waterhouse's sister, was the first of the three accused to appear at the trial.

Q: Do you know the Reverend Thomas Cole?

A: He spake too much.

This was an apposite enough remark. Thomas Cole, who with "Master Foscue" (Sir John Fortescue) presided at an earlier stage of the trial, was noted at the time for his eloquence, as his entry in the *Dictionary of National Biography* confirmed.

Q: Who put you to the question?
A: Master Gerard . . . Queen's attorney.

This too was perfectly correct. The prosecutor at the trial was none other than the royal Attorney-General Gilbert Gerard, a surprisingly important figure to be involved in the trial of simple village women.

Q: What makes them think you are a witch?
A: 'Tis Agnes.
Q: Agnes? Who is Agnes?
A: The child lies.
Q: How old is Agnes?
A: [after a pause, mumbling] . . . perceive she's twelve.
Q: Do you know who she is? What is her second name?
A: Brown. Agnes Brown.
Q: What did the child Agnes say that you did?
A: She said . . . She *lies!*
Q: What did she say that you did?
A: I bring a black dog to fear her.
Q: Why did she say it?
A: She lies . . .
Q: Why is she lying?
A: I know not . . . my mother has the black dog. She has the black dog . . . not I . . .
Q: Is your mother a witch?
A: Aye.

All this Keeton found to be quite correct. In Joan Waterhouse's trial her chief accuser was indeed a somewhat unpleasant twelve-year-old called Agnes Brown. One day while her mother was out, Joan allegedly went to Agnes Brown to ask her for some bread and cheese. When this was refused, Joan returned home and

called out from under her mother's bed a creature called Sathan
who assumed the form of a black dog to frighten Agnes Brown
and subsequently haunt her. According to the charges against
Elizabeth Francis and Mother Waterhouse, they used the same
Sathan in the forms of a cat and a toad for various murderous en-
terprises. Agnes, Joan's mother, was found guilty of witchcraft
and hanged within three days. Joan and Elizabeth were acquitted,
although years later Elizabeth Francis was to be retried and
found guilty on similar charges.[3]

What to Keeton was so impressive about Joan's information
was not only that it corroborated factual details, but also that her
whole performance—if it *was* a performance—was seemingly beyond the capabilities of even the finest actress. Consistently during her regression Jan held out her hands with the fingers curled
up as if in intense pain, eventually compelling Keeton to ask,
"Why do you hold your hands like that?"

A: They're burnt!

Q: They burnt your hands?

A: Mmmh! [apparently reliving the anguish over again] 'Tis a
rod of iron . . .

Joan was referring to the ordeal of trial by fire, where the victim
was required to grasp a bar of hot iron. Keeton then asked
whether she was tortured. Joan's reply was another expressive
"Mmmmh!" followed by more pained breathing.

Q: How were you tortured?

A: Pins and . . .

Q: Pins to find your witch mark? Did they find one?

A: No, sire.

Q: Did they find a witch mark?

A: I have no witch mark . . . *No imp sucked from me.*

This too was perfectly comprehensible from known sixteenth-century practice. Every witch was supposed to have a spot on her
body which was insensitive to pain,[4] so suspects were stripped,
shaved of their body hair, and then pricked all over with pins in
an attempt to find that spot. At the same time, the searchers
would look for the supernumerary nipple—the extra nipple by

which a witch was said to suckle demons. This was the explanation of Joan's "No imp sucked from me."

So intense was Jan's emotional state that, without asking as
many questions as he might otherwise have done, Joe Keeton
brought her out of the hypnotic trance. As he discovered, however, once Jan was safely back in the twentieth century, her whole
attitude toward hypnosis had been changed by the Joan Waterhouse experience. She wanted nothing more to do with past-life
adventures. A subject of the passive-observer type, she could remember all the events described in detail, and is still terrified by
the experience. Three years have now passed since this regression,
but nothing would persuade her to be regressed again. She refused
to have her full name disclosed in connection with the case, and
refused to be photographed for the Keeton book *Encounters with
the Past*, although she kindly consented to a long and frank interview with me.

The Waterhouse trial happens to be the first one recorded in
what became a whole series of chapbooks of sixteenth- and seventeenth-century witch trials. In the Library of the Archbishop of
Canterbury at Lambeth Palace, London, is preserved the only surviving original copy of the tiny black-letter chapbook recording
the Waterhouse trial.[5] This provided useful corroboration of Jan's
information. For instance, Jan had a vivid post-hypnotic memory
of her sixteenth-century mother, Agnes Waterhouse, standing beside her in the dock. Jan was shocked by her appearance because
the woman's face was "disgustingly spotted," and "she looked too
old to be my mother."[6] The chapbook specifically gives Agnes
Waterhouse's age as sixty-four, which means that she must have
given birth to Joan at the surprisingly late age of forty-six and
would indeed have looked exceptionally old as a mother to the
eighteen-year-old Joan. Furthermore, the same chapbook
specifically attests to Agnes Waterhouse's facial spots. Asked by
Attorney-General Gerard "When did thy cat suck of thy
blood?", Agnes' reply was a defiant "Never!" Perry Mason style,
Gerard then asked for the kerchief covering much of the woman's
face to be pulled back. As the chapbook records the moment:
". . . and then the jayler lifted up the kercher on her head, and
there was diverse spottes on her face and one on her nose." Jan

also remembered under hypnosis the exceptionally hot and oppressive atmosphere in the courtroom, which is consistent with what is known of the dates of the trial, July 26 and 27.

Jan herself is convinced that the experience must have been some form of past-life memory—after all, she "saw it in her mind's eye." She has said emphatically that, to the best of her conscious recollection, she had never seen, read, or heard anything of the Chelmsford Witch case until the whole highly emotional story poured out from her under hypnosis. "I remember at school finding extreme difficulty in absorbing facts about Napoleon, never mind some village twit called Joan Waterhouse, so I can honestly say I had never heard of her,"[7] she told me. Joe Keeton's integrity is also beyond question—but can the memory really be all it seems and all Jan herself clearly thought it?

The period in which Jan's regression was set is of particular interest from the point of view of language. Sixteenth-century English was very different from that spoken today, and the tape recording of Jan's regression shows a period flavor to her English, employed spontaneously, and remarkably consistent in its quality. As Joan she gave her age as "nigh on my eighteenth year," and addressed Keeton consistently as "sire." Other apparently archaic expressions she used in a fluent and natural manner are evident from the excerpts from the transcript of the regression: "I know the child not well," "a black dog to fear her," "No imp sucked from me," and so on. But listening to the tape recordings made of Jan's regression, even the uninitiated can pick out the faint background tones of her native South Merseyside accent, as if it had not been quite buried by the Joan personality. This gives rise to some doubts, so does Joan's speech really stand up to expert investigation?

For the answer to this, Stanley Ellis at the School of English at Leeds University very kindly agreed to listen to the tape recordings of the Joan Waterhouse regression. He has made a lifetime's study of both the variations among English regional accents as they exist today, and the variations in spoken English as they have occurred through the centuries. He acknowledged before hearing the tapes that he would be delighted to come across anyone, in any circumstances, using genuine sixteenth-century speech

—or indeed that of any other historical period. On listening to Jan's regression, however, to his own regret he came to the unhesitating conclusion that, even allowing for Jan's own accent to show through, there was nothing about Joan's speech content which suggested a genuine sixteenth-century speaker at work, let alone one from Essex. In his opinion, Joan's archaisms beyond doubt were the sort used to convey period flavor in books and in period dramas on radio and television; they could in no way be reconciled with the manner in which the real sixteenth-century Joan Waterhouse would have spoken.

This suggests that, after all, Jan must have acquired her knowledge of the Chelmsford Witch trial from some perfectly ordinary twentieth-century source, such as a book, a magazine article, a radio or television drama. But what? Tracking down what might have inspired her is virtually impossible. The only sure method would be to rehypnotize her in the manner employed by Dr. Reima Kampman. Very understandably Jan has refused further hypnosis at any price. We do, however, have independent means of checking that Jan obtained her material from a twentieth-century source, for although I have not commented on it so far, the circumstances surrounding the date of the Waterhouse trial are very unusual. Early on in the regression Jan very positively and precisely gave the year in which she found herself as "the year of our Lord fifteen hundred and fifty-six." This would have put her trial during the reign of Mary, two years before that of Elizabeth, which began in 1558. To confirm that 1556 was indeed the year, some while later during the regression Joan was quite deliberately asked the name of the reigning king or queen. Joan answered, "It's not a king."

Q: Who is it?
A: It's Elizabeth.
Q: Oh . . . not . . . not Mary?
A: Elizabeth.

This discrepancy clearly troubled Joe Keeton's wife Monica, intently following the details of the regression. After some questioning of Joan on other matters, she again asked her directly the year in which she found herself:

A: The year of our Lord fifteen hundred . . . five six.

Q: Fifteen fifty-six . . . and yet you say Elizabeth is on the throne. Has she been on the throne for long?

A: No.

Q: I thought it was Mary. What's happened to Mary?

A: Why do you ask me?

Q: Because I thought Mary was on the throne. Is she not?

A: *You too say I lie.*

This controversy may seem unimportant, yet it is crucial to our understanding of the origins of the whole Joan Waterhouse saga in Jan's mind. For historically there can be no doubt that the Waterhouse trial took place, not in July 1556, as stated by Joan, but in July 1566, well within the reign of Elizabeth. This date is given in the Lambeth Palace chapbook and is independently confirmed by contemporary records of the cases heard at Chelmsford Assizes, which specifically list those of Joan and Agnes Waterhouse being heard in 1566.[8] Furthermore, Justice John Southcote, Attorney-General Gilbert Gerard, and the Reverend Thomas Cole were all worthies of the establishment scene during the reign of Elizabeth, not Mary.[9]

Even in the light of this information such a dating error might seem minor enough, but Jan's "mistake" is more significant than at first appears. The Lambeth Palace chapbook is the only surviving original copy, and in the latter half of the nineteenth century the British Philobiblon Society, specialists in reproducing updated limited editions of rare books, decided to republish the sixteenth-century chapbook in modern type as part of the eighth volume of their *Miscellanies*.[10] A nineteenth-century typographer carefully transcribed from the front page of the original the sixteenth-century English words:

> The examination and confession of certaine
> Wytches at Chensforde in the Countie of Essex
> before the Quenes maiesties Judges,
> the xxvi daye of July Anno . . .

But instead of transcribing the date 1566, as given in the original, he set 1556, a discrepancy which went unnoticed at the proofreading stage and, indeed, unnoticed even after the publication of the book. With only one copy of the original, and that difficult to gain access to (even today the Lambeth Palace Library is rather like Fort Knox), anyone interested in the case inevitably consulted a Philobiblon Society copy. For the date of the trial it was quite natural to refer to the front page. As a consequence, several serious writers of the early part of this century inadvertently repeated the wrong date, among these Margaret Murray in *The Witch Cult in Western Europe*, published in 1921,[11] and C. L'Estrange Ewen in his appendix to *Witch Hunting and Witch Trials*, published in 1929.[12] More minor authors following these compounded the error, with the result that even Peter Moss's recent *Encounters with the Past*, directly referring to Jan's regression, has accepted 1556 as the correct date,[13] when it can be proved that it is not.

We may not be able to pinpoint exactly the source from which Jan obtained her Joan Waterhouse memories—it may have been a comparatively minor radio play or a story from a girl's comic that would be a needle-in-a-haystack task to identify—but since Joan's historical information is so accurate in all other respects, we can be virtually certain that her single mistake derives from someone writing of the trial *after* the error by the nineteenth-century typographer. Given the independent findings of Stanley Ellis and all that we have hitherto learned of the mechanics of past-life regressions, Jan's Joan Waterhouse may be confidently attributed to nothing more out of the ordinary than something she has read or heard—in other words, the cryptomnesic mechanism discussed in Chapter 7.

Jan is a normal, healthy, well-balanced girl with no particular interest in the occult, though she acknowledges a ready enjoyment of the ordinary horror film at the cinema. But almost as far back as she can remember, anything involving witchcraft has terrified her. Whatever our source, therefore, it seems to have been responsible not only for Jan's hypnotic regression but also for her conscious phobia. Nor does its influence end there. The Joan experience had very real side-effects upon Jan. Besides taking on the personality of Joan Waterhouse during the regression, seeing herself in a sixteenth-century body and speaking in a sixteenth-century voice, Jan told me that for weeks after the regression by Joe Keeton she suffered mild but nevertheless alarming bouts of repetition of the Joan Waterhouse condition. Some were merely minor feelings of disorientation and dissociation. Others were more specific. For instance, while she was with her boyfriend at a club in Manchester one night, she found herself saying, in a strange voice, something to the effect that her drink was like poison. As Jan expressed it, she "did not feel right" and attributed this to the hypnosis.

One can scarcely avoid detecting in this a hint of the multiple personality symptoms with which we have now become familiar from the cases of Chris Sizemore, Sybil, and others. While it would be quite unreasonable to suggest that Jan might be suffering from anything even approaching the serious disturbances of the latter, there are justifiable suspicions that whatever brought into being the Joan Waterhouse memories created a mild, normally quiescent, form of the condition, which the hypnosis exacerbated. If this is the case, hypnotists carry a heavy burden of responsibility when they suggest to their subjects they are back in past lives. Whatever the answer, as a rare example of a regression personality traceable in historical records, the Joan Waterhouse case should have provided the most positive evidence in favor of reincarnation. Instead, as detailed scrutiny has revealed, it has done the very reverse. It may, of course, be argued that it is set too long ago. Let us therefore turn to a case of another reliably documented past-life personality, this time set firmly within living memory.

CHAPTER 13

Elsie and the
Cain Family Picnic

IN THE YEAR 1895 a master draper called John William Cain[1] from the Isle of Man set up a shop at 85 Chapel Street in the Lancashire town of Salford. He and his wife Margaret worked hard, and with the passing of years they and their son Harry and four daughters Annie, Florrie, Elsie, and Lily all became well known and well liked in the Salford community—attending the local Methodist chapel regularly, participating in local government, above all giving customers of their well-stocked drapery shop a cheerful welcome and efficient service. As local folklore ran, "If Cain's didn't have it, it was no use going anywhere else." When John Cain died in 1935, his son Harry Cain took over the running of the business, but although he carried on in the traditional manner its heyday had passed. Not long after the birth of their daughter Mona, Harry's wife Doris was found to be suffering from multiple sclerosis, and in 1937 she died from this. Then in 1939 the Flat Iron Market,[2] a colorful gathering of stallholders very close to the Cains' shop, was moved to another site, depriving the drapery business of much of its passing trade. Although World War II brought with it a valuable contract for supplying local blackout material, in 1948 Harry Cain shut up shop for the last time.

Harry's daughter Mona had by now grown up and on visits to her father they would sometimes look back on the old happy days at 85 Chapel Street. It was on one such occasion that father and daughter happened to be discussing the earliest incidents each could remember. As Mona told Harry, what she thought to be her earliest memory was a clear mental picture she had of a Cain family picnic that, so she believed, must have happened when she was about two years old, which would have been in 1927. In her mind's eye she could see Harry and her mother Doris there, together with her aunts Annie and Florrie (who were, of course, Harry's sisters), and their respective husbands, Bert and Tom. She could recall the food for the picnic laid out on a white cloth with a green check border, set on top of a dark-green traveling rug, fringed on two sides, plain on the others. The picnic stood out so forcefully in her memory because there had been a commotion in the neighboring field, and she could remember herself in a white dress running across to this field as fast as her tiny legs could carry her, to discover her mother Doris lying unconscious, her back against a tree trunk, after being thrown by a pony.

Mona's memory was received with disbelief by Harry. He remembered the incident well. The accident had happened in the way Mona had described, and all the details, such as the appearance of the cloths laid out for the picnic, were absolutely correct. Doris, who was five months pregnant at the time, had lost consciousness and on admission to hospital was found to have suffered a miscarriage, the dead fetus being that of a perfectly formed baby boy. Harry and Doris were told by the doctors that there was no reason why they should not have another child, but it would be best for them to wait for a year or so. This they did, and the daughter born to them two years later, in May 1925, was none other than Mona herself. She simply could not have remembered the picnic because at the time of it she had not even been conceived.

Being staunch Wesleyan Methodists, the Cains had no interest in matters of the occult, but nevertheless Mona, a thoroughly level-headed and practical-minded individual, remained puzzled by the clear memories that in all logic could not belong to her. She married, moved to Birmingham, and today as Mona Reynolds is employed as a nurse in a Birmingham hospital. But during

1977, like Jan of the Chelmsford Witch case, she heard of Joe Keeton via a television program, and, in the hope that it might throw some light on her unexplained memories, volunteered for regression at one of Keeton's group hypnosis sessions in Birmingham. The result was astonishing, and not at all what Mona expected. She proved to be an excellent hypnotic subject, regressing vividly back to the days of her earliest childhood. Then Keeton instructed her, "Drift off to sleep. Drift off to sleep. Now go back to times before you were born. Go back. Go back." Immediately Mona was back at the picnic of her childhood memory. In the opening moments she could be heard in great agitation calling out, "Doris!" and "Watch it!", as if she was actually at the scene, seeing her father and uncles struggling to aid her injured mother. Keeton, intrigued, inquired her name.

"Elsie, Elsie," was the reply, immediately followed by more agitated instructions to the invisible companions trying to help her mother: "*Oh, don't be silly! Don't be s . . . be careful with her!*"[3]

With remarkable naïveté one of those attending this particular regression session of Keeton's asked, "Are you enjoying the picnic, Elsie?"

A: No. No.

Q: Why?

A: No. Accident. *Why do you have to worry me when we've got this on our mind?*

Q: Who's had the accident, Elsie?

A: My sister-in-law.

Q: What's her name?

A: Doris.

Q: She's married to your brother, is she?

A: Yes, Harry's got . . . [flustered] *We've got no time to worry about you. We're worrying about Doris.* I don't know where Harry's took her. He put her in the car.

Q: Why are you worrying about her?

A: She's hurt herself. She's . . . she's fell.

Q: What did she fall from?

A: [angrily] . . . I was in the other field. But she's hurt herself.
She's hurt herself. We know she has.

Q: Which hospital has he taken her to?

A: *I don't know. I don't know.* [Very angry] *I've got no time
to worry about this. I don't know why you're . . . messing me
about!*

Q: And what are you going to do now?

A: I'm taking Mother home.

Q: And where does Mother live?

A: In Salford . . . at the shop.

Q: What shop is it?

A: A drapery shop of course.

Q: What's it called?

A: Cain's.

When Mona was brought out of hypnosis she proved to be a
somnambulistic type of subject, unable to remember anything she
had said while in the hypnotic state. But when Keeton and the
others who had attended the session told her that she consistently
referred to herself as Elsie and talked about the Cain drapery
shop, she realized with some astonishment that she must have
been producing memories of her own aunt Elsie Cain, Harry's
sister, whom she had never known because, as she explained, Elsie
had died before she, Mona, had been born.

Joe Keeton recognized immediately the importance of having
found in Mona one of the rare examples of a past life of someone
who demonstrably once lived, and who had died in comparatively
recent times. The case was particularly impressive because of
Mona's liveliness and spontaneity in reply to questions. While
many subjects' responses under regression tend to be labored and
sluggish, Mona spoke of the picnic incident with all the emotion
and breathlessness of the deceased Elsie, present at the scene.
Whenever Keeton visited Birmingham he therefore encouraged
Mona to return for further regressions on other aspects of Elsie's
life in order to build up more information. Given the suggestion
that she was back in her earliest years, Elsie vividly recreated the
Cain family domestic scene. Elsie's brother Harry Cain (who was,
of course, Mona's real-life father) emerged as a bit of a bully,

spitefully knocking down wooden bricks which Elsie and her sisters had built up, and smashing Elsie's china doll Clara by throwing it across the room. Her recall of her three sisters Annie, Florrie, and Lily was more affectionate. She particularly remembered the fine singing at the piano of her eldest sister Annie, and the long curls and pretty blue eyes of her youngest sister Lily. There was also the family's tailless Manx cat, Marmalade. ("Cats with tails are not intelligent," remarked the young Elsie.) There was a fat girl called Elsie Morris living next door, with whom Elsie played. She spoke also of her happy days at Gravel Lane Primary School, situated on the same road as the chapel attended by the Cains. And it was chapel, in the form of Salford's austere but well-supported Gravel Lane Wesleyan Methodist gathering, that, according to Elsie, clearly dominated most of the Cains' nonworking lives. The family had their own pew and attendance was punctilious:

Q: Do you go dancing, Elsie?
A: No. We belong to the chapel.
Q: How many times do you go to the chapel a week?
A: Four times on a Sunday.
Q: Four?
A: Four. I go on Thursday night with mother, 'cos she's in . . . Mother's in the choir. Then we go to Sunday School in the morning on a Sunday. Then we go into the chapel after Sunday School. Then we have lunch. We go to Sunday School in the afternoon. And we go to chapel with Dad and Mother at the night time.

By her late teens, as hypnosis revealed, Elsie was mildly resenting her parents' prohibition of her wearing makeup, but it was through chapel that she seemed to have met her husband-to-be, vividly recalling, at Keeton's instructions, the day of her wedding:

Q: Who are you marrying, Elsie?
A: Albert.
Q: How old is Albert?
A: Thirty.
Q: Have you known him for long, Elsie?

A: I met him at church . . . at chapel. He sings in the choir.

Q: What does he do for his living?

A: He works in the garage.

Q: Where is the garage that Albert works, Elsie?

A: Down the bottom of Chapel Street. Near the River Irwell, where the bridge crosses over.

Q: This is in Salford, is it?

A: In Salford.

Q: What does he do?

A: He repairs the wheels on trams, and things like that. This . . . these cages he tells me, that go at the front of trams to keep the . . . the road clear if anything falls on the tram line.

A fatal illness struck Elsie down not long after her marriage, and she recalled her last moments with particular vividness. Gone was her familiar chirpiness; every word was spoken with difficulty and accompanied by terrible rasping breathing:

Q: Where are you, Elsie?

A: In bed.

Q: What's the matter?

A: Don't feel very well.

Q: What's the matter then?

A: Hot.

Q: How old are you now? Perhaps we can help you.

A: [panting] Twenty-seven.

Q: What is the matter with you, Elsie?

A: Don't know.

Q: Any pain?

A: Chill.

Q: Have you got a bad cough? [Noise of difficult breathing.] Finding it difficult to breathe?

A: [whispering] Yes.

Q: Does . . . does this happen often?

A: [whispering] Yes.

Q: How long have you been poorly, Elsie?

A: [panting] A week, two weeks.

Q: Is it summer? Or winter?

A: [panting] I don't know.

Q: You don't know? . . . Where's your husband?

A: [barely audible] Gone to get the doctor.

Q: Doctor who?

A: Don't know.

Q: Are you by yourself?

A: Mother's here.

Q: Ah, that's a good job. Have you had the doctor?

A: [faintly] Yes.

Q: What did the doctor say it is? [Breathing.] Bronchitis, did he say?

A: As . . . As . . . As . . .

Q: Drift off to sleep. Drift off to sleep. Come forward five minutes. Where are you, Elsie? [Gasping and noisy breathing.]

Keeton did not obtain an answer to his question and at this point he gently brought Mona out of her regression. For Joe Keeton, the information that the historical Elsie Cain died not long before Mona's birth seemed vindication of his idea that from death to conception is to all intents and purposes instantaneous. For Mona herself, hearing from those who observed her the familiar family details she related under hypnosis, the idea that the dead Elsie was somehow speaking through her seemed the only logical explanation. However, she remained puzzled that her original memories were quite distinctly of herself as a two-year-old running across the grass at the picnic.

In a family such as the Cains' there would clearly have been limitless opportunities for Mona to learn information about Elsie in the cryptomnesic manner discussed in Chapter 7. Furthermore, some details, such as the family's staunch Methodism, would have been as true as of Mona's childhood as they were of Elsie's. So can we separate in Elsie's memories the information Mona might have been able to acquire via normal family conversation from information which could only have come from the dead Elsie herself?

Mona readily agreed to be interviewed at her pleasant home in the Northfield district of Birmingham, and proved a frank and objective informant. In order to distinguish the details of which Mona had no conscious knowledge I had prepared a questionnaire setting out every item of factual information Elsie had given under hypnosis. Mona cooperated by providing what information she could, from her best recollection of the family. Even at this stage the results were astonishing, for it quickly became apparent that much of Elsie's information was quite inaccurate when compared with what Mona knew perfectly well in normal consciousness. This was something Mona herself had not realized hitherto because, as a somnambulistic type of subject, she had no post-hypnotic memory of her regressions. For instance, at the day of her marriage, Elsie gave her husband's name as Albert. She also separately gave his surname as Brown. As Mona consciously knew perfectly well, the real Elsie's husband was, in fact, called Norman Doyle. But there was a weird logic to her choice of this fictitious name, for Elsie's eldest sister Annie had married an Albert Bailey and her youngest sister Lily had married a Tom Brown. The invented husband's name was a strange amalgam of the two, bearing an uncanny resemblance to the sort of twisting of real names and real individuals' roles that sometimes happens in dreams. Another example was Elsie's memory of her father, John William Cain. During the same regression in which she described her marriage, Elsie said that he died of cancer when he was twenty-one and her brother Harry's name then went up over the shop. But, in fact, John William Cain did not die until Christmas Day 1935, thus outliving his daughter. This was again well known to Mona in normal consciousness, since John Cain was her grandfather, and she was nearly ten years old in 1935.

Elsie's inaccuracies in such major factual items for which the waking Mona knew perfectly well the correct answers are clearly serious, but when I began to check the accuracy of Elsie's information on details about which Mona had *no* conscious knowledge, the whole case fell apart. Under regression Mona gave Elsie's date of birth as October 12, 1896. The conscious Mona had no idea whether this was accurate, nor any means of checking this herself from family records, since her father had died in 1973 and so far as she knew all other relevant family members, including Norman Doyle, were also dead. My only resort, therefore, was a visit to the General Register Office of Births, Marriages and Deaths at St. Catherine's House, London, where a search for Elsie in the registers for 1896 revealed an immediate problem. No Elsie Cain of Salford could be found for the entire year and a search of the registers for the year either side was similarly fruitless. It was the same with Elsie's marriage. From the hypnotic information, and from what Mona knew of her family's history, this should have taken place around the year 1923, yet there was nothing in the registers for that date. The registers were also searched for information relating to Elsie's death, which, from the hypnotic information and so far as Mona herself was aware, should have occurred around 1924 and certainly not later than May 1925, when Mona herself was born. No death record for Elsie could be traced to this period.

Questioned on the difficulty, Mona acknowledged that her conscious knowledge of dates was vague, but there could be no doubt that Elsie Cain had existed at roughly this time. Nevertheless, the lack of corroboration presented a serious obstacle. I wrote a letter to the Manchester *Evening News,* not mentioning hypnotic regression, but merely inquiring if any readers had memories of the Cain family of Salford, and in particular of Elsie and her husband Norman Doyle. The letter appeared on Saturday, November 17, 1979, and produced a voluminous response. It became clear that the hypnotic Elsie had been five years too early in her reckoning of her birth. Elsie had been born not in 1896, but in 1901. The St. Catherine's House Register of Births for that year confirmed 1901 was the year, but the date was not October 12, as Elsie had stated, but July 24. It could be said that under hypnosis, not knowing the real Elsie's date of birth, Mona's Elsie, albeit unconsciously, had blithely invented one five years in error, and of entirely the wrong month and day.

As more and more details of the real life of Elsie Cain emerged, so the same pattern recurred. Dates and ages were sometimes inconsistent with each other in the regressions, and invariably disagreed with the real facts. For instance, Mona's Elsie gave

18. Elsie Cain as a young woman. She was the third of John William Cain's four daughters and died at the age of twenty-six.

19. Mona Reynolds today. Under regression she assumes the personality of her deceased aunt Elsie Cain.

20. Mona under regression as Alice Simmonds. Note the contorted expression, an example of facial change and assumed only for this personality.

¶ Ione Waterhouſe, daughter to the
mother Waterhouſe, beinge of the
age of. rbiii. yeres, and erami-
ned, côfeſſeth as foloweth.

¶ The ende and laſt confeſ-
ſion of mother Waterhouſe at her
death, whiche was the
rrir. daye of July.
Anno, 1566.

Mother Wa=
terhouſe.

21. Joan Waterhouse and
her mother Agnes, from
the sixteenth-century
chapbook recording their
trial for witchcraft.

The Examina=
tion and Confeffion of cer= taine Wytches at Chenffozde in the Countie of Effex, befoze the Quenes maieftties Iudges, the xxbi. Daye of July.∴.
ANNO. 1566,

22. *Above:* The original front page of the Lambeth Palace Library chapbook, showing the correct date for the trial. *Below:* The typographer's error from the nineteenth-century Philobiblon Society edition, from which many later writers consulted the trial record.

THE   EXAMINA-
tion and confeffion of cer- taine Wytches at Chensforde in the Countie of Effex before the Quenes maiefties Judges, the XXVI daye of July Anno 1556

23. James IV, King of Scots, from a contemporary portrait in the Scottish
National Portrait Gallery.

24. A. J. Stewart, who believes herself to be the reincarnation of James IV.

25. The disputed Holbein portrait, which A. J. Stewart identifies to be herself as James.

26. A painting by Hugo van der Goes showing James III kneeling and a tiny figure, thought to be the future James IV, behind.

27. The head of the James IV figure seen under infrared. This clearly shows this part of the painting to be original to the work, and undoubtedly by Van der Goes himself. A.J.'s story of the picture's creation must therefore be wrong.

28. Nadia's drawing of a horse and rider done when she was approximately five years and six months old.

29. Nadia's drawing when she was approximately eight and a half years old, showing the decline in skill.

30. An ordinary six-year-old's drawing of a horse and rider.

her husband's age at the time of their marriage as thirty, her own as twenty-seven. The marriage certificate, dated April 5, 1926, proved otherwise. Norman Doyle at the time of his marriage was twenty-five years old, the real Elsie twenty-four. Mona's Elsie was also wrong about her husband's occupation. She described him as some kind of garage mechanic, who repaired trams in a building at the bottom of Chapel Street, yet even on this her hypnotic information was quite wrong. The real Elsie's marriage certificate says that Norman was a metal merchant like his father, their business being carried out at the Doyles' premises at 93 Great Clowes Street, which by no stretch of the imagination can be described as the bottom of Chapel Street. Nor can the description "metal merchant" be twisted into perhaps including the odd vehicle repair; local information confirms that they were essentially commodity dealers, without the slightest connection with mechanical repairs or the city's trams.

And so the inaccuracies continue: Mona's Elsie said that the name of the minister at the Gravel Lane Wesleyan Methodist Chapel was Jones. The Chapel itself closed in 1967–68, but Salford residents, together with local archive sources, produced many names of ministers of the real Elsie's time, among these the Reverend Augustine Harry Kellaway, who married Norman and Elsie, the Reverend Mudie Draper, the Reverend Dyson, the Reverend Phelps, and several others. But no Reverend Jones. It also emerged that, unknown to Mona, Elsie's youngest sister Lily is still alive and living in Northern Ireland. Lily, now seventy-five, even named her daughter Elsie in memory of her dead elder sister. Lily was able to provide the information that although the family had indeed once owned a Manx cat, this was called Tiddles and not Marmalade. Lily was able to deny emphatically that anyone by the name of Elsie Morris had lived next door to the Cains. Perhaps most crucial of all, she cast considerable doubts on the real Elsie Cain ever having been at the picnic at which Mona's mother Doris suffered her fall. Lily is quite sure that she herself was not there, and so far as she can recollect Elsie would either have been with her, or in the early stages of courting Norman Doyle.

The most important information of all, however, came to light with the true circumstances surrounding Elsie's death. Although

Mona Reynolds was regressed to Elsie by Joe Keeton on many occasions, she never mentioned having had a child. There was a
simple explanation for this: the present-day Mona had not the
slightest idea that Elsie had ever had a child. She knew that Norman Doyle had a daughter but assumed this was from his second
marriage. Yet one of the first letters to arrive from the Manchester *Evening News* was from a Mrs. Brenda Walklate of Gor-
ton, Manchester, stating that her maiden name had been Doyle,
and that she was the only daughter of the real Elsie and Norman
Doyle. It was, in fact, the birth of the baby Brenda, back in 1927,
that shortened what remained of Elsie Doyle's life, for as a result
of a complication arising from the birth Elsie contracted puer-
peral septicemia, one of the last mothers in the country to do so
before the infection was more or less eliminated. Mrs. Walklate's
information enabled me to trace Elsie's death certificate at St.
Catherine's House, which showed that Elsie did not die from
asthma or bronchitis as the regression suggested, but from a pul-
monary embolism as a secondary complication arising from the
septicemia. Furthermore, the same death certificate recorded that
she died at the Doyles' home, 93 Great Clowes Street, Lower
Broughton, not the Cains' home in 85 Chapel Street where, according to the regression, Elsie and her husband had been allowed to set up marital quarters. But by far the most intriguing
detail to emerge from the death certificate was the date of the
real Elsie's death. This was not shortly before Mona Reynolds'
birth in May 1925, as Mona had hitherto quite genuinely
believed, but November 27, 1927, two and a half years *afterward*.
In other words, Elsie, from whom Mona was theoretically reincarnated, did not die until two and a half years after Mona was
born.

So what can have induced Mona to assume the demonstrably
false Elsie personality under hypnosis? There is also the question
of what activated the original memories that led Mona to seek
hypnosis by Joe Keeton. This is likely to be integrally linked with
the Elsie personality, because the picnic was the very first item
which Elsie remembered under hypnosis, and furthermore the details do tally. It occurred to Joe Keeton to check this out at an
early stage, and at one of the sessions at which Mona produced
the Elsie character Keeton quite deliberately suggested to her that

she was back at the picnic scene just a few minutes before the accident occurred. Fortuitously Elsie described herself "helping Mother put the table."

Q: . . . What are the others doing?
A: I don't know. Messing around with some horses or something.
Q: Are they? [Laughter.] Have you got a tablecloth?
A: Yes.
Q: What color is it?
A: White, of course.
Q: Oh. Have you got a rug to sit on?
A: Not to sit on. We put a rug under the cloth.
Q: What color is the rug?
A: Um . . . dirty color. I don't know. Browny green color.
Q: What sort of dress are you wearing, Elsie?
A: Me? It's . . . er . . . cotton, white. It's got a blue . . . blue band round the middle.

All the mental images—the white cloth, the rug, the white dress —are clearly the same as in Mona's waking memories before a single regression by Joe Keeton. So although the data is admittedly limited, it may be reasonably inferred that both varieties of memory, the hypnotic and the nonhypnotic, had a common origin. But in what? Some form of genetic inheritance from one or other of Mona's parents might tentatively be suggested, since both to Doris and to Harry the picnic accident would inevitably have been a traumatic experience. But there is no scientific evidence for such a mechanism and even if there was, why, in relation to the incident, was Mona's conscious body image that of herself at the age of two, and her hypnotic body image that of the deceased Elsie—both these images being demonstrably false? Is there some as yet undetected point of connection, and/or some alternative explanation?

I remembered the work of Dr. Reima Kampman with Niki and others, and an attempt was made to resolve the mystery. Observed by me, Joe Keeton regressed Mona, not back into her past-life Elsie personality, but to the earliest moment in her present life in which she had heard of her mother's accident at the picnic. The experiment took place on February 16, 1980 with the full co-operation of both Joe Keeton and Mona, but it was only a qualified success because Mona found herself seemingly around the age of two and only able to communicate in very limited phrases. However, she did manage to convey that she was hiding under a table at her parents' home while some form of discussion was going on between her mother Doris and her grandmother Margaret Cain. The exact topic of discussion the infant Mona found impossible to explain in words. It may well be that at the real age of two she was able to understand more than she was able to express. But if we look to family circumstances, there were two major and traumatic events which must inevitably have shattered the close-knit and hitherto relatively trouble-free Cain family at about this time. One was the death of Elsie so shortly after childbirth at the tragically young age of twenty-six, leaving behind a young daughter, and the other was the first medical diagnosis of disseminated or multiple sclerosis in Mona's mother Doris Cain. Mona is quite positive that the family, whether rightly or wrongly, directly attributed this illness in Doris to the shock and miscarriage following the fall at the picnic. While we can only guess at the possible dominance of one, other—or perhaps both—of these events in the conversation between Doris and her mother-in-law the day the infant Mona hid under the table, what we do know is one key phrase which Mona managed to repeat from Grandma Cain: "No more picnics!"

This is perhaps the closest we can get to determining a conceivable trigger for the conscious and the hypnotic memories haunting the mind of Mona Reynolds. While a particularly traumatic story learned via a book, TV or radio program seems to have led to Jan's unconscious identification with Joan Waterhouse, in Mona it seems to have been this crucial conversation overheard under the table that led to her equally unconscious identification with Elsie. The results of the two traumas were very different. Jan's seems to have been strongly cryptomnesic, reproducing perfectly the key facts with little discernible invention. A possible explanation of this is that she was perhaps older at the time, and received the material in a highly concentrated and sophisticated form. Mona's, by contrast, would seem to have been largely hidden observer inspired, having a loose foundation in certain basic information relating to Elsie and the Cains' family life, but otherwise of largely invented material. This was perhaps because Mona was so very young at the time, and her source was the far less satisfactory one of loose fragments of conversation.

Whatever, the result in both Mona and Jan is that hypnotic regression produced in them past-life personalities with striking similarities to the characteristics of the multiple personality condition. Mona's Elsie personality is not only a very individual entity in her own right—she is as unlike Mona herself as Chris Costner was unlike the conscious Chris Sizemore. Quite untypical of everything I know of the conscious Mona (and according to those who remember her, quite untypical of the real-life Elsie), Mona's hypnotic Elsie could be bitchy, even about Mona's own parents. Of Doris, Mona's mother, in relation to the picnic accident she remarked, "I think she only wants to attract attention to herself."

"Don't you like Doris?" Keeton asked her.

"I think . . ." she replied, "I think Doris has got ideas that Harry's not spending enough time looking at her. So she's . . . I think she's doing this on purpose."

While Mona, as Elsie, exhibited little voice or facial change, this was not the case with an otherwise lightly sketched personality which Joe Keeton regressed Mona to in a life preceding that of Elsie Cain. Alice Simmonds from Cambridge was a wine merchant's daughter crippled by a carriage wheel at the age of eight. Regressed to this personality, Mona's whole face twisted and contorted (plate 20), assuming a quite different muscular tension from her normal relaxed and placid expression. Curiously, when Joe Keeton regressed her to a life even earlier than that of Alice Simmonds, Mona exhibited, surprisingly, a totally isolated passive-observer type of recall. She seemed to see herself standing on a mound surrounded by a herd of horses which she was directing; she was dressed in some strange open-sided garment which chafed her legs. An otherwise unproductive regression, it suggested that the same individual may have regressions of both the somnambulistic and passive-observer variety.

But while a few details on Mona Reynolds remain imprecise, we have yet again nothing but confirmation for the view that past lives recalled under hypnosis are mere unconscious, self-induced illusions, as real and as unreal as the personalities of an Eve, a Sybil, or a Billy Milligan. What of past lives recalled without hypnosis? We saw in the earliest chapters some of the weaknesses relating to Ian Stevenson's cases, and in Chapter 11 the apparent fallaciousness of Edward Ryall's John Fletcher. But are there not cases in which *consciously* remembered past-life individuals are traceable in historical records? Such cases, as in those of the hypnotic variety, are rare, but there are known examples and these should be given the same consideration. Accordingly, for one of the best of these, never before treated with the seriousness it deserves, we now turn to what is one of the most extraordinary to be considered in this book.

CHAPTER 14

The Woman
in the Iron Chain

IN AUGUST 1967, a thirty-eight-year-old redhead Ada Stewart, a successful BBC playwright and scriptwriter under her maiden name of Ada F. Kay, settled down for the night at a house in which she was a guest at Jedburgh, in the border region between England and Scotland. Hardly had she shut her eyes when, with an almost audible click of consciousness, she found herself seeing what seemed to be a sixteenth-century battlefield in action before her. Just a few yards away was a cluster of horsemen whom she knew to be the English enemy. One was on a white charger bearing a battle standard. Immediately in front of her were men with long-staved weapons, and her head seemed to be going from side to side following a movement she identified as desperate slashing and parrying with a sword. Her next sensation was of an explosion in her head, then, in her own words:

> [I was] lying on my back staring up at what seemed like a tunnel of staves and blades, and beyond them . . . hands and merciless faces of men intent on killing me. My left arm I raised to cover my head, to ward off the blows. All the hate of the world was concentrated on me at that moment, *and*

nobody was stopping it. I howled, a howl of pure animal terror, as the blades thrust down upon me . . .[1]

The howls Ada Stewart let out at that moment were not simply
sixteenth-century. They were very audible to the twentieth century, and brought her host running from an adjoining room to
find out who was attacking her. Instead of any intruder, he found
merely his guest, alone, in a state of shocked self-revelation. For
although she had suffered more than a few shifts of consciousness
of the same type before, now she knew with an overwhelming cer-
tainty just what it was she had seen—and, even more important,
who she was. Before they had gone to bed that night she and her
host had made plans to visit Flodden Field the next day, just an
hour's drive away and the site of the battle in 1513 in which King
James IV of Scotland, with the flower of the Scottish Army, was
defeated and killed by an English defense force under the Earl of
Surrey. Ada Stewart now knew that the scene which had flashed
before her consciousness was that of Flodden's most critical moment, and that the mental images of the individual who so
valiantly defended himself, then helplessly saw himself on the receiving end of the English staves and blades, was none other than
the king himself, James IV. Somehow Ada had James IV's memories, and she felt the only explanation was that she had been the
Scottish king back in the sixteenth century. And certainly, whatever the truth of the matter, something of the former Ada F. Kay
the playwright "died" that night, and an entity she now recognized as James emerged and increasingly took over her waking
thoughts, her actions, even the way she dressed.

For readers unversed in Scottish history perhaps some word is
needed about James IV.[2] He was one of the most attractive of
Scotland's kings, which made his death at Flodden the more poi-
gnant. From his portraits he stares out as a virile, clean-cut young
man who did not assume the normal jewel-encrusted trappings of
royalty; he was unspoiled by the overindulgence that so debili-
tated the English counterpart of his later years, Henry VIII.
James came to the throne in 1488 at the age of fifteen, after a
swift and effective coup in which his father James III was murdered by a group of rebel Scottish nobles unwilling to tolerate further his loathsome favoritism and lack of interest in Scotland's

real needs. Although James IV was too young to have had any real control over the events which led to his father's death, the affair shocked him deeply and marked his personality indelibly. As a permanent reminder of his personal burden of responsibility —from which he felt no priest, not even the Pope, could absolve him—he wore an iron chain around his waist for the rest of his life. He had extra links added to this on occasion, and to remedy the deficiencies exhibited by his father he threw himself into the affairs of kingship with extraordinary vigor, earning new loyalty from his hitherto troublesome Gaelic-speaking subjects in the northern parts of the kingdom, improving general educational standards, encouraging the new Renaissance arts of printing and medicine, and building the *Great Michael*, Europe's largest and most impressive warship. Instead of the aloofness adopted by his father, James IV made himself readily approachable even to his most lowly subjects. Resolute in setting his country's needs before his own, he heartbreakingly rejected the love of his life, the beautiful Margaret Drummond, in favor of a diplomatically more advantageous marriage with Margaret Tudor, the plump and somewhat bad-tempered daughter of King Henry VII of England. Sadly, with the passing of years, this English alliance did not have the desired effect. When Henry VIII, Margaret's brother, succeeded his father and adopted an aggressive attitude toward France, James felt impelled to warn Henry he was interfering with the European balance of power. Henry ignored his brother-in-law and landed an army on French soil, and James saw no alternative but to attack England from the north. Being the sort of king he was, when faced with the Earl of Surrey's defense force at Flodden Edge he insisted on going into battle, on foot, at the head of his troops, a practice which had long been abandoned by other European kings because of its dangers. And while the Earl of Surrey saw his task as winning the battle by any available tactics, James tried to behave according to the old-fashioned medieval codes of chivalry. The result, aided by England's superior weaponry, was the defeat and death of James at Flodden, a fate as undeserved by James as it was tragic for his kingdom. Perhaps the saddest aspect of all was that the Scots were never able to bury James with the honor they regarded as his due. After his corpse, covered in wounds, had been conveyed to London for

Henry VIII's inspection, Henry, instead of either returning it to
the Scots or arranging decent burial in London, had it left in a
lumber room at a monastic establishment in Sheen. The body
had been properly embalmed, and in the course of time workmen
hacked off James's still well-preserved head, and one of Elizabeth I's glaziers Lancelot Young kept this for many years as a
curio. Young eventually passed it over to St. Michael's Church in
Wood Street, London, but the clergy merely threw it into their
charnel house, which was burned to the ground during the Great
Fire of London.[3] It is not known what happened to James's torso.
The Scots nursed the legend that James had not really died on
the battlefield of Flodden, and that one day, when his country
needed him most, he would come again like England's King
Arthur.

We now have to face the question of whether James is indeed
come again in the form of still youthful fifty-two-year-old A. J.
Stewart,[4] or whether, like so many of the cases we have studied,
this woman also has been taken over by a past-life illusion. A. J.
Stewart very kindly granted me a first interview at her Edinburgh
flat in May 1978, and the experience was certainly out of the ordinary. Below natural red hair and striking features A.J., as she likes
to be known, was dressed in black, the costume plain except for a
white collar and cuffs, and at her throat a neat gold brooch
emblazoned with a black falcon.[5] Black shoes and black stockings
completed the ensemble, and at her waist was the Jamesian
chain, though in gilt. The flat itself was very tastefully decorated
with white walls, black doors, and antique black furniture, together with drawings and prints of personalities of James IV's
court. An iron chain was visible in a cabinet. A perhaps discor-
dant element was her heavy smoking (clearly not abandoned
from the old BBC scriptwriting days), and it was impossible not
to note her tendency to look upward and sideways with her
eyes. Yet her responses to questioning were open, lucid, and
straightforward, without the slightest hint of irrationality or
evasiveness.

As she described then, and as she has since revealed more fully
in a published autobiography *Died 1513—Born 1929*, she was
born Ada F. Kay in Tottington, Lancashire, on March 5, 1929. Her

father, Ernest Kay, was a very bookish schoolmaster whose special interest was history. From an early age she claims to have seen in her mind's eye strange historical flashbacks involving old-fashioned square-rigged sailing ships, foreign envoys at court, and the like. She also claims that she constantly pestered her parents to take her to Scotland. But although Scotland was no insuperable distance from where her parents settled at Thornton Clevelys in Lancashire, she did not achieve her ambition until her late teens when she joined the Auxiliary Territorial Service, and propitiously received a Scottish posting. The effect of this first visit was dramatic. The flashback historical scenes that intermittently haunted her throughout childhood intensified and, naïvely consulting an Army psychiatrist about these, she found herself very abruptly discharged and sent back to England. It took a few weeks of severe depression before she managed to gain a new grip on life, but when she did the improvement seemed set fair to last. From 1949, when she was twenty, she began to write a stream of plays: *The Man Came Too Soon*, *Warp and Weft* (later *Red Rose for Ransom*), *The Devil's Children*, *The Shadowed Star*, *So Runs the World Away*, and *Cardboard Castle*, which took her into the world of the professional theater. With *The Man from Thermopylae* in 1956 she received an invitation from the BBC to join their central TV script section in London.

Not only was she successful in this field at a particularly exciting time when television was developing as a mass medium, but with her striking red hair and 37-23-37 figure she found no shortage of male admirers and in 1957 she married Peter Stewart, a newly qualified London architect. For the first few years, as the couple busied themselves in their chosen vocations, the "working Stewarts"—as they became known—enjoyed a relatively trouble-free marriage, financially well-rewarded, and unsuspecting of the troubles that lay ahead. Then in 1959 her scriptwriting took her to Glasgow, her first significant return to Scotland since her discharge from the A.T.S. There is a certain obscurity surrounding this visit, but the most significant aspect is that she found a love of Scotland had been rekindled in her which she could no longer ignore. She began to take up what became an increasingly permanent residence in Edinburgh, and although there was a brief return to Peter, the fatal fascination for Scotland inexorably drew her back, to result in a slow, steady erosion of both her marriage and her writing career in the next few years.

First, once she was resident in Edinburgh, her financial fortunes deteriorated as her lack of deep knowledge of Scottish affairs diminished her potential job opportunities. Far worse, however, was the increasing intrusion of her historical flashbacks. She would momentarily see the Firth of Forth in a sixteenth-century rather than a twentieth-century setting. She would find herself answering questions put by sixteenth-century people who fleetingly appeared to her. Browsing at a shoe shop, she would see not the twentieth-century racks of shoes, but heaps of clearly more ancient ones lying abandoned on a desolate battlefield. On one occasion, during an interview for a job as a wardrobe mistress, she suddenly felt, to her considerable embarrassment, that she was wearing a heavy sixteenth-century gold shoulder chain, when in reality she was wearing nothing of the kind. These experiences were accompanied by a serious neglect both of her physical welfare and of her living accommodations. When her parents visited her in Edinburgh in 1965, they found her in the most appallingly squalid conditions, spending days on end in a darkened room and seemingly unable even to feed herself. Within two days her father, who had been suffering from a bowel disorder before he arrived, collapsed and had to be taken to Edinburgh Royal Infirmary for an emergency operation, requiring a month's convalescence in the city afterward. When her parents eventually returned to Lancashire her incursions into her private sixteenth-century world increased still further, seriously hampering the professional scriptwriting assignments she was still receiving. Despite all this, it needs to be emphasized that Ada had not yet actually identified herself as James IV. She claims that she did not come across anything about James during her schooldays and only read about him for the first time when trying to give herself a crash course in Scottish history for one of her abortive job interviews. At this stage nothing impelled her to associate him with her strange mental problems. Even when she began to write a play about him in January 1966 she did not realize the identification immediately, though there were certain telltale signs when she encountered seemingly insuperable difficulties in her research. She suffered new bouts of depression partly due to hormonal pills prescribed for a menstrual irregularity, and actually attempted suicide by swallowing salts of sorrel, a very poisonous combination of potassium acid oxalate and oxalic acid. Earlier she had felt an irresistible compulsion to acquire a black sweater and black theatrical tights and had begun to wear this garb, first for Saturday night literary parties, then as a working costume, and then more frequently still. A friendly psychiatrist she met at a party advised her for her own good to return to London. But the grip of Scotland, and with it her flashback condition, was already too strong. As her suspicions that somehow she might be James IV grew, when the final revelation of Flodden occurred at Jedburgh that August night in 1967 there could be no turning back. On that night the former playwright Ada F. Kay effectively "died," to be replaced by the new James personality, increasingly to be seen on the streets of Edinburgh in her black Hamlet-like apparel.

Although the Ada who once was never finished the play about James IV, with the encouragement of the London literary agent Spencer Curtis Brown the new personality turned to the idea of an autobiography of herself as James, composed of all the fragments of what she took for the king's memories floating in her head and set in chronological order according to the historically recorded facts about James's life. This, drastically reduced from her original 258,000 words, was published in 1970 under the title *Falcon—the Autobiography of His Grace James IV, King of Scots*, presented by A. J. Stewart.[6] Had it been left uncut, it might have had a cathartic effect; instead, it had exacerbated her condition. While as a personality James had ostensibly taken over, terrible recurring traumas imply that this was by no means total. Sometimes A.J. found only sixteenth-century words had any meaning for her, and she was unable to read. On other occasions she found herself unable to speak for days on end. There were repeated bouts of depression, particularly around James's "dying time," September 9, the anniversary of Flodden.[7] Despite all this, it should be emphasized that she managed to lead a perfectly well-adjusted existence for long periods, and in 1978 produced her very detailed and lucid autobiography, *Died 1513—Born 1929,* recording her twentieth-century life up to the Jedburgh incident in 1967. Today, by her own description, she is "completely contained by the title A. J. Stewart, and the James IV personality interchanges naturally with the Ada F. Kay personality who wrote *The Man from Thermopylae.*"[8] When giving interviews or lectures she tends to wear the formal black and white she wore as James, but for the rest of the time in town or country she lives comfortably in twentieth-century tweeds or other inconspicuous clothing. While once she would have insisted that the playwright Ada F. Kay is dead, today she can find satisfaction that *The Man from Thermopylae* has recently been chosen for publication in the Scottish Society of Playwrights Scottish Classics series under her old name of Ada F. Kay.

One of the first questions must be: Just how much of her story can we believe? Unlike many past-life subjects who cloak themselves and their subjects with anonymity, A. J. Stewart has been refreshingly different and open to investigation. In *Died 1513—Born 1929* she quotes the real names of individuals with whom she has come into contact in the course of her life: her former husband Peter Stewart, today a senior partner in a very successful London architectural practice; one of her TV associates, James Brabazon, now a senior producer with the Granada network; Dr. David Stevenson, Senior Lecturer in International Community Health at the Liverpool School of Tropical Medicine, among many others. When I contacted them these people invariably proved willing and able to confirm the essential truthfulness of A.J.'s account of her life, insofar as each became involved with it. Whatever the nature of the James IV memories, to her they have been all too real, and with few compensating advantages.

The next question is: Can A.J. somehow really be the historical James IV? The question is by no means easy to answer, because by any standards A.J. is a highly intelligent and literate woman, well used to tackling historical source material and therefore as likely as anyone to have acquired correct historical information. She has made no attempt to hide the fact that before she identified herself with James, she went to most major available

sources on his history to research the play she originally intended
to write about him. Although, as is to be expected, some aspects
of her account go beyond the data provided by the history books,
in no sense do these step beyond the bounds of credibility. A typical case in point is A.J.'s interpretation of James's motives in
building his huge ship the *Great Michael*. All history knows of
James in connection with this ship is that he planned her as the
largest ship of her time, lavishing considerable personal attention
on her, and denuding Fife of many of its fine oaks so that the
ship's walls could be built ten feet thick. He seems to have been
specifically concerned to make these resistant to almost any conceivable cannon fire, as the Scottish historian Pitscottie attests:

> . . . when the ship passed to the sea and was lying in the
> roads the king caused to shoot a cannon at her, to essay if
> she were strong; but I heard say it damaged her not, and did
> her little scathe.[9]

History also knows that when he set out on his ill-fated land inva-
sion of England, James dispatched the *Great Michael* under the
command of Lord Arran, but the exact purpose of this mission
has never been made clear, because whatever his orders Arran
hopelessly bungled the enterprise. What is therefore fascinating
about A.J.'s account of James is that according to her he planned
that the *Great Michael* should sail up the Thames to London
and pound Henry VIII's Thames-side palaces as an exercise in
bloodying the English king's nose. When this possibility was
discussed with Caroline Bingham, the well-respected biographer
of Scotland's kings and, since the publication of *Falcon*, one of
A.J.'s friends, Caroline confirmed that this explanation was by no
means inconceivable, for the *Great Michael* was unquestionably
the largest and most powerful ship of its time, and arguably constructed for just such a feat. Caroline also acknowledged that she
could find no serious fault with A.J.'s other information on James,
and was of the opinion that somehow A.J.'s memories must be
those of the real James, whatever the underlying mechanism.

So is there some means, quite independent of straight historical
sources, of checking A.J.'s memories as James? As it happens, just
the right circumstances do seem to apply in respect of her

remarks on a painting in the Scottish National Gallery in Edinburgh (plate 26). This painting, by the brilliant late-fifteenth-century Flemish artist Hugo van der Goes, depicts James III kneeling in prayer in the company of St. Andrew, with a tiny figure in royal robes behind him who is generally identified as the future James IV. Art historians have sometimes expressed doubts as to the identity of this figure, but when A.J. saw the painting she made a remark which carried with it all the authority of the original James:

> When I first saw an illustration of it in 1968 I said, "Oh no, that's not the way it was originally." It was just my father [James III] and St. Andrew. I had myself [James IV] painted in later, as an act of penance, kneeling behind him. That is me at fifteen in my coronation robes over my funeral black, with my poor lank hair in need of washing. If I remember correctly there was a vine painted where I now kneel because my mother was at that time pregnant.[10]

According to A.J. the James IV figure was to be identified with James because, among other details, it featured "my hands." Here we have an explicit mental image statement by A.J., and an issue of some considerable interest. Van der Goes died in 1482, six years before James IV succeeded James III, so if A.J. was right the James IV figure in his coronation robes must have been overpainted by another artist after Van der Goes's death. If this is the case, then X-ray and infrared photography should show up the differences of this handiwork and reveal the underlying vine.

As it happens, X-ray and infrared photography were carried out on the painting in question in the early 1970s by Stephen Rees-Jones of the Courtauld Institute of Art. His work has been documented in an excellent artistic monograph, *Hugo van der Goes and the Trinity Panels in Edinburgh*, by the art experts Colin Thompson and Lorne Campbell.[11] This reveals that there is indeed evidence of overpainting of the James III portrait, and infrared shows up a slightly different likeness below. As Van der Goes is not known ever to have visited Scotland, the interpretation is that he more than likely painted James III back in his studio in Bruges, using drawings sent from Scotland. The vain

James III, on receiving the picture, proved dissatisfied with the likeness and employed an inferior local artist to overpaint the original, thus accounting for the retouching in this instance.

But under X ray the area of the James IV figure shows not the slightest trace of any underlying vine. Instead, the infrared (see plate 27) shows that the under drawing of the likeness is original to the painting and from a skillful hand unmistakably that of Van der Goes himself. This view is supported by the likeness of the James IV face and hands to those of the Virgin in Van der Goes's Portinari altarpiece. A.J. has to be wrong both about the James IV figure being a later addition and about it being painted at the time of James's coronation. In short, in this instance at least, A.J.'s mental images and memory are an illusion.

There is a similar state of affairs in connection with another adult portrait sometimes thought to be that of James, listed in the Scottish National Gallery's catalogue as number 1929. Early authors of books on James IV[12] have not only featured this portrait as his likeness, they have identified the artist as Holbein. A.J. has pointed out remarkable facial similarities between this portrait and herself (see plates 24 and 25) and has quoted memories of being painted by a pleasant artist called Holbein who came specially to Edinburgh for the task. Yet from the evidence of art historians this again can only be regarded as false. The famous Hans Holbein the Younger, born in 1497, would have been a mere youth of sixteen at James's death, and the style is in any case wrong for both him and his father, Hans Holbein the Elder. As confirmed by Mr. Hugh Macandrew, Keeper of the Scottish National Gallery,[13] the portrait in question is neither of James nor painted by either Holbein. The sitter has still not been identified, but the artist belonged to the Flemish school rather than the German school of the Holbeins.

While it would be quite unfair to dismiss A. J. Stewart's undoubtedly sincere belief in her identity as James IV on the basis of these artistic revelations, another angle of investigative inquiry reveals further cause for disquiet. When I received the very first handwritten letter from A.J., the individuality of her handwriting was a source of astonishment and interest. It is a highly decorative script with the strong impression of a period character to it.

She has had this style at least since 1970, as the following example from that year makes clear:

Had A.J. always written in this style, or was it the adoption of the James personality after 1967 which created such a period character? Samples of A.J.'s early writing as Ada showed that the latter was the case, as in the following example, dated May 1967, a mere three months before the night at Jedburgh.

So if the A. J. Stewart personality, purporting to be that of James IV, has had such a dramatic effect on A.J.'s handwriting, is there any trace of the original James IV's handwriting in her present-day script? By fortunate chance there is an example of the historical James IV's handwriting among the National Manuscripts of Scotland, in the form of an autograph letter written by James to Henry VIII when the two kings were still on friendly terms. A facsimile[14] of this is given below.

The letter is ended with the words "with ye il hand of your cousyng" (in your cousin's own handwriting), and signed "James Rex." But it is obvious, even at a casual glance, that there really is no clear resemblance between this and A.J.'s present-day script, despite its period character. It may be argued that to expect this would be asking too much. A.J. has never claimed the two handwritings to be identical, and when challenged on any similarly doubtful point has invariably referred to interference of the twentieth-century Ada's consciousness with that of the sixteenth-century James, occasionally creating an understandably inaccurate admixture of the two. While I accept this, nevertheless it is surely logical that if A.J. is James, and if, as she claims, James's mind lies behind her experiences to the extent of visibly altering her handwriting, then something of the original James's handwriting should surely be detectable in A.J.'s script. Even if this is not discernible to the layman, it should surely be so to the handwriting expert. Yet is it? For advice on this problem I again called on the aid of Dr. Vernon Harrison, the specialist referred to earlier in connection with the Carol Dow handwriting. Apprised of the full complexities of the issue, Dr. Harrison made the most careful comparison of the two scripts to see if any of the features of the script of the real James could be detected in that of A.J. Dr. Harrison also studied A.J.'s pre-1967[15] handwriting from the same point of view. As a member of the British Society for Psychical Research, Dr. Harrison may be regarded as sympathetic to consideration of out-of-the-normal happenings, but his view was nevertheless emphatic and unequivocal.

> . . . there really is nothing in common between the writing of James IV and that of A. J. Stewart, before or after breakdown [1967]. James has a clear and characteristic script, and your subject does not imitate it either in its obvious features like the delta "d" or in the more subtle matters of slope and spacing. "A.J.'s" letters are not written by James, *even if he is struggling to master an unfamiliar brain and nervous system.* [my italics][16]

For a variety of reasons, therefore, A.J.'s identification of herself with the historical James IV is by no means unimpeachable, though there is not the slightest case for any conscious fraudulence on her part. I have already remarked how honest and open she has been to investigation, and this opinion is in no way mitigated by the art historical and graphological evidence.

How then are we to interpret her? Once her medical history, as recorded in *Died 1513—Born 1929*, is studied, certain characteristics, familiar from earlier chapters, become apparent. We know, for example, she was barely in her teens before she was suffering from blinding headaches and "fainting spells," mysterious bouts of near unconsciousness diagnosed at the time as "nervous vagal instability." These bouts returned during her time with the A.T.S. and contributed to her swift discharge. We observed precisely the same teenage physical symptoms in multiple personality cases such as Chris Sizemore, Sybil, Billy Milligan, Dr. Lechler's Elizabeth, and others. Insomnia, black depressions, suicide attempts, hysterical losses of comprehension and speech—all these are persistently reported by A.J., and all these are equally persistently found in classic multiple personality cases. But they are merely the warning signs.

One characteristic common to both multiple personality and past-life regression cases is that of facial change, the alteration of the whole set of the countenance according to the personality adopted. A.J. has quite spontaneously described an occurrence of this during her writing of the Margaret Drummond episode in *Falcon*. According to her, at a particularly traumatic stage she began uncontrollable alternations of consciousness from the sixteenth century to the twentieth century and back again. These were so severe that she had to be driven by a friend from Edinburgh to Kent to receive proper care. As she has described it to me:

> . . . I went down there and I was sedated for three weeks and they had to address me as "Your Grace" or as "Ada" according to the change of my face. It was as bad as that.[17]

She also refers in her writings to a "dead look" facial expression, which was particularly remarked on by her mother. This seems identifiable with the facial blank of the multiple personality condition and the between-lives hypnotic regression states.

Another multiple personality characteristic exhibited by A.J. is that of body image. As early as her late teens, on the train journey taking her back to Lancashire after her discharge from the A.T.S., she describes seeing in the mirror of the train's toilet compartment the image of herself with a masculine-looking face, longer and older than her real face, and with points of sapphire around the head—a classic example, merely with a historical twist, of the change of body image experienced by multiple personality sufferers. Another instance of this, before she actually began to affect the wearing of sixteenth-century costume, occurred when she felt herself wearing an anachronistic gold shoulder chain at the time of her wardrobe mistress interview. And when she actually switched to being A. J. Stewart these problems intensified. When I interviewed her in Edinburgh she confessed a perpetual problem of not knowing what to wear, not in the normal feminine sense, but of "Who am I today?" Only a dressing gown "a long robe . . . that fits both of me" did not cause a quarrel between the personalities.

Perhaps one final instance of the multiple personality condition in A.J. may be quoted—that of her reaction, at the age of eight, to being bullied by a gang of four fourteen-year-old youths who had taken her hostage. According to her own account in *Died 1513—Born 1929*, suddenly:

> . . . fear left me. All I saw were those grinning white teeth, half as tall again as I was, and the red mist gathering. A voice came from me, deep and quiet—almost amused, quite unlike my own: I heard it say, "I will give you *this!*"—and up streaked my clenched fist propelled by a force which almost lifted me off the ground. What happened after that I am not sure, until I found myself on the far side of the gate surrounded by the dumb-struck faces of my comrades. Nearby three young men had lost all interest in us while they commiserated with their leader, who was spitting out blood and some bits which had been his front teeth.[18]

All the elements of multiple personality cases may be detected in this passage: the stress situation, the inner voice, different from her own, the uncharacteristic violent action, seemingly not from herself, the disruption of self-awareness.

Are we then to conclude that A. J. Stewart is merely another case of multiple personality? If she is, her assumption of the personality of a deceased historical figure must, at the very least, make her an intriguing variation on the cases of Claire Brenner, Chris Sizemore, Sybil, and Billy Milligan. But such an interpretation still obliges us to suggest some way in which she might have been exposed to historical material by which she unconsciously chose to identify herself with James, and also some accompanying stress which might have sparked in her the multiple personality condition. Identifying either satisfactorily is by no means easy. For instance, even trying to trace how far back in her twentieth-century life she might have had James IV experiences is by no means straightforward. According to her own account she regaled her parents with what she would interpret as James's memories from as early as she first learned to talk. But we cannot ignore the possibility that her memory of these memories may be a later and illusory assumption, in the same way that Chris Sizemore's Jane believed she had been to Furman University.

Assuming, however, that the memories did occur at a very early stage, there are circumstances of her early childhood that could conceivably explain them. From the point of view of stress, on her own admission her preschool years were acutely lonely. Her parents' home was in a relatively isolated position in a rural area and did not provide her with a single child companion, so that at the age of four she actually pleaded with her parents to be allowed to go to school. It was before the age of television, she was not allowed to play with her father's books, and her most important source of interest seems to have been the radio. In *Died 1513* she describes how she illicitly twiddled the knobs of the family wireless to listen to Scottish regional radio programs.[19] Could she have listened to some program or programs about James which she unconsciously wove into an imaginary companion figure of the same kind as Sybil's Victoria Antoinette Scharleau? This must at least be accounted a possibility. A further possibility takes us to the period immediately preceding her teenage years, a stage in her life which—again on her own admission—was "hideously unhappy."[20] She is by no means explicit on the exact source of unhappiness, but some early bullying, the onset of World War II, her parents' acceptance into their home of an older evacuee girl of unclean habits—all these may have played a part. At this period we also find her directly involved with a literary source undeniably associated with James IV. This is *Marmion*, a long narrative poem written by Sir Walter Scott in the early nineteenth century. It is set in Scotland in the reign of James IV and is particularly concerned with the events leading to Flodden. She was given *Marmion* in class as a set book at the age of twelve. For reasons that are tantalizingly unclear, the very sight of this book caused her intense trauma. According to her own account, it "brought me out in goose pimples. I hurried back to my desk and frantically buried it beneath every other book that I could lay my hands on . . ."[21] And as she has gone on to state in one of the most significant passages in *Died 1513*:

> . . . I never did discover what *Marmion* was about because I missed those lessons. I was always ill; in the beginning with

migraine, and latterly with a strange cardiac manifestation
which began that term. A couple of times I tried to get out
the book, and on each occasion . . . my vision blotted out so
that I thought I was about to faint and I asked to be excused
. . . All through that year its presence in my desk was a
nightmare . . .[22]

This episode is almost classically in the multiple personality
mold: the migraine, the blotting out of vision, the sensation of
being about to faint. It is also worthy of note that most published
editions of *Marmion*, and almost inevitably any school set-book
version, are accompanied by Sir Walter Scott's detailed historical
notes on James, the events of his reign, and the personalities of
his court.

While it might be thought that we need look no further for
the source of the James memories, it needs to be stressed that A.J.
herself insists to this day that she has never read the poem. She
also insists that although her father's library included two complete sets of Scott's Waverley Novels, he possessed nothing in the
way of Scott's poetical works, so she could not possibly have read
the poem at home. However, there are some crucial questions to
be asked. On any interpretation of A.J.'s James memories, why
her hysterical reaction to *Marmion*? Even if she is the reincarnation of James, by what means could the dead king have
acquired a knowledge of the poem's contents when this was not
published until more than three hundred years after his death?
Although she has no conscious memory of having read *Marmion*
and Scott's notes at school, could she not have done so in the
guise of another personality, as Sybil did, losing two years of
schooltime memories as a result of multiple personality traumas?
Marmion cannot by any stretch of the imagination account for all
her James memories, but there is clearly more to her reactions to
the poem than we as yet understand, and it is to be remarked
that from this time on the young Ada began to have dream fantasies of fifteenth- and sixteenth-century people and places that she
wove into youthful, never-published novels.

A final potentially significant phase of A.J.'s life is the time in
her mid-thirties when she actually tried to write the play about
James IV. Since at this period she went about consulting every

available source on his reign (disagreeing with most of them), it is easy to see how she might have fueled her memories. But were there at this time circumstances of personal stress that might have been sufficient for her to split consciousness in the multiple personality manner? Significantly, as she herself has acknowledged, she can remember neither when nor how the idea of writing about James first consciously entered her mind. It seems to have been before the middle of January 1966, when she heard that her father had cancer of the lung, and a few months after the legalities of her divorce had been completed. Although the events of her life at this time come within the period described in *Died 1513*, there are certain deeply traumatic personal aspects which have become known to me, at least in part. For very understandable reasons A.J. has omitted these from her account, yet they may conceivably be crucial to our understanding of how the James personality emerged. What is certain is that sometime between the years 1965 and 1969 A. J. Stewart switched from hardly having heard of James IV to expending more than a quarter of a million words writing his autobiography. How this happened and her traumas during the years that followed are for her to describe in due time, as indeed she intends to do. Much may then be clearer.

So far, however, multiple personality is the only explanation we have suggested for her James memories, and it would be entirely unfair not to suggest others also worthy of serious consideration. Some attention must be accorded, for instance, to the undeniably intense historical proclivities of A.J.'s father, the schoolmaster and headmaster Ernest Kay. A.J. insists that his special interests were English history and local history, and that like most Englishmen he had virtually no knowledge of Scotland's kings before the Union. Also, as she has disclosed, he totally refused to accept her identification of herself as James until he had read her book *Falcon*, published just before he died. She never learned what it was in the book which might have caused him to change his mind because he died in Scotland on his way to tell her. Nevertheless, could he at some stage in his voracious historical reading have come across an account of James that somehow fused in his unconsciousness and became transmitted to A.J. before she was born in the manner we have suggested for some of the more credible

Ian Stevenson cases? This is a possibility, although at best a tenuous one, that should be taken into consideration.

The only possibility that commends itself to A.J. herself is that she really is James IV reincarnate. And despite the serious grounds for doubt that we have mentioned earlier in the chapter, we do have to acknowledge that there is no obvious single work of history or historical novel to which her memories can be traced, and that in many details of James's life—such as the original plan for the *Great Michael* expedition—her insights are original to her. We also have to acknowledge—the disputed Holbein aside—that physically she does bear some resemblance to historical portraits that are indisputably of James. And on straight historical grounds no less an authority on Scotland's history than Caroline Bingham finds A.J.'s identification with James both reasonable and convincing. The possibility that A.J. might be a genuine case of mind-out-of-time memory—working perhaps via the multiple personality condition—cannot as yet be entirely ruled out.

Over all, if there is any genuine case of an individual possessing memories of a past life, then A.J. more than anyone has adopted the right approach to bring this within the orbit of human knowledge. Arthur Guirdham has cloaked his informants in an impenetrable anonymity. The historical novelist Rosemary Hawley Jarman, who has hinted at possible mind-out-of-time factors having inspired her *We Speak No Treason*, set in the time of Richard III, has refused to discuss these on the grounds she might be thought a crank.[23] By contrast, A. J. Stewart has commendably laid herself wide open. She has unquestionably had the mental experiences she interprets as those of the deceased James. But whether this is a stress-induced amalgam of unconsciously remembered reading or listening, skillfully embellished by a brilliant hidden observer, or somehow the real historical personality, must be for the reader to decide.

CHAPTER 15

The Evidence Reassessed

As THIS BOOK is being prepared for press a case has just been published which, although it does not directly involve past-life experiences, supports to an astonishing degree the interpretations that I have made. This is *The Story of Ruth*,[1] an account by psychiatrist Morton Schatzman of a twenty-five-year-old American woman patient pseudonymously named Ruth who came to his London practice suffering from terrifying hallucinations. In the hallucinations Ruth would see her father and hear him speak to her, even though at the time he was alive and well three thousand miles away in the United States. She would be able to smell his body, sometimes soapy as if he had just had a bath, sometimes reeking of stale sweat as if he had not washed for days. She would be able to feel him, as on one occasion when she hallucinated him getting into bed beside her. His clothes and general appearance would vary in a totally naturalistic way between one appearance and the next, and if she saw him move around the room she would hear his clothes rustle and his figure would have a shadow and even a reflection in the mirror. These visions could be seen by no one but Ruth. Their incidence, the fear they generated, and the problems they caused for her marriage not unnaturally

made her feel she must be going insane. It was in these circumstances that she sought psychiatric help.

Had Ruth consulted someone else in Schatzman's profession
she might have been routinely diagnosed a schizophrenic and put
on a course of tranquilizers or fluphenazine. Schatzman, however,
was impressed by all the apparent sensory accompaniments to her
visions and her otherwise well-balanced and rational personality.
Furthermore, on routine questioning he learned that she had
some sound justification for harboring traumatic fears relating to
her father, who was a sinister and mentally unstable former con-
vict. On one occasion when she was ten years old he had tried to
rape her in a particularly brutal manner, and on another he fired
a shotgun at her. Memories of such traumas in other patients all
too often become repressed and appear unconsciously via psycho-
somatic illnesses and the like. The interesting feature of Ruth was
that she retained *conscious* memories of the incidents and in waking consciousness was experiencing images she might otherwise
have encountered unconsciously during dreams.

This analogy with dreams gave Schatzman his idea for a bold
and innovative method of treating Ruth. He knew from psychological studies that the Senoi tribe of West Malaysia practiced a
method of "turning" bad dreams. For instance, if someone had a
recurring nightmare of being chased by a tiger, the Senoi theory
was that the next time the individual experienced this he or she
should try to face the tiger and thereby vanquish their fear of it.
Following this line of thinking, Schatzman adopted the policy
not of discouraging Ruth's visions but of positively encouraging
them, so that by learning to produce them on command she
could become aware that they were nothing but her own unconscious creation.

This idea proved extraordinarily effective. Under supervision
from Schatzman, Ruth produced in his presence not only visions
of her father, but also doubles of Schatzman and even of her own
self. As she grew more adept she even became able to hallucinate
deliberately. For instance, she could make herself see the light in
the room being switched on and off. Although Schatzman was
naturally able to see none of these phenomena he carefully followed Ruth's detailed description of everything and built up an
increasingly clearer scientific evaluation of what Ruth was actu-

ally seeing and hearing in her own mind. Of course, when Ruth hallucinated her father sitting in a chair talking to her, no amount of photography or tape recording was able to capture what she described being there. Furthermore, when Ruth hallucinated a light being switched on, her eyes showed nothing of the retinal change that would occur if a real light was switched on. She was unable to read by this hallucinated light the title of a book handed to her. Schatzman even tried having individuals theoretically sensitive to psychic phenomena sitting in the room and trying to see Ruth's visions at the same time that she did, again without success. From all these tests there could be no doubt that Ruth's visions were purely illusions in her own mind.

But for Schatzman the most fascinating and instructive experiment was one carried out in association with Peter Fenwick, psychiatrist and neurophysiologist at St. Thomas's Hospital, London.[2] At Fenwick's laboratory electrodes were attached to Ruth's scalp and the waves of electrical activity from different areas of her brain synthesized and monitored via a visual display screen known as an oscilloscope. To provide a consistent input of signals to Ruth's brain a television screen was set before her showing a checkerboard on which every second or so the white squares changed to black and the black to white and vice versa. Once a consistent pattern from her brain's reaction to this was discernible via the oscilloscope, Ruth was asked to hallucinate her daughter Heather sitting on her lap and blocking her view of the screen. Immediately the oscilloscope's pattern changed just as it would if a real person had come between Ruth and the screen. The experiment was repeated with several variations, always with the same result. Scientifically the oscilloscope was confirming that Ruth was quite genuinely seeing in her mind that which all along she claimed to see even though the vision had absolutely no reality. This is a striking result, and it confirms that whether hypnotized or not hypnotized, it is possible for the mind to see an illusion as real. As soon as Ruth realized that her visions were illusory and self-generated, they ceased.

While Ruth's case may appear exceptional, there are grounds for believing similar phenomena to those she experienced are present in a variety of walks of life, almost invariably associated with strong emotions. For instance, a *British Medical Journal* survey[3] carried out in mid-Wales in 1971 found that out of 295 widows and widowers interviewed, some 137 or nearly 50 per cent reported having seen, heard, spoken to, or been touched by their dead spouse. It would seem more than likely that these experiences too were of the widows' and widowers' unconscious creation. Similarly, there has recently occurred in the British law courts the case of a thirty-nine-year-old estate agent accused of lurid sexual adventures with a schoolgirl under the age of consent.[4] According to a diary the girl kept at the age of fourteen, during a nine-month period the agent made love to her in a sauna, in his car, at his office, and in flats and houses he was selling for his company. The girl's story convinced parents, police, and lawyers to the extent that after eighteen months of legal preliminaries the agent found himself on trial at Durham Crown Court. There he was able to establish, thankfully owing to his own well-kept diary, that he had unimpeachable alibis for some of the occasions the girl claimed he had been with her. His counsel was able to show how some of the purple passages from the girl's diary could be traced to pages from Harold Robbins' novels *The Betsy* and *The Lonely Lady*, and how the whole affair seemed to have arisen because the girl, who had developed a crush on the agent, felt rebuffed when dropped from baby-sitting for his family. For us the case is significant because there is no evidence the girl was anything other than convinced by her story herself. The Wakefield psychiatrist Dr. Stephen Shaw has explained her state of mind:

> In some individuals the dividing line between fantasy and reality becomes very blurred. And examples *par excellence* are immature children, particularly girls. Added to this is that at fourteen they are sexually restrained—they are guarded more harshly by their parents than are boys. And that means that their fantasies can become more enmeshed and develop until they spill over and become such a part of their lives that they assume a "reality."[5]

From cases such as these it is evident that unconsciously generated fantasies are a phenomenon stretching far beyond the past-life claims on whose validity or otherwise this book has been concentrated. The very prevalence and naturalness of the tendency to fantasize, a point emphasized by Dr. Shaw, makes it doubly imperative that no past-life claim should be considered seriously without the fullest information on the subject's identity and psychological background. Yet if many of the reincarnation claims can be explained by the same mechanisms that affected Ruth and the sauna-case girl, can they all?

It needs to be stressed that even if every past-life case so far presented could be proved to be a fantasy, reincarnation might nevertheless exist, working in a manner that has yet to be detected. Furthermore, while I believe I have offered justifiable grounds for rejecting many of the cases discussed in this book, others remain. Of A. J. Stewart, for instance, although I have advanced strong reasons for skepticism that she is some form of reincarnation of James IV, I have to acknowledge peculiarities to her case (such as her facial resemblance to undisputed portraits of the historical James) for which there is no easy explanation. Of John Pollock and his daughters, if everything happened the way he has described, including the twins' reliving of their dead sisters' memories, then I have to recognize that something not yet within the understanding of twentieth-century science would seem to have been at work.

In respect of Dr. Ian Stevenson, I continue to maintain that he has not been critical enough of the reliability of his subjects' testimony,[6] a view which would seem yet more justified in the light of recent press reports of a child claiming to be the reincarnation of the Indian Prime Minister Indira Gandhi's late son, Sanjay Gandhi. But even if large numbers of Ian Stevenson's cases are rejected, there remain others, including some with the mysterious birthmarks, which cannot be explained. A case which most convinces me that there is something to Stevenson's arguments is one which, ironically, he himself has never investigated. The subject of the case is a child of Polish parents living in Britain, one Nadia, who in 1974 when she was six years old came to the attention of Nottingham University psychologists Elizabeth Newson and Lorna Selfe.[7] Although at the time clumsy, overlarge for her age, and almost totally lacking in normal speech development, it was found that from the age of three Nadia had been producing drawings of vitality, depth, and three-dimensionality with perspective and foreshortening handled in a manner normally found only in the mature artist.[8] Her favorite theme was an eighteenth-century horse and rider (plate 28), an exceptionally powerful image with curious accompaniments such as a small animal running down the horse's saddle, an unidentifiable half-circle shape at the base of the horse's neck, and a grotesque face just behind the rider's foot, all of which recur in a variety of versions. Although the source of many of Nadia's pictures, which she never copied directly, was her collection of Ladybird children's books, the origin of this is so far untraceable.[9]

Like the more credible of Ian Stevenson's cases, such as Kumkum, she exhibited a state of delirium, appearing "a different person" during her drawing bouts, at the end sometimes lapsing into "a staring reverie lasting for several minutes," and on other occasions talking "jargon to herself, with no one able to understand what she was saying."[10] Again in the manner of the Stevenson child cases whose past-life memories faded after the age of six, so too Nadia's drawing skills declined from that age on, and by the age of eight-and-a-half a now rare horse and rider drawing shows none of her earlier exceptional qualities (plate 29).[11] Lorna Selfe in her psychological study of Nadia has not suggested reincarnation as an explanation for her strange state of mind, and I would similarly hesitate to do so. But Nadia's case offers the most striking and reliably attested evidence for an unlearned skill of any that I have come across, and while it remains an enigma I cannot entirely rule out the possibility that some form of genuine mind-out-of-time mechanism was in play.

There remain the cases of past lives remembered under hypnosis. Long hours spent attending regressions and listening to recordings of them persuades me to no more charitable view than that if there is any genuine past-life material to such cases, it is so rare that I have yet to find an example that remains convincing once investigated in depth. Of course, in all areas of the subject more research is needed. But in respect of hypnotic past-life regressions this is perhaps an appropriate point to enlarge on a warning only hinted at in earlier chapters. Both in the United States and in Britain, thousands every year volunteer for, and some indeed pay for, trips (not altogether dissimilar from those of the LSD type) into what many fondly imagine to be real past lives. There is no legislation setting out the conditions under which these may be carried out. The hypnotist does not have to be qualified, a doctor does not have to be in attendance, and special safeguards do not have to be employed. While such considerations may be thought unnecessary, and the practice of past-life regression—illusory or otherwise—harmless enough, this view is by no means supported by some instances in which positive harm has been caused, and others in which positive harm could have been caused.

One example of the latter happens to involve John Pollock, the father of the twins referred to in Chapter 1. As recently as 1978, eager to find out what identity he might have had in previous lives, John Pollock volunteered for hypnotic regression at the hands of the former Scarborough MP Wilf Proudfoot. Among several somewhat dubious past lives he produced one of a definite historical character, Dr. Nehemiah Bradford,[12] a surgeon of the late eighteenth and early nineteenth century who lived at Frenchay near Bristol. Pollock had himself heard of Bradford because early in his life he lived in Bristol and actually dreamed of and then visited the still-existing house in which Bradford once lived on Frenchay Green. John Pollock, however, was quite unprepared for the revelations he made under hypnosis as Bradford. After describing Bradford's prosperous surgical career, married to a wife named Rachel Brewiss, John Pollock was moved forward in time by Proudfoot to the surgeon's old age. Asked his circumstances, he informed the hypnotist that his wife had recently died, and he was living in the house alone, apart from a young servant girl toward whom he admitted an infatuation. Progressed further on in time, he said he was now completely alone, and proved reticent about what had happened to the servant girl until, pressed by Proudfoot, he confessed that, unable to control his passions toward her, he had raped her, then murdered her. Asked what he had done with the body, he said he had waited until there was a fresh grave dug in the nearby churchyard and then dragged the corpse to this under cover of darkness, burying it on top of the new interment so that the already disturbed soil would effectively disguise his handiwork. He described how he told neighbors that the girl had gone away to work elsewhere, and how he lived on alone in the house until his death, his crime never detected.

A passive-observer type of subject, John Pollock saw these macabre adventures of himself as Bradford so vividly that he was even able to draw for me the precise spot in Frenchay churchyard where he had buried the body. He was so convinced by it all that it never even occurred to him to check if the details matched with historical reality. Yet, as recent inquiries have revealed, the hypnotic Bradford's story is no more attributable to the memories of the real Dr. Nehemiah Bradford than any of the others we have come across. Born in 1749 and a friend of vaccine pioneer Edward Jenner,[18] the historical Dr. Bradford married no Rachel Brewiss but Susannah Rogers, "an agreeable young lady with a handsome fortune,"[14] who became the surgeon's wife at St. James's, Bath, on January 18, 1786. The house of which Pollock dreamed and had his hypnotic memories was not that in which Bradford spent his last years, this being the smaller Manor Cottage to which the surgeon moved on retirement.[15] As for the story of his wife having died before him, local records[16] reveal that while Dr. Bradford, aged eighty-seven, died on December 31, 1835, his wife, aged sixty-nine, did not die until September 12, 1837, nearly two years afterward. There is no way in which the hypnotic Bradford's story may be reconciled with the identifiable events and personalities of the real Bradford's life. The details John Pollock got right, that Bradford was a surgeon living in Frenchay in the late eighteenth and early nineteenth century, were those he knew from his boyhood in Bristol. The material he invented seems to have been based partly on the fact that at the time of the regression John Pollock's own wife Florence had recently died, and partly on a local legend about grave-robbing in Frenchay which Pollock may well have heard in his youth. There is to this day in the ground of Frenchay's Unitarian Chapel a massive granite gravestone said to have been erected to deter the Resurrectionists—those who in the eighteenth century used to rob freshly dug graves to supply surgeons with much needed cadavers. There was also in the eighteenth century a Captain Read of Frenchay falsely accused of murdering his Negro servant for dissection by a Dr. Thomas Mountjoy. John Pollock's strange hypnotic tale may well have been a twisted amalgam of these two.[17]

These altogether illusory memories could have had a harmful psychological effect on John Pollock. With his strong Catholic and pro-reincarnationist views, John Pollock was not unnaturally disturbed by the idea that he had raped and murdered in a previous life, with not even the expiation of having been punished for his crime. He sat up with me until three o'clock in the morning, chain-smoking and playing and replaying his tape-recorded confession of his past-life misdeeds. The whole grisly hallucination of what he had done was to him very, very real. Fortunately, he enjoys the support of the two refreshingly no-nonsense twin daughters, has recently remarried, and no lasting harm appears to have been done. But in another man the revelation of the Bradford regression might have led to severe depression or worse.

The aftereffects of some other cases in Britain do not exactly make comforting reading. It is on record that Arnall Bloxham's Jane Evans fainted after one particularly traumatic regression, feeling so unwell for days afterward that her husband insisted she should never be regressed again. As mentioned in our chapter on the Chelmsford Witch case, the Merseyside girl Jan found herself so profoundly disturbed after reliving the terrors of the witch trial that she too refused to have anything further to do with another past-life regression. Dr. Tom Troscianko and his wife spent a particularly uncomfortable night after both were regressed by Joe Keeton.

In the United States, the stories of the mental disturbances that can follow hypnotic regressions are even more alarming, with, in some cases, hypnotists finding themselves powerless to return a subject to the present day, the subject remaining in an altered state of personality for several days or more before regaining their normal personality. For instance, after a series of regressions conducted by her doctor husband, the subject of the Jensen xenoglossy case began spontaneously relapsing into the past-life personality, in exactly the manner of those suffering from multi-

ple personality, causing very real fears of a permanent "possession." This still-living American woman is deeply concerned that
her identity should not be revealed, but from my own contacts
with the case, more extensive than it has been possible to discuss
in this book, it is obvious that she is still seriously psychologically
disturbed. In the case of Mrs. Dolores Jay and her Gretchen
memories, not only has she suffered nightmarish dreams following
the hypnotic experiments, she even began experiencing waking
hallucinations of Gretchen, in a manner similar to Morton
Schatzman's subject Ruth and her visions of her father.

It also deserves mention that in the wake of the Bridey
Murphy affair one distraught mother wrote to Virginia Tighe to
say that her son had just committed suicide, leaving a note saying
that he could not wait to find out if he would be reincarnated.
Most extreme of all, one of the lesser-known aspects of the
Guyana tragedy, in which 912 of the followers of the religious
"prophet" James Jones committed mass suicide, is that in the
final moments—when it is just possible that some of the followers
might have balked at their leader's instructions to take the fatal
potion—one of Jones's aides, Don Macelvane, made this appeal:

> "Uh—what I used to do before I came here, uh, let me tell
> you about it: It might make a lot of you feel a little more
> comfortable. Sit down and be quiet, please. One of the
> things I used to do, I used to be a therapist; and the kind of
> therapy that I did had to do with reincarnation and past-life
> situations. And every time anybody had the experience of
> going into a past life, I was fortunate through Father [James
> Jones] to be able to let them experience all the way
> through their deaths, so to speak. And everybody was so
> happy when they made that step to the other side."[18]

With that assurance 912 men, women, and children, together
with their leader, went to their deaths in the Guyana clearing
under Jones's tragically mocking placard, "Those who do not
remember the past are condemned to repeat it."

Such, then, are the lessons to be learned from the dabblings in
past-life regression, and the dangers to be faced by those who continue to practice it. In warning of these dangers I find myself, in
this instance at least, in total accord with Dr. Ian Stevenson. Be-

cause of the numerous inquiries he receives on the subject at his office in Charlottesville, he has drawn up a carefully worded circular, of which the following is a particularly telling extract:

> I am not now engaging in experiments with hypnotic regression to "previous lives." I do not recommend hypnotists to persons who wish to have this experience. I do not approve of any hypnotist who makes promises to clients that suggest they will certainly return to a real previous life under his direction. I do not approve of anyone who charges fees for acting as a hypnotist in such experiments.[19]

I can only add a sincere "Amen."

I am conscious that for some readers this book may be a cause of disappointment or even disbelief, since so many reincarnation claims have, after a review, proved unconvincing. However, though we may certainly have less assurance than before that there is such a thing as reincarnation, one very positive underlying message of this book should by now have become obvious: the sheer magnitude of the potentialities of the human mind.

For too many decades, psychology has been too rooted in the thinking of the so-called behaviorist school, concentrating its attention on the more ready-to-hand mechanical properties of the brain insofar as they can be learned from animals, rather than on some of the far more fundamental issues of mind, consciousness, and personality. From what we have learned, there is far more to each of us than mere machines thrown up by chance in the course of evolution. How and why is it, for instance, that within us, beyond the reach of our normal consciousness, we retain the complete recording track of our existence, as has been so ably demonstrated by Dr. Wilder Penfield? What precisely is the nature of the "hidden observer," with its extraordinary creative properties, so carefully researched by Stanford's Professor Hilgard? What power is it within us that can so dramatically change our voices, accents, vocabularies, handwriting, even brainwave characteristics to bring about the multiple personality phenomena noted by Dr. Morton Prince? Above all, what within our minds can so affect our bodies that there can be spontaneously produced the "stigmatic"-type phenomena observed by Britain's Dr. Moody and Germany's Dr. Lechler?

Here, to borrow a memorable simile of President John F. Kennedy's, is a "new ocean" upon which we must sail—with hypnosis, properly used, a most powerful means of navigating our voyage. For of one thing we can be sure: We are each of us passengers in the exploration of a vast universe within ourselves, a dynamic, ever-restless kaleidoscope of images, ideas, dreams, emotions, and more, the complexity and extent of which we have scarcely as yet even begun to grasp . . .

Notes and References

CHAPTER 1

1. From the publisher's blurb of L. Ron Hubbard's *Have You Lived Before This Life?*, Scientology Publications, 1978.

2. G. M. Glaskin, *Windows of the Mind*, Arrow Books, 1974, and *Worlds Within*, Arrow Books, 1978.

3. See Harold Lief, "Commentary on Dr. Ian Stevenson's 'The Evidence of Man's Survival after Death,'" *Journal of Nervous and Mental Disease*, Vol. 165, No. 3, September 1977, p. 172.

4. The United Kingdom figure derives from a 1979 Gallup Poll, based on a nationally representative sample of 918 adults and published in the *Sunday Telegraph* April 15, 1979.

5. Dr. Ian Stevenson, "The Evidence for Survival from Claimed Memories of Former Incarnations," *Journal of the American Society for Psychical Research*, Vol. 54, pp. 51–71 and 95–117.

6. Dr. Ian Stevenson, *Twenty Cases Suggestive of Reincarnation*, American Society for Psychical Research, 1966. A second edition, revised and enlarged, was subsequently published by the University Press of Virginia in 1974.

7. Dr. Ian Stevenson, *Cases of the Reincarnation Type: Vol. 1, Ten Cases in India; Vol. 2, Ten Cases in Sri Lanka;* and *Vol. 3, Twelve Cases in Lebanon and Turkey*, all published by the University Press of Virginia, 1975, 1977, and 1980, respectively. The last volume was received too late to be encompassed within this present study.

8. The factual details concerning the Pollock case derive from the author's firsthand interviewing and correspondence with John Pollock, together with the following: Alan Bestic, "My Girls Are Back from the Dead," *Woman's Own*, September 8, 1979; *Credo*, a British documentary television program shown on the ITV network, Sunday, February 11, 1979; *Daily Express*, May 6, 1957; Hexham *Courant*, May 10, 1957, July 19, 1957, October 17, 1957, October 10, 1958.

9. From an interview with Alan Bestic, op. cit.

10. Ibid.

CHAPTER 2

1. See in particular Dr. Ian Stevenson, "The Explanatory Value of the Idea of Reincarnation," *Journal of Nervous and Mental Disease*, Vol. 164, No. 5, May 1977, pp. 305–26, and "Research into the Evidence of Man's Survival After Death," *Journal of Nervous and Mental Disease*, Vol. 165, No. 3, September 1977, pp. 152–70.

2. Ian Stevenson, *Twenty Cases Suggestive of Reincarnation*, (revised edition), University Press of Virginia, 1974, p. 39.

3. Ibid., p. 261.

4. Stevenson, "The Explanatory Value of the Idea of Reincarnation," p. 319.

5. Stevenson, "Some Questions Relating to Cases of the Reincarnation Type," *Journal of the American Society for Psychical Research*, Vol. 68, 1974, p. 409.

6. Stevenson, *Ten Cases in Sri Lanka*, University Press of Virginia, 1977, pp. 15–42.

7. Stevenson, *Twenty Cases*, pp. 91–105.

8. Ibid., p. 101.

9. Stevenson, *Ten Cases in Sri Lanka*, pp. 235–80.

10. The instance referred to is the case of Jasbir, which Stevenson suggests may alternatively be attributable to possession.

11. In the cases on the table marked with an asterisk the distances are based on the known locations of conception. In most other cases the place of conception and the place of birth may be assumed to have been identical.

12. Stevenson, *Twenty Cases*, p. xi.

13. Francis Story, *Rebirth as Doctrine and Experience*, Buddhist Publication Society, 1975, pp. ix–xv.

14. Ibid., p. 236.

15. Peter Blythe, *Hypnotism, Its Power and Practice*, Arthur Barker, 1971, p. 132. For further information on Henry Blythe and the Mary Cohen case see Chapter 5 of the present work.

16. Story, op. cit., pp. 240 and 242.

17. Ibid., p. 241.

18. Stevenson, *Twenty Cases*, p. 109.

19. Stevenson's Introduction to Story, op. cit., p. xiii.

20. From a document kindly made available to me by the British Society for Psychical Research.

21. Stevenson, *Ten Cases in India*, University Press of Virginia, 1975, p. 2.

22. That of Kumkum Verma. See *Ten Cases in India*, pp. 206–40.

23. Ibid., pp. 332, 333.

24. Ibid., p. 100.

25. Ibid., p. 310.

26. Ibid., p. 131.

27. Stevenson, *Twenty Cases*, p. 95.

28. Stevenson, *Ten Cases in India*, p. 95.

29. Stevenson, *Ten Cases in Sri Lanka*, p. 37.

30. Ibid., p. 241.

31. Stevenson, *Ten Cases in India*, pp. 206–40.

32. The pica condition is the desire for unusual items of food that often occurs during pregnancy. From the Latin *pica*, a magpie.

33. Dr. Ian Stevenson, "The South-east Asian Interpretation of Gender Dysphoria: An Illustrative Case Report," *Journal of Nervous and Mental Disease*, Vol. 165, No. 3, September 1977, p. 203.

34. Ibid., p. 202, note 3.

35. Stevenson, *Twenty Cases*, pp. 231–41.

36. Dr. Michele Clements, "What a Fetus Hears an Adult Remembers," *General Practitioner*, April 13, 1979, p. 38.

37. Dr. Carl Sagan, *The Dragons of Eden*, Hodder & Stoughton, 1978, p. 148: "Full term newborn babies spend more than half their sleep time in the REM (rapid eye movement) dream state. In infants born a few weeks premature the dreamtime is three-quarters or more of the total sleep time. Earlier in its intra-uterine existence the foetus may be dreaming all the time."

38. I asked Stevenson whether I might be allowed for the purposes of this book a single birthmark photograph, or even the sight of a single photograph. Both requests were refused.

39. Dr. Harold I. Lief, "Commentary on Dr. Ian Stevenson's 'The Evidence of Man's Survival After Death,'" *Journal of Nervous and Mental Disease*, Vol. 165, No. 3, September 1977, p. 171.

CHAPTER 3

1. The basic details of the Rosemary case as presented in this chapter are derived from A. J. H. Hulme and F. H. Wood, *Ancient Egypt Speaks*, Rider, 1937; F. H. Wood, *This Egyptian Miracle*, John M. Watkins, 1955; and from correspondence with Dr. Wood's literary executor, Mr. Ray Donovan of Blackpool.

2. Hulme and Wood, *Ancient Egypt Speaks.*

3. In fact, as has been noted by Egyptologist John Ray, the Old Perfective was in current use at Nona's alleged eighteenth-dynasty period, and survived for several centuries after that. For Hulme it was easy enough to pick up from the standard book of Egyptian grammar by A. H. Gardiner, first published in 1927.

4. Battiscombe Gunn in *Journal of Egyptian Archaeology* 23, 1937, pp. 123, 124.

5. It is to be acknowledged that according to Genesis 12:16, an Egyptian pharaoh contemporary with Abraham gave the patriarch camels as a gift. However, the passage gives no suggestion of the animal being used for domestic transport.

6. It is fair to point out that I have concentrated on the fallacy of what has hitherto seemed the prime strength of the Rosemary case—that the "Egyptian" was vouched for by an accredited Egyptologist. Dr. Wood later in life came to recognize Hulme's deficiencies, learned Ancient Egyptian himself, and went on to accumulate nearly five thousand of Rosemary's utterances which he regarded as authentic Egyptian. I have not investigated this later work.

7. I am indebted to the Librarian of the Lever Library, Miss V. M. Wells, for assistance with trying to trace details of Howard's career with Lord Lever. The only clear reference occurs in the 1916 volume of *Progress*, the Lever Brothers' house magazine, in which Howard was said to be giving free monthly lectures at Hulme Hall.

8. The Howards' first known residence in the South was in Brighton at 33 Norfolk Square, the address quoted in the documents of their purchase of Eagle's Way. The conveyance of Eagle's Way took place on October 16, 1923. I am indebted to the present-day owners, Mr. and Mrs. Harper, for kindly allowing me to inspect the title deeds.

9. One strong possibility is that Howard married into the Hulme family, and for social reasons took on his wife's name. His wife's will is in the name of Florence Elizabeth Hulme, there being a significant omission of the name Howard. But birth and marriage certificates for the couple have proved difficult to trace (although the author's researches have been by no means exhaustive), and there may well be more to the affair than has yet been unearthed. It is to be noted that Ivy Beaumont, whom we now know to have been the medium Rosemary, was a beneficiary in Florence Hulme's will.

10. The basic details of this case as presented in this chapter are derived from Arthur Guirdham, *The Cathars and Reincarnation*, 1970; *We Are One Another*, 1974; and *The Lake and the Castle*, 1976, all published by Neville Spearman. I am also grateful to Dr. and Mrs. Guirdham for interviews and correspondence.

11. It is to be observed that precisely these same symptoms are characteristic of multiple personality cases (Chapters 8 and 9) and A. J. Stewart (Chapter 14), in all of whom the bouts of unconsciousness occurred during early teens. Epileptic fits also tend to manifest at about this same age.

12. Guirdham, *The Cathars and Reincarnation*, p. 89.

13. Guirdham, *We Are One Another*, pp. 13 and 14.

14. This was made at a luncheon meeting in Bath on April 3, 1978. At this stage I also had in mind hypnotic experiments for Mrs. Smith's Cathar memories to be reawakened under controlled conditions, similarly unacceptable to Guirdham. For different reasons I have subsequently come to agree with Guirdham's antipathy toward hypnotic experiments.

15. Luncheon meeting at Guirdham's home, May 8, 1979.

16. Telephone conversation, April 26, 1979. It has since been learned that whoever Miss Mills was, she too is now dead.

17. Letter sent July 10, 1979.

18. My letter of May 9, 1979, of which this suggestion was the major element, was answered by Guirdham on May 21, 1979, but with the suggestion ignored.

CHAPTER 4

1. A proper history of hypnosis has yet to be written. But for a brief, amusing introduction, from which the opening data of this chapter were derived, see Professor L. R. C. Haward, "Hypnosis in the Service of Research," an inaugural lecture given on February 14, 1979, and available as a printed pamphlet from the Department of Clinical Psychology, University of Surrey.

2. Quoted in Morey Bernstein, *The Search for Bridey Murphy*, Hutchinson, 1956, p. 251. Unfortunately Bernstein does not quote the *Lancet*'s date.

3. See, for instance, Dr. A. A. Mason, "A Case for Congenital Icthyosiform Erythrodermia of Brocq Treated by Hypnosis," *British Medical Journal*, August 23, 1952, pp. 422 and 423; also Dr. Richard Dreaper, "Recalcitrant Warts on the Hand Cured by Hypnosis," *Practitioner*, Vol. 220, February 1978, pp. 305–10.

4. See, for instance, Theodore X. Barber, "Suggested ('Hypnotic') Behaviour: The Trance Paradigm Versus an Alternative Paradigm" in Erika Fromm and Ronald E. Shor's *Hypnosis: Research Developments and Perspectives*, Paul Elek Ltd., 1972, pp. 114–82.

5. The following account has been built up from M. Kleinhauz, I. Horowitz, and Y. Tobin, "The Use of Hypnosis in Police Investigation," *Journal of the Forensic Science Society*, No. 17, 1977, pp. 77–80; and the report of the bus bombing itself in the *Jerusalem Post*, July 19, 1976.

6. See Brian R. Clifford and Ray Bull, *The Psychology of Person Identification*, Routledge & Kegan Paul, 1978, p. 21.

7. Shaun Usher, "The Trance That Traps Criminals," *Daily Mail*, November 13, 1980.

8. In Britain publicity has been given to the use of hypnosis in connection with the case of the so-called M5 Rapist (*Western Daily Press*, March 21, 1979) and the disappearance of Genette Tate (*Daily Mail*, October 27, 1978). But Professor Haward of the University of Surrey told me in 1979 that he has been consulted by British police over as many as twenty cases in the course of a year.

9. Kleinhauz, Horowitz & Tobin, op. cit., p. 79.

10. Martin T. Orne, "The Mechanisms of Hypnotic Age Regression: An Experimental Study," *Journal of Abnormal and Social Psychology* 46, 1951, pp. 213–25.

11. Ibid., p. 221.

12. L. Gidro-Frank and M. K. Bowersbuch, "A Study of the Plantar Response in Hypnotic Age Regression," *Journal of Nervous and Mental Disease* 107, 1948, pp. 443–58.

13. See Barber, op. cit., p. 144.

14. David B. Cheek, "Maladjustment Patterns Apparently Related to Imprinting at Birth," *American Journal of Clinical Hypnosis* 18, October 1975, pp. 75–82.

15. Denys E. R. Kelsey, "Phantasies of Birth and Prenatal Experiences Recovered from Patients Undergoing Hypno-Analysis," *Journal of Mental Science* 99, 1953, pp. 216–23.

16. Broadcast on BBC Radio 4, May 2, 1979, producer John Theokaris, hypnotist Leonard Wilder. The program was an edited version of six two-hour hypnotic sessions.

17. Bernstein, op. cit.

18. In the original book the pseudonym Ruth Simmons was used. I have chosen to use the subject's real name, since this was subsequently publicly revealed.

19. According to the original edition her birthplace was Iowa, but later and presumably more accurate editions quote Madison, Wisconsin.

20. Bernstein, op. cit., p. 108.

21. In the original transcript those listening thought she said "Friday" and recorded it as such. The true name was, however, "Bridey," as subsequently became clear.

22. For information on this and the activities of other U.S. newspapers in connection with the Bridey Murphy case, I am indebted to the excellent article by Professor C. J. Ducasse, "How the Case of *The Search for Bridey Murphy* Stands Today," *Journal of the American Society for Psychical Research* 54, 1960, pp. 3–22.

23. William J. Barker, interview with Virginia Tighe published in Part IV of a six-installment series, "How Bridey Changed My Life," Denver *Post*, October 1956.

24. Ducasse, op. cit., p. 18.

CHAPTER 5

1. Helen Wambach, *Reliving Past Lives: The Evidence Under Hypnosis*, Hutchinson, 1979.

2. See Peter Moss with Joe Keeton, *Encounters with the Past: How Man Can Experience and Relive History*, Sidgwick & Jackson, 1979; also Monica O'Hara, *New Hope Through Hypnotherapy*, Abacus, 1980.

3. Kathryn Hill, "'I've Lived Before' Claims Film Star," Bristol *Evening Post*, February 23, 1978.

4. The Vince Hill, Faith Brown, and Diane Solomon claims all derive from hypnotic regressions conducted by Leonard Wilder and reported by Maureen Lawless, "Hypnotist's Amazing Experiment: Did These Stars Live Before?", *News of the World*, April 22, 1979.

5. Jess Stearn, *The Search for a Soul: Taylor Caldwell's Psychic Lives*, Doubleday & Company, Garden City, N.Y., 1973.

6. Because of the nature of the phenomenon, these figures merely form a rough guide to the most generally accepted view. There are some hypnotists who claim that under hypnosis everyone can remember past lives.

7. Henry Blythe, *The Three Lives of Naomi Henry*, Frederick Muller, 1956, p. 71.

8. *The Bloxham Tapes,* documentary narrated by Magnus Magnusson and shown on BBC TV December 19, 1976. Arnall Bloxham died in December 1980.

9. Jeffrey Iverson, *More Lives Than One?*, Pan paperback edition, 1977, p. 52.

10. Ibid., p. 137.

11. Derived from my own interview with Graham Huxtable in Swansea, June 12, 1979.

12. Moss with Keeton, op. cit., p. 103.

13. Mentioned by Sue Atkins to Gordon Rattray Taylor and quoted in his article "Fact or Fiction? The Scientific View of Keeton's Results," *Now!* magazine, September 28, 1979.

14. Moss with Keeton, op. cit., p. 71.

15. Iverson, op. cit., p. 140.

16. Moss with Keeton, op. cit., p. 88.

17. Ibid., p. 66.

18. Ibid., Chapter 7.

19. Iverson, op. cit., p. 109.

20. Moss with Keeton, op. cit., p. 83.

21. Information provided by Joe Keeton.

22. Information provided by Joe Keeton. A dramatized documentary of the Kitty Jay regression was produced by Westward Television during 1980.

23. Dr. Ian Stevenson, *Xenoglossy: a Review and Report of a Case,* University Press of Virginia, 1974.

24. For sources on this regression see Dr. Ian Stevenson, "A Preliminary Report on a New Case of Responsive Xenoglossy: The Case of Gretchen," *Journal of the American Society for Psychical Research,* Vol. 70, January 1976, pp. 65–77; the Reverend Carroll E. Jay, *Gretchen I Am,* Wyden Books, 1977; and an investigation by Peter Greig in the *Daily Mail,* January 23 and 25, 1975.

CHAPTER 6

1. Helen Wambach, *Reliving Past Lives: The Evidence Under Hypnosis,* Hutchinson, 1979, pp. 70–77.

2. *Now!,* September 21, 1979, p. 20.

3. "It is my belief that we are able to pass on memories to our fu-

ture descendants—just as we can pass on all sorts of other characteristics and personality traits through our genes." Interview with
Crüssell quoted in the *Kentish Independent* newspaper February
8, 1979.

4. This is a feature meriting further study. An experiment conducted by the Birmingham (England) *Mail* in which the same
subject was regressed by both Joe Keeton and Leonard Wilder
was hampered by Wilder's difficulties in achieving a suitable
depth of trance.

5. From the unpublished manuscript "Reincarnation: Myth or
Fact? Research into Reincarnation" by H. & D. Arnall Bloxham,
kindly lent to the author.

6. See, for instance, James Graham-Campbell and Dafydd Kidd,
The Vikings, British Museum Publications, 1980, p. 115: ". . .
the iron helmet from Gjermundbu. This Norwegian find is the
only complete Viking helmet known to survive. In shape it is little more than a rounded cap with a nose- and eye-guard, like
monstrous spectacles. No horns, and no wings, such as are frequently and mistakenly provided by all too romantic modern
imagination! The truth of this is confirmed by the many contemporary pictures of helmets, from those on the Gotlandic stones to
those of the Middleton and Sigtuna warriors."

7. Jeffrey Iverson, *More Lives Than One?*, Pan edition, 1977, Chapters 4 and 5.

8. See R. B. Dobson, *The Jews of Mediaeval York and the Massacre
of March 1190*, St. Anthony's Press, York, 1974.

9. Iverson, op. cit., pp. 45, 46.

10. Iverson, op. cit., pp. 44, 45. Jeffrey Iverson and Magnus Magnusson have suggested explanations for these difficulties, but they
remain problematic.

11. One of Edna's more curious mistakes was to refer to Charles II's
wife as Anne Marie when in reality she was Catherine of
Braganza. It is of course possible to argue that Anne Marie may
have been Charles's pet name for his wife, and one that never
reached the history books. For other of Edna's mistakes see Peter
Moss with Joe Keeton, *Encounters with the Past*, Sidgwick &
Jackson, 1979, pp. 140 and 141.

12. For a published example of this, see Moss with Keeton, op. cit.,
p. 30.

13. I attended a regression in Bromley at which this personality was
produced, and made a tape recording.

14. Historically, the name seems to be found only in the counties of Essex and Suffolk (see P. H. Reaney, A *Dictionary of British Surnames*, Routledge & Kegan Paul, 1958, p. 257). According to Orriss his great-grandfather was a Suffolk saddlemaker.

15. See G. O. Rickwood, "A Battalion Officer's Jacket 44th East Essex Regiment c. 1811," *Journal of Army Historical Research* XXIX, 1951, pp. 115, 116.

16. *War Office List of All the Officers of the Army & Royal Marines*. See especially the volume for March 13, 1815, pp. 257–59.

17. Moss with Keeton, op. cit., pp. 111, 112. The extract quoted has been abridged from a more extended original.

18. Ibid., p. 94.

19. I owe this information to Father Joseph Crehan, S.J.

20. Father Joseph Crehan, S.J., letter to *Now!*, October 18, 1979.

21. Moss with Keeton, op. cit., pp. 96, 97.

22. Hans Eysenck, *Now!*, September 28, 1979, p. 101.

23. From a letter to Derek Crüssell, July 5, 1979.

24. Dr. Troscianko is on the staff of the Brain and Perception Unit at Bristol University Medical School and agreed to be regressed by Joe Keeton purely for experimental purposes.

25. Dr. Ian Stevenson, "A Preliminary Report on a New Case of Responsive Xenoglossy," p. 71.

26. Ibid., p. 70.

27. Dr. Ian Stevenson, *Xenoglossy: a Review and Report of a Case*, University Press of Virginia, 1974, p. 58.

CHAPTER 7

1. For some background to this see Vance Packard, *The Hidden Persuaders*, Penguin Books, 1960, p. 41.

2. For background to the life and work of Dr. Wilder Penfield, see Sir John Eccles, F.R.S., and William Feindel, "Wilder Graves Penfield 1891–1976," *Biographical Memoirs of Fellows of the Royal Society*, Vol. 24, pp. 473–513; also Penfield's own works, including *The Excitable Cortex in Conscious Man*, Liverpool University Press, 1958; (with Lamar Roberts) *Speech and Brain Mechanisms*, Princeton University Press, 1959; (with Phanor Perot) "The Brain's Record of Auditory and Visual Experience: a Final Summary and Discussion," *Brain* 86, IV, 1963, pp. 595–696, and *The Mystery of the Mind*, Princeton University Press, 1975. Dr. Penfield died on April 5, 1976.

3. In Penfield's papers on the case she is referred to as M.M. The account of her operation has been built up from Penfield's descriptions of it in the works listed above.

4. Penfield in *Brain*, p. 687.

5. Penfield, *Speech and Brain Mechanisms*, p. 53.

6. Dr. Henry Freeborn, "Temporary Reminiscence of a Long Forgotten Language during the Delirium of Broncho-Pneumonia," *Lancet*, June 14, 1902, pp. 1685–86.

7. Erika Fromm, "Age Regression with Unexpected Reappearance of a Regressed Childhood Language," *International Journal of Clinical and Experimental Hypnosis*, Vol. 18 (2), 1970, pp. 79–88.

8. G. Lowes Dickinson, "A Case of Emergence of a Latent Memory Under Hypnosis," *Proceedings of the Society for Psychical Research* Vol. 25, 1911, pp. 455–67.

9. Jeffrey Iverson, *More Lives Than One?*, Pan edition, 1977, p. 138.

10. Milton V. Kline, *A Scientific Report on "The Search for Bridey Murphy,"* Julian Press, New York, 1956.

11. Edwin S. Zolik, "An Experimental Investigation of the Psychodynamic Implications of the Hypnotic 'Previous Existence' Fantasy," *Journal of Clinical Psychology*, Vol. 14, 1958, pp. 179–83.

12. See Reima Kampman, "Hypnotically Induced Multiple Personality," *Acta Universitatis Ouluensis*, Series D, Medica No. 6, Psychiatrica No. 3, 1973; "Hypnotically Induced Multiple Personality: an Experimental Study" in *International Journal of Clinical and Experimental Hypnosis*, July 1976, Vol. 24 (3), pp. 215–; and (with Reijo Hirvenoja) "Dynamic Relation of the Second Personality Induced by Hypnosis to the Present Personality" *Hypnosis at Its Bicentennial*, ed. Fred H. Frankel and Harold Zamansky, Plenum Publishing Corporation, 1978, pp. 183–88.

13. Kampman, *Acta Universitatis Ouluensis*, p. 35.

14. Kampman, *Hypnosis at Its Bicentennial*, pp. 184, 185.

15. For Kampman's references to this subject see Appendix Kampman's contribution to the *Acta Universitatis Ouluensis* "Dynamic Relationship of Multiple Personality Induced by nosis to Present Personality," a lecture given by Kampman Hirvenoja at the 7th International Congress of Hypnosis an chosomatic Medicine, Philadelphia, Pennsylvania, July 1–3, Kampman does not identify the girl involved, and the nam is therefore at my own conjuration.

16. Kampman, *Hypnosis at Its Bicentennial*, p. 186.
17. Ibid.
18. Ibid.
19. Fromm, op. cit., p. 82.
20. *Now!*, September 21, 1979, p. 39.

CHAPTER 8

1. Richard Hodgson, "A Case of Double Consciousness," *Journal of the Society for Psychical Research*, 1891–92, pp. 221–57.
2. The term "outward self" is inevitably a loose one. It is used here for the permanent personality (if there is such a thing), as distinct from possessing entities or subpersonalities whose existence may be more transitory. Of course, at any given moment any one of these personalities may be "out," effectively replacing the outward, permanent self.
3. Few studies of this classic case identify the subject by her real name. I owe this identification to Dr. George E. Gifford, Jr., ed., *Psychoanalysis, Psychotherapy, and the New England Medical Scene, 1894–1944*, Science History Publications, New York, 1978, p. 232. Claire Brenner subsequently became the wife of Boston psychiatrist George A. Wakeman, one of Morton Prince's assistants.
4. Morton Prince, *The Dissociation of a Personality*, first published by Longmans, Green, 1905; reprinted as a paperback by Oxford University Press, 1978.
5. Corbett H. Thigpen and Hervey M. Cleckley, *The Three Faces of Eve*, McGraw-Hill, New York, 1957.
6. Chris Sizemore and Elen Pittillo, *Eve*, Victor Gollancz, 1978.
7. Corbett H. Thigpen and Hervey M. Cleckley, "A Case of Multiple Personality," *Journal of Abnormal and Social Psychology*, 49, 1954, p. 137.
8. For a fuller description of this episode, see Sizemore and Pittillo, op. cit., p. 255.
9. For a full list of the opposites, see Thigpen and Cleckley, *Journal of Abnormal and Social Psychology*, pp. 141, 142.
10. Ibid., p. 142; also Sizemore and Pittillo, op. cit., p. 261.
11. Thigpen and Cleckley, *Journal of Abnormal and Social Psychology*, p. 145.
12. Sizemore and Pittillo, op. cit., p. 324.

13. Flora Rheta Schreiber, *Sybil*, Penguin, 1975.

14. Ibid., p. 51.

15. Information on this case has been built up from detailed reports in the *Citizen Journal* and the *Dispatch* of Columbus, Ohio, published on October 28, 1977, October 5 and 6, 1978, and December 10, 11, and 12, 1979. The reports of October 5 and 6, 1978, were in their turn based on a psychiatric report on Milligan drawn up by psychiatrist Dr. George Harding of the Harding Hospital, Worthington, Ohio.

16. From Harding's report as quoted in the Columbus *Dispatch*, October 5, 1978.

CHAPTER 9

1. Morton Prince, *The Dissociation of a Personality*, Oxford University Press, 1978 edition, pp. 106–7.

2. Ibid., p. 105.

3. Flora Rheta Schreiber, *Sybil*, Penguin, 1975, p. 347.

4. Shaun Usher, "Can This Boy Be Ten Different People?" *Daily Mail*, October 24, 1978.

5. Prince, op. cit., p. 158. For the sake of consistency I have substituted "Claire Brenner" for the pseudonymous "Miss Beauchamp" of the original text.

6. Cleckley and Thigpen, *Journal of Abnormal and Social Psychology*, 49, 1954, p. 149.

7. Although it would be out of place to argue for it in a study of this kind, there seems a case for believing that all hypnotic regressions, including normal regressions to present life childhood, are in effect inductions of the multiple personality condition. Don's knowledge of Japanese only in his childhood "self" or subpersonality would seem a excellent example of this, and many of the anomalies of hypnotic regression would be more readily understandable by a multiple personality explanation. Of course far more research is needed into what exactly multiple personality is.

8. Chris Sizemore and Elen Pittillo, *Eve*, Victor Gollancz, 1978, p. 432.

9. For a good general introduction to abreaction with a listing of medical literature on the subject (although now rather dated), see Dr. William Sargant, *Battle for the Mind*, William Heinemann, 1957, Chapter 3.

10. Dr. Robert Moody, "Bodily Changes During Abreaction," *Lan-

cet, Vol. II, December 28, 1946, p. 934, and Vol. I, June 19, 1948, p. 964.

11. See Father Germanus, *The Life of Gemma Galgani*, trans. A. M. Sullivan, O.S.B., Sands & Co., 1914, p. 69; also K. E. Schmöger, *Life of A. C. Emmerich* (Eng. trans.), Vol. I, Academy Library Guild, 1954, p. 4.

12. Father Herbert Thurston, S.J., *The Physical Phenomena of Mysticism*, Burns, Oates & Washbourne, 1952, Chapter 7. Although not published until after Father Thurston's death, this book was written during the 1930s.

13. For biographies of Teresa Neumann, see particularly Anni Spiegl, *The Life and Death of Therese Neumann of Konnersreuth*, trans. Susan Johnson, Eichstatt, 1973; Johannes Steiner, *Therese Neumann von Konnersreuth*, Verlag Schnell & Steiner, Munich, 1967.

14. Thurston, op. cit., p. 112.

15. Ibid., p. 114.

16. Alfred Lechler, *Das Rätsel von Konnersreuth in Lichte eines neuer Falles von Stigmatisation*, Elberfeld, 1933. The English translations were kindly made for the author by Mrs. Iris Sampson of Backwell, near Bristol.

17. Ibid., p. 17.

18. Ibid., p. 18.

CHAPTER 10

1. G. Lowes Dickinson, "A Case of Emergence of a Latent Memory Under Hypnosis," *Proceedings of the Society for Psychical Research*, Vol. 25, 1911, p. 464.

2. Julian Jaynes, *The Origins of Consciousness in the Breakdown of the Bicameral Mind*, Houghton Mifflin, 1976, p. 23.

3. Brian Hitchen, "A Bullet from a Horse Pistol in My Shoulder," *Now!*, September 28, 1979, p. 98.

4. Colin Wilson, *Mysteries*, Hodder & Stoughton, 1978, pp. 302–3.

5. Professor Ernest R. Hilgard, *Divided Consciousness*, John Wiley, New York, 1977.

6. Ibid., p. 196.

7. Ibid., p. 196.

8. Ibid., p. 197.

9. Ibid., p. 198.

10. Ibid., p. 198.
11. Peter McKellar, *Mindsplit*, Dent, 1979, p. 81.
12. Ibid., p. 82.
13. Ibid., p. 129.
14. Professor Ernest R. Hilgard, "A Neodissociation Interpretation of Pain Reduction in Hypnosis," *Psychological Review*, 1973, pp. 396–411; E. R. and J. R. Hilgard, *Hypnosis in the Relief of Pain*, William Kaufmann, Inc., California, 1975.
15. Thomson Prentice, "Defending My Homeland from the English," *Now!*, September 28, 1979, p. 98.

CHAPTER 11

1. For information on Leonard Wilder's early work in past-life regression, see Peter Underwood and Leonard Wilder, *Lives to Remember*, Robert Hale, 1975.
2. The register consulted was the second register, 1678 to 1812. The only name remotely resembling that given by David Rolfe was a Philip Augustine, son of George Augustine, who died January 19, 1712. But there seemed no evidence to link the individual with the personality described by David Rolfe.
3. On May 4, 1970.
4. Edward Ryall, *Second Time Round*, with an Introduction and Notes by Dr. Ian Stevenson, Neville Spearman, 1974.
5. For a detailed review of some of the superficial mistakes in *Second Time Round*, see Renée Haynes, *The Seeing Eye, The Seeing I*, Hutchinson, 1976, pp. 182–87; *Theta*, Vol. 6, No. 4, 1978; and *The Christian Parapsychologist*, Vol. 3, No. 4, September 1979, pp. 136–37, together with a rejoinder by Dr. Ian Stevenson, *Theta*, Vol. 7, No. 4, 1979, pp. 8–9.
6. See entry under "Shakers," *Oxford Dictionary of the Christian Church*, ed. F. L. Cross, Oxford University Press, 1957. It is, of course, possible that the term was in use earlier, but I have found no evidence of this.
7. For an excellent description of the battle, with sources and references to Godfrey, see Peter Earle, *Monmouth's Rebels—The Road to Sedgemoor 1685*, Weidenfeld & Nicolson, 1977.
8. Ryall's references to the date and features of the house occur principally on pp. 39 and 66 of *Second Time Round*.
9. This is reproduced opposite p. 161 of *Second Time Round*.

10. Marjorie and C. H. B. Quennell, *A History of Everyday Things in England*, first published 1919 by B. T. Batsford. Figure 15 occurs on p. 27 of the 1954 edition.
11. Ryall, op. cit., p. 24.
12. Ibid., p. 110.
13. Ibid., pp. 176–77.

CHAPTER 12

1. This and all subsequent extracts from Jan's Joan Waterhouse regression derive from a tape recording made at the time by Joe Keeton.
2. *Encyclopaedia of Witchcraft and Demonology*, Octopus Books, 1974.
3. For background sources on the trial, see Wallace Notestein, *A History of Witchcraft in England from 1558 to 1718*, Oxford University Press, 1911; also C. L'Estrange Ewen, *Witch Hunting and Witch Trials*, Kegan Paul, 1929.
4. See, for instance, Edgar Peel and Pat Southern, *The Trials of the Lancashire Witches*, David & Charles, Newton Abbott, England, 1972.
5. *The examination and confession of certaine wytches at Chensforde in the Countie of Essex before the Quenes maiesties Judges the XXVI day of July, anno 1566* "imprynted at London by William Powell for Wyllyam Pickeringe . . . 1566" This was published in three parts, two on August 13, the third on August 23, 1566. The pamphlet gives extracts of the confessions and an account of the court interrogations, and there is every reason to believe it is an accurate account of the trials described. The Lambeth Palace library copy bears on the binding the initials R. B. for Richard Bancroft, Archbishop of Canterbury, who died in 1610.
6. This and the subsequent post-hypnotic information was given to me by Jan in an interview conducted at her home on November 6, 1978.
7. Letter to the author, October 25, 1979.
8. *Calendar of Assize Records, Essex Indictments Elizabeth I*, ed. Prof. J. S. Cockburn, H.M.S.O., 1978. Joan Waterhouse appears as entry 263 (p. 46), her mother Agnes as entry 274.
9. John Southcote (1511–1585) was Justice of the Queen's Bench from 1563 to 1584 and is described as "a judge of the highest reputation." Gilbert Gerard was Serjeant in 1558, Attorney-

General in 1559, and Master of the Rolls in 1581. He died in 1593.

10. Philobiblon Society, *Miscellanies* Vol. VIII, one of a set of volumes published between 1877 and 1884.

11. Margaret Murray, *The Witch-Cult in Western Europe*, Oxford University Press, 1921.

12. C. L'Estrange Ewen, op. cit., p. 317.

13. Peter Moss with Joe Keeton, *Encounters with the Past*, Sidgwick & Jackson, 1979, p. 8.

CHAPTER 13

1. For background on the Cain family during the early years of this century, I am deeply indebted to the numerous Manchester residents who responded to my appeal for information in the Manchester *Evening News*. Among these should be mentioned Miss V. McElroy, Mr. V. Rhodes, Tom Williams, F. Hampson, Leslie Byrom, Mrs. D. Barlow, Mrs. Beatrice Williamson, John Euston, Mrs. Eileen Coleman, Mrs. Irene Peters, and Fred Cain Bailey.

2. For a fascinating pictorial introduction to old Salford, with early photos of the Flat Iron Market, see Alan Smith, A.L.A., *Salford as It Was*, Hendon Publishing Company, 1973.

3. This and all subsequent extracts from Keeton's regressions of Mona derive from tape recordings made at the time.

CHAPTER 14

1. *Died 1513—Born 1929, The Autobiography of A. J. Stewart*, Macmillan, 1978, p. 306. This has now been reissued under the title *King's Memory: The Autobiography of A. J. Stewart*, William MacLellan Embryo, 1981.

2. For an excellent short biography see Caroline Bingham, *The Stewart Kingdom of Scotland, 1371–1603*, Weidenfeld & Nicolson, 1974; also G. Gregory Smith, *The Days of James IV*, David Nutt, 1900.

3. For the original references to these misadventures relating to James's body, see John Stow, *A Survey of London*, 1598 and 1603.

4. She adopted the name A. J. Stewart from 1970, the time of the publication of her James biography, *Falcon*, purely at the instigation of her publisher, who pointed out to her that copyright can-

not be owned by a dead medieval king. According to her own account, in a note to the author:

> I refused to allow the name Ada F. Kay to appear because I was too well known by that name as a playwright. So I suggested that we ascribe authorship (under the lines "presented by") to me beneath my lawful name Stewart, which I had never used as a writer. This would cover the copyright problem. The initials A. J. occurred simultaneously to everyone at the meeting because a) it sounded anonymous, b) it had the slightly masculine inflection which fitted the autobiography of a man, c) my initial "F" had for years been mistaken for a "J", and it all fitted rather nicely the "James" who was the real author of the book.

5. A plummeting black falcon is believed by A.J. to have been James's battle standard for the Flodden campaign. This gave rise to the title *Falcon* of her autobiography as James.

6. *Falcon—the Autobiography of His Grace James IV, King of Scots,* presented by A. J. Stewart, Peter Davies, 1970.

7. This information was given during interviews and correspondence with the author.

8. An explanation given in correspondence with the author.

9. R. Lindesay of Pitscottie, *The Historie and Chronicles of Scotland,* ed. A. J. G. Mackay, Scottish Text Society (3 vols.), Edinburgh, 1899–1911, p. 107.

10. Personal communication to the author, May 22, 1979.

11. Colin Thompson and Lorne Campbell, *Hugo van der Goes and the Trinity Panels in Edinburgh,* Trustees of the National Gallery of Scotland, 1974.

12. See, for instance, Agnes Mure Mackenzie's *The Rise of the Stewarts,* A. Maclehose, 1935, and the frontispiece to Christine Orr's *Gentle Eagle,* 1937.

13. Personal communication to the author, May 22, 1979.

14. From *Facsimiles of National Manuscripts of Scotland* selected under the direction of the Rt. Hon. Sir William Gibson-Craig, Bart., General Register House, Edinburgh, 1872, Part III, facsimile IX.

15. It should be noted that both according to A.J. and as confirmed from datable samples, the actual change in handwriting took place not in 1967 but in 1970, after the publication of *Falcon.*

16. Letter to the author, November 7, 1979.

17. Tape-recorded interview with the author, May 22, 1979.

18. *Died 1513*, p. 38. For a particularly pertinent multiple person-ality parallel to this, see Ludwig, Brandsma, Wilbur, Benfeldt, and Jameson, "The Objective Study of a Multiple Personality," *Archives of General Psychiatry*, Vol. 26, April 1972, pp. 298–308. Describing a multiple personality case of a colored man by the name of Jonah, the authors record on p. 300:

> When Jonah was about 9 or 10 years old, a gang of white boys decided to beat him up after school just "for sport." They proceeded to pummel Jonah with their fists, and he be-came absolutely terrified that he was going to die. At this point Jonah lost consciousness and Usoffa Abdulla (a war-rior-like subpersonality) emerged. Usoffa fought so viciously and vehemently that he purportedly almost killed a couple of the boys. From that moment on Usoffa has maintained a constant vigilance over Jonah to insure his safety.

19. *Died 1513*, p. 26.

20. Letter to the author.

21. *Died 1513*, p. 57.

22. Ibid., p. 58.

23. Interview with journalist Marcelle Bernstein, 1971.

CHAPTER 15

1. Dr. Morton Schatzman, *The Story of Ruth*, Duckworth, 1980.

2. Ibid., pp. 270–75.

3. W. Dewi Rees, "The Hallucinations of Widowhood," *British Medical Journal*, October 4, 1971, pp. 37–41.

4. See British national newspapers for the week of September 16–20, 1980.

5. Judy Graham, "The Sex Adventures That Never Were," London *Daily Mail*, September 20, 1980.

6. As this book goes to press, I have just received a copy of Dr. Stevenson's latest book, *Cases of the Reincarnation Type*, Vol. 3, *Twelve Cases in Lebanon and Turkey*, University Press of Vir-ginia, 1980. This records of Stevenson on the flyleaf: "He now believes that unreliability of the informants is the most likely al-ternative explanation for reincarnation, but he does not believe that this explanation adequately accounts for all the features of the stronger cases." This suggests that Stevenson's views may be coming closer to my own.

7. Lorna Selfe, *Nadia—A Case of Extraordinary Drawing Ability in an Autistic Child*, Academic Press, 1977.

8. As recorded on videotape by the Nottingham psychologists, Nadia began a drawing of a horse, not with the outline of the head—as virtually all children and most untrained adults would —but with the neck, in the manner of a trained artist. Similarly, while everything else about her was clumsy, her whole hand-eye coordination was far in advance of that of the normal five- to six-year-old. As observed by Lorna Selfe:

> . . . her lines were firm and without unintentional wavering. She could stop a line exactly where it met another despite the speed with which the line was drawn. She could change the direction of a line and draw lines at any angle towards and away from the body. She could draw a small but perfect circle in one movement and place a small dot in the center. (Selfe, op. cit., p. 8)

9. It is perfectly possible that some normal source will be discovered for this picture. But that still leaves unexplained Nadia's extraordinary unlearned abilities.

10. Ibid., p. 6.

11. Ibid., pp. 129–31.

12. A tape recording of this regression was played to the author by John Pollock and the content of the regression noted from this.

13. See John Baron, *Life of Edward Jenner*, Henry Colburn, 1838.

14. *Felix Farley's Journal*, as quoted in C. H. B. Elliott, *Winterbourne Gloucestershire*, 1936, p. 111.

15. C. H. B. Elliott, op. cit., p. 120.

16. These are available at Frenchay Church, care of the Reverend Barry Trotter.

17. I owe this latter information to Mr. John Lucena of the Frenchay Preservation Society.

18. These notes were tape-recorded at the time and published by David Blundy, "The Jonestown Tape," *Sunday Times Magazine*, November 25, 1979, p. 43.

19. Ian Stevenson, "Hypnotic Regression to Previous Lives—A Short Statement," a circular distributed by the Division of Parapsychology, Department of Psychiatry, University of Virginia Medical Center.

Cryptomnesia—
A Special Postscript

When I first wrote this book, for the British hardback edition *Mind Out of Time?* (Victor Gollancz, London, 1981), I regarded the task of tracing the actual literary and other sources of subjects' alleged reincarnation memories as too much of a "needle in a haystack" exercise to be practicable. The listing of historical novels in library catalogues rarely gives clues to their subject matter, and radio and TV historical dramas that may have been broadcast twenty or thirty years ago are similarly virtually impossible to trace, particularly when the all-important title and author of the work are unknown.

In the face of such difficulties I reckoned without the assiduousness of BBC writer and presenter Melvin Harris of Essex, England. An enthusiastic browser in secondhand bookshops, Melvin Harris during the last year has tracked down several historical novels that either influenced or directly inspired what have hitherto been regarded among reincarnationists as particularly convincing cases of "past-life" memories.

Undoubtedly the most important and conclusive of Melvin Harris' finds so far has been the discovery that the novel which inspired Jane Evans' "Livonia" regression (see pages 66–67 and 83–84) is without doubt German-born Louis de Wohl's *The Living Wood*, published as a hardback by Victor Gollancz in 1947 and subsequently republished as a paperback in Elek Books' Bestseller Library (under the title *The Empress Helena* in 1960). The following is a comparison between

Jane Evans' regression, as published in Jeffrey Iverson's *More Lives Than One?* (Pan Books, London, 1977), and Louis de Wohl's *The Living Wood:*

JANE EVANS' REGRESSION	DE WOHL NOVEL
1. The regression is set in Roman Britain in the late fourth century A.D. It focuses on events in the lives of the Roman legate Constantius, his wife "the domina" (p. 50) Helena, and Constantine their son. Their story is told by Jane Evans as "Livonia," wife of Titus, one of Constantine's tutors.	1. The first half of the novel is set in Roman Britain in the late fourth century A.D. It focuses on events in the lives of the Roman legate Constantius, his wife "the domina" (p. 65) Helena, and Constantine their son. Their story is told by de Wohl.
2. An early episode features the young Constantine in the garden of the family's Eboracum villa, being taught use of weapons by "military tutor" (p. 48) Marcus Favonius Facilis.	2. An early episode features the young Constantine in the garden of the family's villa, being taught use of weapons by "military tutor" (p. 38) Marcus Favonius Facilis.
3. At the family's villa Constantius is visited by one Allectus, bringing him an urgent summons to return to Rome. Allectus is given a meal. Livonia says she does not like Allectus. She twice remarks on his eyes: "very cold eyes, cold eyes" (p. 51).	3. At the family's villa Constantius is visited by prefect Allectus, bringing him an urgent summons to return to Rome. Allectus is given a meal. De Wohl describes Helena's instinctive hatred of Allectus, twice remarking on his eyes: "a pair of cold gray eyes" (p. 42) and "eyes always cold" (p. 49).
4. Livonia describes as suspicious the fact that although	4. De Wohl describes Constantius as faintly suspicious

JANE EVANS' REGRESSION	DE WOHL NOVEL
the message Allectus brought to Constantius was supposed to be urgent, he stopped at Gessoriacum to see Carausius, "who is in charge of the fleet."	of Allectus when he learns that although the message he brought was supposed to be urgent, he stopped off at Gessoriacum to see Carausius, "the admiral of the fleet."
5. Constantius appoints Valerius and Curio to be in charge of Britain during his absence (p. 52).	5. Constantius leaves behind Valerius and Curio to be in charge of Britain during his absence (p. 46).
6. Aided by Allectus' treacherous removal of Constantius, Carausius conquers Britain with his fleet (p. 52). Valerius dies but Curio survives (p. 53).	6. Aided by Allectus' treacherous removal of Constantine, Carausius conquers Britain with his fleet (p. 59). Valerius dies (p. 69), but Curio survives to reappear in a later episode.
7. Returning to Constantius' villa, Allectus kills some of the servants but Favonius manages to kill some of Allectus' men. Helena, Constantine, Favonius, Livonia, Titus, and Hilary all flee, traveling by night and eventually reaching Verulam (p. 52).	7. Returning to Constantius' villa, Allectus kills a servant but Favonius manages to fell Allectus and capture some of his men. Helena, Constantine, Favonius, and Hilary (an aide) all flee, traveling by night and eventually reaching Verulam (p. 87).
8. After some years, during which the family stays in Verulam while Constantius is unable to return, Allectus murders Carausius in order to seize power for himself. Rome declares war (p. 53).	8. After some years, during which the family stays in Verulam while Constantine is unable to return, Allectus murders Carausius in order to seize power for himself. He finds Rome's declaration of war in Carausius' hands (pp. 97–102).

JANE EVANS' REGRESSION	DE WOHL NOVEL
9. Helena, anticipating that Constantius will be with the re-invasion force, returns to their original villa. Allectus has occupied this for some time "and the garden is terrible" (p. 54). Constantius sends ahead "beautiful carpets, beautiful material . . ." (p. 54).	9. Helena, anticipating that Constantius will lead the re-invasion force, returns to their original villa. Allectus has occupied this for ten years and "the lawn had become a wilderness" (p. 105). Constantius sends ahead carpets and other beautiful objects (p. 116).
10. Curio arrives at the villa and "looks terrible" (p. 54). He discloses that together with Galerius Constantius has been made a Caesar, and each has married a daughter of the reigning emperors. In order to marry Maximianus' daughter Theodora, Constantius has renounced Helena in the Temple of Jupiter. Constantius is on his way to the villa, bringing Theodora with him (p. 54).	10. Curio arrives at the villa ashen-faced (p. 116). He discloses that together with Galerius Constantius has been made a Caesar, and each has married a daughter of the reigning emperors. In order to marry Maximianus' daughter Theodora, Constantius has repudiated Helena in the Temple of Jupiter. Constantius is on his way to the villa, bringing Theodora with him (p. 118).
11. Shocked by her husband's infidelity, Helena flees the villa and returns to Verulam. There she is introduced to Albanus, a woodcarver and a Christian. Livonia's husband Titus is to be made a priest by one Osius (p. 55).	11. Shocked by her husband's infidelity, Helena flees the villa and returns to Verulam. There she is introduced to Albanus, a woodcarver and a Christian. Helena's aide Hilary has become a priest, ordained by Bishop Osius (pp. 119–20, also 151, 152).
12. Livonia describes walking through streets where Chris-	12. De Wohl describes Helena walking through streets

JANE EVANS' REGRESSION	DE WOHL NOVEL
tian houses burn. The priest Titus is killed. People run, scream. At this stage Livonia seems to meet her end.	where Christian houses burn. The priest Hilary is killed. Soldiers arrive. People run, scream (pp. 155–56). (The novel goes on to recount Constantius' subsequent very moving reconciliation with Helena, Helena and Constantine's conversion to Christianity, and Constantine's eventual mastery and unification of the Roman Empire.)

It is important to note that while Constantine, Helena, Constantius, Allectus, Carausius, and Osius are all characters known to history, although not necessarily in exactly the circumstances portrayed, Hilary, Valerius, and Curio, who all appear in Jane Evans' regression, are entirely fictitious characters invented by De Wohl. The "military tutor" Marcus Favonius Facilis is a similar invention by De Wohl, although in this instance inspired by an indisputably first-century tombstone of a centurion, Marcus Favonius Facilis, preserved at Colchester. Some of De Wohl's devices for injecting a period flavor—e.g., referring to Helena as "the domina"—are repeated in the Jane Evans' regression. Jane Evans also repeats a literary idiosyncrasy of De Wohl—referring to Roman St. Albans by the abbreviated name Verulam (instead of Verulamium), while all other towns are given their full conventional Roman names.

It is of further considerable interest, in the light of the "hidden observer" psychological mechanisms which we discussed in Chapter 10, that for the purposes of the regression Jane Evans invented her own observing character "Livonia," although the name Livonia does occur as a lady-in-waiting, "a charming creature with pouting lips and smoldering eyes," on page 8 of *The Living Wood*. This is precisely the same adaption and inventiveness employed by Cynthia for "Blanche Poynings" (see p. 106).

Aside from "Livonia" and *The Living Wood*, it is to be noted that Thomas B. Costain's *The Moneyman* (Staples Press, London, 1948) provides virtually all background on the life of Jacques Coeur necessary for Jane Evans' "Alison" memories. Another work by the same writer may also have inspired Jane Evans' "Rebecca" memories, but there are other indications suggesting the primary source of this latter was an as-yet-untraced BBC radio play.

In the case of Arthur Guirdham's Cathar "past-life" memories, Hannah Closs's *High Are the Mountains* (Andrew Dakers, London, 1945) features the same period of history, the same locations, and many of the same characters. Further evaluation is in progress.

Such pinpointing of the exact sources of past-life regressions can be a valuable aid to understanding how and why cryptomnesia occurs, and any reader who has positive information of this kind is invited to write to the author c/o the Society for Psychical Research, 1 Adam & Eve Mews, London W8 6UG.

Index

About the Author

IAN WILSON lives in Bristol, England. His best-selling first book, *The Shroud of Turin*, was translated into ten languages and was the subject of an English documentary. The book has become a classic in the literature on the Shroud. For *All in the Mind*, in addition to historical research, Mr. Wilson has drawn on the latest psychiatric findings.